Adventure Guide

THE UNITED METHODIST CHURCH

Baltimore-Washington Conference

Equipping spiritual leaders to transform the world

We seek to be like Christ as we call, equip, send and support spiritual leaders to make disciples and grow at least 600 Acts 2 congregations by 2012.

The Discipleship Adventure

celebrate . connect . develop . serve . share

Edited by BWC Communications Department, printed by Kutztown Publishing Co., Inc. Cover Art: The Amazing Longleat Hedge Maze in Britain contains over 16,000 English Yews and covers an area of around 1.48 acres with a total pathway length of 1.69 miles. Scripture quotations are from the New Revised Standard Version of the Bible, copyright © 1989 all rights reserved.

The Adventure Guide

DAILY DEVOTIONAL

Welcome to the 2012-2013 Adventure Devotional. I am delighted you committed to grow in your faith journey through the daily disciple of Bible reading and prayers. As you read the Scripture passages, reflect on the questions and prayers. You will know hope, find peace and experience God's grace and love. Write down your thoughts and reflections in this book to remind you of how each day's worship brought you closer to God.

As we read the Adventure Devotional together we will celebrate our joys, face challenges, make tough decisions and grow in our faith. I encourage you to share your thoughts with others; a co-worker, a single parent in your church, young adults hungry for God or neighbors next door.

Whether in your church or Café, use this devotional in your small group Bible study and invite others to join you.

Be Adventurous!

John R. Schol

John R. Schol, Bishop
Baltimore-Washington Conference of
The United Methodist Church

Fulton, Maryland

Table of Contents

How to use this guide

The Adventure Guide is an ideal resource for small group Bible studies. It can also be used in meetings with staff, administrative council and committees to ensure that the business of the church is centered firmly in the Word of God. United Methodist Women and United Methodist Men groups can use it to open their gatherings. Sunday school classes can grow deeper in their faith together around the Adventure.

Each participant will need a copy of the guide. A church may wish to buy a dozen or more and leave them in a centralized location for all to use. As the group comes together, participants can be asked to read the Scripture for the day.

The convener can then open the group with a simple, heart-felt prayer calling upon God to be present in the sharing of God's word. One person in the group can then be asked to read the passage aloud, and members are invited to share what they heard God saying in the passage. What in the Scripture passage was meaningful to them? Those who wish may respond in turn.

The convener can then pose the questions presented in the pondering and meditation section. Discussion and the free flowing of ideas should be encouraged as the Scripture takes on meaning in the context of our daily living. When a predetermined time limit has been reached, a volunteer from the group can then lead devotional time using the prayer provided in the Guide.

The Adventure Guide is a tool that allows your group to navigate its agenda with meaning, inspiration and prayer.

SEPTEMBER

BISHOP JOHN R. SCHOL

The readings for the next four weeks use Wisdom literature from Proverbs, the Psalms, James and Jesus' words from the Gospel of Mark. Wisdom literature teaches about God and how to live a virtuous life. The literature is rational, straightforward and by following it, one will have a blessed life.

Today, everyone has advice on how to live. There are books, horoscopes, teachers, sages, who all seek a higher truth or better way. As United Methodist people of faith, we test wisdom by Scripture, reason, tradition and experience. We call this the Wesleyan quadrilateral.

I encourage you to reflect on your own wisdom and the deeper significance of your life in light of the readings. I hope you will play with the ideas, think deeper about them and become wiser about your relationship with God and your relationships with others in the world.

Proverbs 22:1-2; 8-9

A good name is to be chosen rather than great riches, and favor is better than silver or gold. The rich and the poor have this in common: the Lord is the maker of them all.

Whoever sows injustice will reap calamity, and the rod of anger will fail. Those who are generous are blessed, for they share their bread with the poor.

Pondering and Meditating: What we do with our money and how we treat the poor is a common theme throughout the Scriptures. How does your spending and wealth reflect your love for God? How have you shared with the poor in the last week?

Prayer: O Wise God, increase my blessing so that I may be a greater blessing to the poor. Decrease my selfishness so that I will be more generous with my wealth, time and talents. Amen.

Reflection:

Proverbs 22:22-23

Do not rob the poor because they are poor, or crush the afflicted at the gate; for the Lord pleads their cause and despoils of life those who despoil them.

Pondering and Meditating: If you are reading the Adventure Guide, I imagine you are not robbing the poor. But are there other ways we cause harm to the poor? Do you look the other way when you see someone who is poor? Do you offer wages that are unfair to low-income workers? Do you engage in community mission projects that serve the poor?

Prayer: God, give me strength and wisdom to examine my life and how I treat or neglect the poor. Help me and my church to serve the poor. Through Christ Jesus I pray. Amen.

Reflection:

Isaiah 35:4-5

Say to those who are of a fearful heart, "Be strong, do not fear! Here is your God. He will come with vengeance, with terrible recompense. He will come and save you." Then the eyes of the blind shall be opened, and the ears of the deaf unstopped; then the lame shall leap like a deer, and the tongue of the speechless sing for joy. For waters shall break forth in the wilderness, and streams in the desert.

Pondering and Meditating: The Scripture indicates there will be harsh judgment against those who have violated God's justice. Judgment is God's way of making things right. The harshest judgment is reserved for the oppressor. Living streams of righteousness will go to those who have been oppressed.

Prayer: Holy One, may my days be filled with righteousness and my wilderness wanderings spring with streams of obedient living. Amen.

Reflection:

James 2:1-4

My brothers and sisters do you with your acts of favoritism really believe in our glorious Lord Jesus Christ? For if a person with gold rings and in fine clothes comes into your assembly, and if a poor person in dirty clothes also comes in, and if you take notice of the one wearing the fine clothes and say, "Have a seat here, please," while to the one who is poor you say, "Stand there," or, "Sit at my feet," have you not made distinctions among yourselves, and become judges with evil thoughts?

Pondering and Meditating: A sign of our falleness is that we make judgments of people's character based on our own prejudices. This occurs in the church. A sign of godliness is to treat people with dignity and respect. Who do you treat differently? Why? How will you look at people through the eyes of Jesus?

Prayer: Jesus, increase your love in me so that I will increase my love for others. Amen.

Reflection:

Friday, September 7, 2012

James 2:13-17

For judgment will be without mercy to anyone who has shown no mercy; mercy triumphs over judgment. What good is it, my brothers and sisters, if you say you have faith but do not have works? Can faith save you? If a brother or sister is naked and lacks daily food, and one of you says to them, "Go in peace; keep warm and eat your fill," and yet you do not supply their bodily needs, what is the good of that? So faith by itself, if it has no works, is dead.

Pondering and Meditating: We are saved by faith. God loved us even before we loved God. But this is not grace to be abused. Discipleship without service and justice without faith is dead. Faith and works are all part of a disciple's adventure. How have you evidenced faith that involves belief and works this week? What will you do to express your faith by serving others?

Prayer: Jesus, awaken my faith by sending people in need to me. Amen.

Reflection:

Mark 2:32-37

They brought to him a deaf man who had an impediment in his speech; and they begged him to lay his hand on him. He took him aside in private, away from the crowd, and put his fingers into his ears, and he spat and touched his tongue. Then looking up to heaven, he sighed and said to him, "Ephphatha," that is, "Be opened." And immediately his ears were opened, his tongue was released, and he spoke plainly. Then Jesus ordered them to tell no one; but the more he ordered them, the more zealously they proclaimed it. They were astounded beyond measure, saying, "He has done everything well; he even makes the deaf to hear and the mute to speak."

Pondering and Meditating: Healing is a sign that the Kingdom of God is in our midst. Where have you seen healing recently? How are you a part of God's healing?

Prayer: Divine Healer, today I pray for the healing of _____. Come quickly that we may experience your Kingdom in our midst. Amen.

Reflection:

Sunday, September 9, 2012.

Psalm 146

Praise the Lord! Praise the Lord, O my soul! I will praise the Lord as long as I live; I will sing praises to my God all my life long. Do not put your trust in princes, in mortals, in whom there is no help. When their breath departs, they return to the earth; on that very day their plans perish. Happy are those whose help is the God of Jacob, whose hope is in the Lord their God, who made heaven and earth, the sea, and all that is in them; who keeps faith forever; who executes justice for the oppressed; who gives food to the hungry. The Lord sets the prisoners free; the Lord opens the eyes of the blind. The Lord lifts up those who are bowed down; the Lord loves the righteous. The Lord watches over the strangers; he upholds the orphan and the widow, but the way of the wicked he brings to ruin. The Lord will reign forever, your God, O Zion, for all generations. Praise the Lord!

Pondering and Meditating: What do you praise God for this Sabbath day?

Prayer: Praise the Lord, O my soul! Amen.

Reflection:

Proverbs 1:20-23

Wisdom cries out in the street; in the squares she raises her voice. At the busiest corner she cries out; at the entrance of the city gates she speaks: "How long, O simple ones, will you love being simple? How long will scoffers delight in their scoffing and fools hate knowledge? Give heed to my reproof; I will pour out my thoughts to you; I will make my words known to you."

Pondering and Meditating: Wisdom is knowledge combined with experience. It is hard to be wise if you do not study or if you do not broaden your experience. How is your wisdom increasing? How is your understanding and experience of God expanding?

Prayer: Divine Wisdom, help me know enough to see wisdom in others and recognize my own need to understand and experience more of you. Amen.

Reflection:

Proverbs 1:32-33

For waywardness kills the simple, and the complacency of fools destroys them; but those who listen to me will be secure and will live at ease, without dread of disaster.

Pondering and Meditating: This proverb teaches that complacency leads to one's demise. Passive faith, not using wisdom from God, is the destruction of the body of Christ. When is your faith complacent? How will you keep your faith growing and active in the world?

Prayer: Divine Wisdom, help me to see all the ways my life is complacent and renew in me a mind that actively seeks your knowledge. Amen.

Reflection:

James 3:1-6

Not many of you should become teachers, my brothers and sisters, for you know that we who teach will be judged with greater strictness. For all of us make many mistakes. Anyone who makes no mistakes in speaking is perfect, able to keep the whole body in check with a bridle. If we put bits into the mouths of horses to make them obey us, we guide their whole bodies. Or look at ships: though they are so large that it takes strong winds to drive them, yet they are guided by a very small rudder wherever the will of the pilot directs. So also the tongue is a small member, yet it boasts of great exploits. How great a forest is set ablaze by a small fire! And the tongue is a fire.

Pondering and Meditating: Our words speak for God or for evil, to build up or to tear down, to bring joy or to bring pain, to speak wisdom or foolishness. What will you do so that you speak more to build up, to bring joy, to speak wisdom?

Prayer: Divine Wisdom, tame my tongue so that I learn to do more to build up others. Amen.

Reflection:

James 3:9-12

With our tongue we bless the Lord and Father, and with it we curse those who are made in the likeness of God. From the same mouth come blessing and cursing. My brothers and sisters, this ought not to be so. Does a spring pour forth from the same opening both fresh and brackish water? Can a fig tree, my brothers and sisters, yield olives, or a grapevine figs? No more can salt water yield fresh.

Pondering and Meditating: Like the fig tree yielding figs, our words reflect who we are. When we bless, it means blessings dwell within us; when we harm, it speaks of our own pain; when we speak evil of others, it speaks of the evil within us. How do your words speak to who you are?

Prayer: Divine Wisdom, let me be shaped by you so that every word that flows from me reflects your presence in my life. Amen.

Reflection:

Friday, September 14, 2012

Mark 8:27-29

Jesus went on with his disciples to the villages of Caesarea Philippi; and on the way he asked his disciples, "Who do people say that I am?" And they answered him, "John the Baptist; and others, Elijah; and still others, one of the prophets." He asked them, "But who do you say that I am?" Peter answered him, "You are the Messiah."

Pondering and Meditating: Christians are unique because we believe Jesus is the Messiah, a gift for the salvation of the world. It is the wisdom of God that yields such understanding. It takes courage to profess Christ. Is your wisdom leading to greater profession of your faith?

Prayer: Divine Wisdom, reveal to me more of Jesus and give me courage to proclaim Jesus, died, buried and resurrected for my life. Through the Messiah, Christ Jesus, I pray. Amen.

Reflection:

Mark 8:31-35

Jesus began to teach them that the Son of Man must undergo great suffering, and be rejected by the elders, the chief priests, and the scribes, and be killed, and after three days rise again. He said all this quite openly. And Peter took him aside and began to rebuke him. But turning and looking at his disciples, he rebuked Peter and said, "Get behind me, Satan! For you are setting your mind not on divine things but on human things." He called the crowd with his disciples, and said to them, "If any want to become my followers, let them deny themselves and take up their cross and follow me. For those who want to save their life will lose it, and those who lose their life for my sake, and for the sake of the gospel, will save it."

Pondering and Meditating: It's hard to proclaim that our Messiah was a loser. It is hard for us to go around losing our own life in a world that worships winners. It is what makes us different. We win by giving up our desire to be first. How have you recently experienced a loss that became a sign of the resurrected Christ in you?

Prayer: Divine Wisdom, keep me humble so that I never boast of my knowledge, never try to make more of myself than I am, never make Jesus a superstar but a humble servant who gave his life for my own redemption. Through the Messiah, Christ Jesus, I pray. Amen.

Reflection:

Sunday, September 16, 2012

Psalm 116:5-9

Gracious is the Lord, and righteous; our God is merciful. The Lord protects the simple; when I was brought low, he saved me. Return, O my soul, to your rest, for the Lord has dealt bountifully with you. For you have delivered my soul from death, my eyes from tears, my feet from stumbling. I walk before the Lord in the land of the living.

Pondering and Meditating: The psalmist cries out, "you have delivered my soul from death, my eyes from tears, my feet from stumbling." On this Sabbath day, what do you cry out in gratitude for?

Prayer: Divine Wisdom, on this Sabbath day, return my soul, my whole being, to rest in you. Amen.

Reflection:

Monday, September 17, 2012

Proverbs 31:10-15

A capable wife who can find? She is far more precious than jewels. The heart of her husband trusts in her, and he will have no lack of gain. She does him good, and not harm, all the days of her life. She seeks wool and flax, and works with willing hands. She is like the ships of the merchant; she brings her food from far away. She rises while it is still night and provides food for her household.

Pondering and Meditating: Beverly, my wife, told me one day that she needed a good wife. She was lamenting that I was not pulling my weight around the house. Our culture has changed since Proverbs was written of the stereotypical roles of women and men. While culture has changed, biblical values have not. God wants women and men to respect and honor each other. God wants women and men to give to and receive graciously from each other. How does your life reflect biblical values?

Prayer: Just God, help me not to seek but to serve, not to want but to give, not to embellish but to humble myself. Grant me patience and greater humility so that I will serve others. Amen.

Reflection:

Tuesday, September 18, 2012

Proverbs 31:30-31

Charm is deceitful, and beauty is vain, but a woman who fears the Lord is to be praised. Give her a share in the fruit of her hands, and let her works praise her in the city gates.

Pondering and Meditating: Charm and beauty have long been what we want people to see in us. The church tries to lure people in through charm and beauty. All God wants is a humble and authentic people who demonstrate faith in God. What would your life look like if you gave up charm and embraced humility? Gave up beauty and embraced faith?

Prayer: Merciful God, forgive me for all the ways I take you for granted. Forgive me for trying to get by on charm and making myself look better than I am. Strengthen me through my own weakness. Through the perfecter of life, I pray. Amen.

Reflection:

James 3:13

Who is wise and understanding among you? Show by your good life that your works are done with gentleness born of wisdom.

Pondering and Meditating: A criticism of Jesus is that he focused too much on gentleness and meekness for a tough and mean world. Gentleness only gets you stomped on. There is a lot of gentleness in the Bible, and there is quite a bit of harsh judgment. The difference is that God does the judging. The wise recognize our goodness is expressed with bold gentleness. How is a bold gentleness being born through you?

Prayer: God, may I never achieve goodness by harming others and may goodness be born on the wings of humility. Amen.

Reflection:

Thursday, September 20, 2012

James 4:1-3

The conflicts and disputes among you, where do they come from? Do they not come from your cravings that are at war within you? You want something and do not have it; so you commit murder. And you covet something and cannot obtain it; so you engage in disputes and conflicts. You do not have, because you do not ask. You ask and do not receive, because you ask wrongly, in order to spend what you get on your pleasures.

Pondering and Meditating: These are strong words for disciples in the 1st century and relevant words for disciples in the 21st century. The conflict among believers, couched in theological terms, tends to arise out of the things we want to preserve. The non- and nominally religious move further and further away from the church because our controversies seek to address institutional issues rather than the spiritual hunger and the immense poverty within the world. How will you focus your discipleship on the deep spiritual hunger of the non- and nominally religious and the poverty in our world?

Prayer: Forgive me, God, for my over reaction to worship changes, new ministries and personality conflicts. Allow your grace and wisdom to guide me and my church as we live the Gospel of Jesus Christ. Through Jesus Christ, I pray. Amen.

Reflection:

Friday, September 21, 2012

James 4:7-8

Submit yourselves therefore to God. Resist the devil, and he will flee from you. Draw near to God, and he will draw near to you. Cleanse your hands, you sinners, and purify your hearts, you double-minded.

Pondering and Meditating: Resist the devil. One of the great challenges is that the devil is often disguised as our friend. War sometimes is portrayed as a friend to our security and then has not led to any measurable peace. Money has been disguised as a solution but only led to more problems. Love has been disguised as mutual affection and led to lust, envy and abuse. How do you determine if something is of God or evil?

Prayer: God, I am sometimes slow to learn. Make your way plain. Correct me when I choose the way of the devil rather than your way. Amen.

Reflection:

Mark 9:30-32

The disciples went on from there and passed through Galilee. Jesus did not want anyone to know it; for he was teaching his disciples, saying to them, "The Son of Man is to be betrayed into human hands, and they will kill him, and three days after being killed, he will rise again." But they did not understand what he was saying and were afraid to ask him.

Pondering and meditating: "And they were afraid to ask him." Why do you think the disciples were afraid to ask Jesus about his death? What would you ask Jesus?

Prayer: Jesus, help me never to be afraid to ask the questions that will change my heart, sharpen my mind, or engage me in the urgent needs of our time. Amen.

Reflection:

Sunday, September 23, 2012

Mark 9:33-37

Then they came to Capernaum; and when he was in the house he asked them, "What were you arguing about on the way?" But they were silent, for on the way they had argued with one another who was the greatest. He sat down, called the twelve, and said to them, "Whoever wants to be first must be last of all and servant of all." Then he took a little child and put it among them; and taking it in his arms, he said to them, "Whoever welcomes one such child in my name welcomes me, and whoever welcomes me welcomes not me but the one who sent me."

Pondering and Meditating: When have you wanted to be first? Why is being first important to you?

Prayer: God, help me to welcome the children, the vulnerable, those new to the faith, those society pushes to the margins. Help me to change my life so that they will always be ahead of me. Through Christ Jesus, who became last so that I could have a place in the Kingdom. Amen.

Reflection:

Esther 7:1-3

So the king and Haman went to feast with Queen Esther. On the second day, as they were drinking wine, the king again said to Esther, "What is your petition, Queen Esther? It shall be granted you. And what is your request? Even to the half of my kingdom, it shall be fulfilled." Then Queen Esther answered, "If I have won your favor, O king, and if it pleases the king, let my life be given me — that is my petition — and the lives of my people — that is my request.

Pondering and Meditating: Esther risked her own life before the king to save the life of the Jews. She was a messiah of God. What have you risked recently for the salvation of others?

Prayer: God, anoint me to stand up for the most vulnerable. Challenge me to risk more for the sake of the Gospel. Through your anointed one, Jesus Christ, I pray. Amen.

Reflection:

James 5:13-14

Are any among you suffering? They should pray. Are any cheerful? They should sing songs of praise. Are any among you sick? They should call for the elders of the church and have them pray over them, anointing them with oil in the name of the Lord.

Pondering and Meditating: Do you find we are not very good at asking for help, and are especially bad at asking for healing? Where has your growth and health suffered because you were afraid to ask for help?

Prayer: God, help me. Help me not to rely only on myself when there are supernatural powers waiting to be unleashed through the disciples around me. Amen.

Reflection:

James 5:16-20

Therefore confess your sins to one another, and pray for one another, so that you may be healed. The prayer of the righteous is powerful and effective. My brothers and sisters, if anyone among you wanders from the truth and is brought back by another, you should know that whoever brings back a sinner from wandering will save the sinner's soul from death and will cover a multitude of sins.

Pondering and Meditating: We have been confused, sometimes by Scripture, that disease and problems are caused by the sins of those who suffer. Sometimes our own sin creates our own disease. Sometimes it is the sins of others that creates our disease. And sometimes our disease is caused by a fallen world. At all times, we should pray for the forgiveness and healing of ourselves, others and our world. Whose forgiveness will you pray for today?

Prayer: Forgive me, God, for the times I let you down. Amen.

Reflection:

Thursday, September 27, 2012

James 5:19-20

My brothers and sisters, if anyone among you wanders from the truth and is brought back by another, you should know that whoever brings back a sinner from wandering will save the sinner's soul from death and will cover a multitude of sins.

Pondering and Meditating: Bringing back people who have wandered from the faith pleases God. We sometimes confuse bringing back someone to church and bringing someone back into relationship with God. These are two different things. It is the relationship with God that is most urgent. It is in the community of believers where the person can be nurtured and challenged to grow their relationship with God. Who are you praying for and leading back into a relationship with God?

Prayer: God, give me the heart and wisdom to save souls. Amen.

Reflection:

Friday, September 28, 2012

Mark 9:38-41

John said to him, "Teacher, we saw someone casting out demons in your name, and we tried to stop him, because he was not following us." But Jesus said, "Do not stop him; for no one who does a deed of power in my name will be able soon afterward to speak evil of me. Whoever is not against us is for us. For truly I tell you, whoever gives you a cup of water to drink because you bear the name of Christ will by no means lose the reward

Pondering and Meditating: "We tried to stop him," the disciples boasted. This is the institutional church, trying to put boundaries and restrictions on the power of God to transform lives. How do you limit the power of God with your family, friends and fellow disciples?

Prayer: May your wisdom be unleashed within me, God, so that I know the difference between binding the Gospel and setting it free. Amen.

Reflection:

Mark 9:42-45

"If any of you put a stumbling block before one of these little ones who believes in me, it would be better for you if a great millstone were hung around your neck and you were thrown into the sea. If your hand causes you to stumble, cut it off; it is better for you to enter life maimed than to have two hands and to go to hell, to the unquenchable fire. And if your foot causes you to stumble, cut it off; it is better for you to enter life lame than to have two feet and to be thrown into hell.

Pondering and Meditating: Jesus never wanted someone to be inhibited from being in relationship with God. It was so offensive to Jesus that he said it was better that you lose your life than cause someone to stumble. He also said that if anything causes you to sin, it is better to get rid of it. Does your church create stumbling blocks for others to come into relationship with Christ? What do you need to get rid of so that you keep a strong relationship with Jesus Christ?

Prayer: God, reveal to me my own stumbling blocks that keep me and others from a meaningful relationship with you. Amen.

Reflection:

Sunday, September 30, 2012

Psalm 124

If it had not been the Lord who was on our side — let Israel now say — if it had not been the Lord who was on our side, when our enemies attacked us, then they would have swallowed us up alive, when their anger was kindled against us; then the flood would have swept us away, the torrent would have gone over us; then over us would have gone the raging waters. Blessed be the Lord, who has not given us as prey to their teeth. We have escaped like a bird from the snare of the fowlers; the snare is broken, and we have escaped. Our help is in the name of the Lord, who made heaven and earth.

Pondering and Meditating: What Psalm is on your heart today? What joy within you is bursting for a Psalm of Praise to God?

Prayer: For life, for my church and the purpose you have given to my life, O God, I thank you. Amen.

Reflection:

OCTOBER

Rev. Miguel A. Balderas

This month we will celebrate World Communion Sunday, Children's Sabbath and Laity Sunday. If we want to be consistent, we have to reflect and meditate in a contextual way, that is to say, consider the community in which we live and the celebrations that are a part of our traditions. World Communion Sunday gives all Christians an opportunity to celebrate as one body in Christ. It provides the opportunity to be a great family regardless of cultural traditions, language, skin color, sex-gender or age. All of us will be celebrating the great family that we are in Jesus Christ. This reminds us that we are all equal as God's creations. Children's Sabbath and Laity Sunday help us to recognize the importance of our children, youth, young adults and the laity within the Methodist movement. We must remember that the movement to which we belong is a movement of the Holy Spirit, which reminds us that we are all equal in the presence of our Lord. I invite you, when you do your reflection, to seriously consider the context in which you live and where God has called you to serve. Listen to the voice of God and dare to take specific action for the building of God's Kingdom here and now.

Job 2:3-10

The Lord said to Satan, "Have you considered my servant Job? There is no one like him on the earth, a blameless and upright man who fears God and turns away from evil. He still persists in his integrity, although you incited me against him, to destroy him for no reason." Then Satan answered the Lord, "Skin for skin! All that people have they will give to save their lives. But stretch out your hand now and touch his bone and his flesh, and he will curse you to your face." The Lord said to Satan, "Very well, he is in your power; only spare his life." So Satan went out from the presence of the Lord, and inflicted loathsome sores on Job from the sole of his foot to the crown of his head. Job took a potsherd with which to scrape himself, and sat among the ashes. Then his wife said to him, "Do you still persist in your integrity? Curse God, and die." But he said to her, "You speak as any foolish woman would speak. Shall we receive the good at the hand of God, and not receive the bad?" In all this Job did not sin with his lips.

Pondering and Meditating: When people speak of us, can they say, just like they said of Job, that we are blameless, upright, afraid of God and turn away from evil? Or when a situation becomes difficult, do we act like Job's wife trying to persuade others to complain and to move away from God?

Prayer: My God, help us to be humble, righteous, honest, afraid of you. Deliver us from the temptation to become angry with you, and use this as a pretext to move away from you. In Jesus Christ we pray. Amen.

Reflection:

Tuesday, October 2, 2012

Proverbs 8:27-31

Genesis 2:18-25

Then the Lord God said, "It is not good that the man should be alone; I will make him a helper as his partner." So out of the ground the Lord God formed every animal of the field and every bird of the air, and brought them to the man to see what he would call them; and whatever the man called each living creature, that was its name. The man gave names to all cattle, and to the birds of the air, and to every animal of the field; but for the man there was not found a helper as his partner. So the Lord God caused a deep sleep to fall upon the man, and he slept; then he took one of his ribs and closed up its place with flesh. And the rib that the Lord God had taken from the man he made into a woman and brought her to the man. Then the man said, "This at last is bone of my bones and flesh of my flesh; this one shall be called woman, for out of man this one was taken." Therefore a man leaves his father and his mother and clings to his wife, and they become one flesh. And the man and his wife were both naked, and were not ashamed.

Pondering and Meditating: How do we relate to the partner that we have chosen to live with? Do we value the blessing of having a family, and are we able to enjoy it? Are we able to live in a mature and healthy relationship without the interference of our parents?

Prayer: Lord, those who are parents give us the wisdom and understanding to walk with our sons and daughters, but not to live their lives. Give them, our sons and daughters, the courage of flying and of living in fullness as we did at that time. Thank you, Father, for your freedom and your love. Amen.

Reflection:

Wednesday, October 3, 2012

Hebrews 1:1-4

Long ago God spoke to our ancestors in many and various ways by the prophets, but in these last days he has spoken to us by a Son,*whom he appointed heir of all things, through whom he also created the worlds. He is the reflection of God's glory and the exact imprint of God's very being, and he sustains all things by his powerful word. When he had made purification for sins, he sat down at the right hand of the Majesty on high, having become as much superior to angels as the name he has inherited is more excellent than theirs.

Pondering and Meditating: Do we understand the way that God acts in this world? Do we accept the authority of Jesus in this world and in our lives?

Prayer: Lord, help us to see in Jesus the accomplishment of your love, and the importance of obeying his words and following his example. Amen.

Reflection:

Mark 10:2-10

Some Pharisees came, and to test him they asked, "Is it lawful for a man to divorce his wife?" He answered them, "What did Moses command you?" They said, "Moses allowed a man to write a certificate of dismissal and to divorce her." But Jesus said to them, "Because of your hardness of heart he wrote this commandment for you. But from the beginning of creation, 'God made them male and female. For this reason a man shall leave his father and mother and be joined to his wife, and the two shall become one flesh. So they are no longer two, but one flesh. Therefore what God has joined together, let no one separate." Then in the house the disciples asked him again about this matter. He said to them, "Whoever divorces his wife and marries commits adultery against her; and if she divorces her husband and marries another, she commits adultery."

Pondering and Meditating: Why are we confused in understanding that women and men are God's creation, and therefore the same? Why have we come to believe that someone is superior to his brother or sister, simply because they are different? Why, in our confusion, do we find it difficult to love the woman, the youth, the elderly, the immigrant, the persecuted, and those who think differently than we do?

Prayer: Lord, it's so easy to assume that we are right and others are wrong. Help us not to make our prejudices bigger than your love, compassion and mercy. In Jesus our Lord we pray, Amen.

Reflection:

Friday, October 5, 2012

Psalm 26

Vindicate me, O Lord, for I have walked in my integrity, and I have trusted in the Lord without wavering. Prove me, O Lord, and try me; test my heart and mind. For your steadfast love is before my eyes, and I walk in faithfulness to you. I do not sit with the worthless, nor do I consort with hypocrites; I hate the company of evildoers, and will not sit with the wicked. I wash my hands in innocence, and go around your altar, O Lord, singing aloud a song of thanksgiving, and telling all your wondrous deeds. O Lord, I love the house in which you dwell, and the place where your glory abides. Do not sweep me away with sinners, nor my life with the bloodthirsty, those in whose hands are evil devices, and whose right hands are full of bribes. But as for me, I walk in my integrity; redeem me, and be gracious to me. My foot stands on level ground; in the great congregation I will bless the Lord.

Pondering and Meditating: We humbly come to God's presence, acknowledging our imperfection, yet we dare to request justice of him. What justice are we talking about? Perhaps it will not be in what we receive, but rather in what we do and give. Justice means we dare to be fair.

Prayer: Dear Father, you who know that in the depths of our being we try to be honest, help us to be just as you have been with us. As the sun shines for everyone in your perfect will, we must love everyone equally. In Jesus Christ we pray. Amen.

Reflection:

Saturday, October 6, 2012

Psalm 8

O Lord, do not rebuke me in your anger, or discipline me in your wrath. Be gracious to me, O Lord, for I am languishing; O Lord, heal me, for my bones are shaking with terror. My soul also is struck with terror, while you, O Lord — how long? Turn, O Lord, save my life; deliver me for the sake of your steadfast love. For in death there is no remembrance of you; in Sheol who can give you praise? I am weary with my moaning; every night I flood my bed with tears; I drench my couch with my weeping. My eyes waste away because of grief; they grow weak because of all my foes. Depart from me, all you workers of evil, for the Lord has heard the sound of my weeping. The Lord has heard my supplication; the Lord accepts my prayer. All my enemies shall be ashamed and struck with terror; they shall turn back, and in a moment be put to shame.

Pondering and Meditating: In the society that we live in, we are always so busy that we forget to see how beautiful and great God's creations are. It seems that we are afraid to enjoy God's creations, as if this was a sin. It makes us feel guilty. Why do we get lost in trivialities and useless disputes and miss the creation and the life God has given us?

Prayer:Your creation praises you and proclaims how great you are, Lord. Help us to praise you every day, and be responsible with your creation, acting in a fair and loving way, because this world is yours and you love us all. You are great, Lord, We want to praise and bless you with our voices and our actions. Amen.

Reflection:

Sunday, October 7, 2012

World Communion Sunday
Hebrews 2:6-12

But someone has testified somewhere, "What are human beings that you are mindful of them, or mortals, that you care for them? You have made them for a little while lower than the angels; you have crowned them with glory and honor, subjecting all things under their feet." Now in subjecting all things to them, God left nothing outside their control. As it is, we do not yet see everything in subjection to them, but we do see Jesus, who for a little while was made lower than the angels, now crowned with glory and honor because of the suffering of death, so that by the grace of God he might taste death for everyone. It was fitting that God, for whom and through whom all things exist, in bringing many children to glory, should make the pioneer of their salvation perfect through sufferings. For the one who sanctifies and those who are sanctified all have one Father. For this reason Jesus is not ashamed to call them brothers and sisters, saying, "I will proclaim your name to my brothers and sisters, in the midst of the congregation I will praise you."

Pondering and Meditating: God put everything under the feet of Jesus. Christ calls us all brothers and sisters. Are we able to call everyone brothers and sisters as Jesus does? Do we proclaim to our brothers and sisters the name of our Lord?

Prayer: Good Father, help us to proclaim among our brothers and sisters the good news of Jesus Christ. Let us not be tempted to be ashamed of others, and let us be proud of our family in Christ without excluding anyone. In Jesus Christ, we pray. Amen.

Reflection:

Monday, October 8, 2012

Job 23:1-9, 16-17

Then Job answered:"Today also my complaint is bitter; his hand is heavy despite my groaning. O that I knew where I might find him, that I might come even to his dwelling! I would lay my case before him, and fill my mouth with arguments. I would learn what he would answer me, and understand what he would say to me. Would he contend with me in the greatness of his power? No; but he would give heed to me. There an upright person could reason with him, and I should be acquitted forever by my judge. If I go forward, he is not there; or backward, I cannot perceive him; on the left he hides, and I cannot behold him; I turn to the right, but I cannot see him. God has made my heart faint; the Almighty has terrified me; If only I could vanish in darkness, and thick darkness would cover my face.

Pondering and Meditating: When we are in difficult situations like Job, what is our attitude in dealing with these situations? Do we become bitter like Job did, and not know where to find God? We need to know that God is everywhere, in every situation that we experience.

Prayer: Dear God, thank you for your loving presence in all the situations we experience; good and bad. Even when we think that you are not with us, you are always there. Help us not to lose the sense of your presence. Amen.

Reflection:

Tuesday, October 9, 2012

Amos 5:6-7

Seek the Lord and live, or he will break out against the house of Joseph like fire, and it will devour Bethel, with no one to quench it. Ah, you that turn justice to wormwood, and bring righteousness to the ground!

Pondering and Meditating: We, as people, are the only ones capable of transforming blessings into curses, justice into unfairness. We are so closed-minded and thinking that we are perfect and better than most. How long before we cease to be vain and pretentious, assuming we do not need to correct or change the way we are? Why are we so stubborn that we do not listen to the advice we seek from the Lord on how to live. Why do we not want to listen?

Prayer: Dear God, help us in our vanity and pride that keeps us from you. We must learn that you speak to us in so many ways. Forgive us, for when we forget or refuse to listen with an open heart and a willing, humble mind. In Christ Jesus we pray. Amen.

Reflection:

Hebrews 4:12-16

Indeed, the word of God is living and active, sharper than any two-edged sword, piercing until it divides soul from spirit, joints from marrow; it is able to judge the thoughts and intentions of the heart. And before him no creature is hidden, but all are naked and laid bare to the eyes of the one to whom we must render an account. Since, then, we have a great high priest who has passed through the heavens, Jesus, the Son of God, let us hold fast to our confession. For we do not have a high priest who is unable to sympathize with our weaknesses, but we have one who in every respect has been tested as we are, yet without sin. Let us therefore approach the throne of grace with boldness, so that we may receive mercy and find grace to help in time of need.

Pondering and Meditating: With the example of Jesus, we have an opportunity to learn how to overcome sin. Christ also gives us insights into understanding the Word of God. Do we dare to follow suit so radically? Or do we just want the benefits of the presence of Jesus, but without any commitment to him? Jesus understands us perfectly because he was fully human like us.

Prayer: Lord, help to realize that what matters most is not so much what we believe, but the way we put our beliefs into action – the way we live and that which we claim to be. Help us in this journey, strengthen us and give us grace as you did with your beloved son. In Jesus' name we pray. Amen.

Reflection:

Thursday, October 11, 2012

Mark 10:17-23

As he was setting out on a journey, a man ran up and knelt before him, and asked him, "Good Teacher, what must I do to inherit eternal life?" Jesus said to him, "Why do you call me good? No one is good but God alone. You know the commandments: 'You shall not murder; you shall not commit adultery; you shall not steal; you shall not bear false witness; you shall not defraud; honor your father and mother.'" He said to him, 'Teacher, I have kept all these since my youth." Jesus, looking at him, loved him and said, "You lack one thing; go, sell what you own, and give the money to the poor, and you will have treasure in heaven; then come, follow me." When he heard this, he was shocked and went away grieving, for he had many possessions. Then Jesus looked around and said to his disciples, "How hard it will be for those who have wealth to enter the kingdom of God!"

Pondering and Meditating: Beyond the moral commandments Jesus moves us to having hearts for God and that is what frees us from everything. We are not tied to anything or anyone, and we dare to follow Jesus in a radical way. How many times has the budget in our homes or churches controlled everything, and we forget that God is Lord and owner of everything?

Prayer: God, thank you for your care for us, even though we sometimes are more concerned about what we do not have and miss the opportunity to do good. In the name of Jesus, Amen.

Reflection:

Friday, October 12, 2012

Psalm 22:1-8

My God, my God, why have you forsaken me? Why are you so far from helping me, from the words of my groaning? O my God, I cry by day, but you do not answer; and by night, but find no rest. Yet you are holy, enthroned on the praises of Israel. In you our ancestors trusted; they trusted, and you delivered them. To you they cried, and were saved; in you they trusted, and were not put to shame. But I am a worm, and not human; scorned by others, and despised by the people. All who see me mock at me; they make mouths at me, they shake their heads; Commit your cause to the Lord; let him deliver — let him rescue the one in whom he delights!'

Pondering and Meditating: The words of despair and loneliness expressed at the beginning of this psalm are tremendous, the same words that Jesus used on the cross. Why is the suffering before an injustice so great that it almost seems that God has abandoned us? Let us think about those who do not have anyone in the midst of this sea of people in our civilized cities. Let us think of the immigrants, crossing the desert to be in a Christian country that describes them as illegal and grants them the status of criminals, making them feel the same agony and loneliness of Jesus. Let us think of all those that we have made feel unwelcome. Their walking alone on a journey is unfair.

Prayer: Father, Jesus cried out on the cross. In his solitude and suffering, he carried all humanity on his shoulders, including our loneliness, suffering and sin. Thank you, Father, because in Jesus we find company, and agony disappears. Thank you. Amen.

Reflection:

Saturday, October 13, 2012

Psalm 90:12-17

So teach us to count our days that we may gain a wise heart. Turn, O Lord! How long? Have compassion on your servants! Satisfy us in the morning with your steadfast love, so that we may rejoice and be glad all our days. Make us glad for as many days as you have afflicted us, and for as many years as we have seen evil. Let your work be manifest to your servants, and your glorious power to their children. Let the favor of the Lord our God be upon us, and prosper for us the work of our hands — O prosper the work of our hands!

Pondering and Meditating: This wisdom is not always easy. The psalmist says, "Teach us to count our days." Do we live our lives wisely? Do we, at times, have the feeling that our lifves have not been productive or ar simply without sense? Do we search and search without finding the happiness that we might find in God?

Prayer: The challenge is to evaluate every day, live the day as if it were our last, recognizing the presence of God in everything we do. To live happy today is a blessing that comes from you, Lord. Help us to recognize it and to continue to accept your teachings. Amen.

Reflection:

Sunday, October 14, 2012

Amos 5:10-15

They hate the one who reproves in the gate, and they abhor the one who speaks the truth. Therefore, because you trample on the poor and take from them levies of grain, you have built houses of hewn stone, but you shall not live in them; you have planted pleasant vineyards, but you shall not drink their wine. For I know how many are your transgressions, and how great are your sins — you who afflict the righteous, who take a bribe, and push aside the needy in the gate. Therefore the prudent will keep silent in such a time; for it is an evil time. Seek good and not evil, that you may live; and so the Lord, the God of hosts, will be with you, just as you have said. Hate evil and love good, and establish justice in the gate; it may be that the Lord, the God of hosts, will be gracious to the remnant of Joseph.

Pondering and Meditating: In the society we live in, it is very easy to act like everyone else, and forget that God knows all our transgressions and sins. No matter what others do, do we seek to do good instead of being like sheep following the others? Do we dare to reject injustice, even if we end up alone?

Prayer: Lord, give us the courage to seek you and to do good without wanting to ingratiate ourselves with the world around us. In Jesus' name we pray. Amen.

Reflection:

Monday, October 15, 2012

Job 38:1-7, (34-41)

Then the Lord answered Job out of the whirlwind: "Who is this that darkens counsel by words without knowledge? Gird up your loins like a man, I will question you, and you shall declare to me. Where were you when I laid the foundation of the earth? Tell me, if you have understanding. Who determined its measurements — surely you know! Or who stretched the line upon it? On what were its bases sunk, or who laid its cornerstone when the morning stars sang together and all the heavenly beings shouted for joy? Can you lift up your voice to the clouds, so that a flood of waters may cover you? Can you send forth lightnings, so that they may go and say to you, 'Here we are'? Who has put wisdom in the inward parts, or given understanding to the mind? Who has the wisdom to number the clouds? Or who can tilt the waterskins of the heavens, when the dust runs into a mass and the clods cling together? Can you hunt the prey for the lion, or satisfy the appetite of the young lions, when they crouch in their dens, or lie in wait in their covert? Who provides for the raven its prey, when its young ones cry to God, and wander about for lack of food?"

Pondering and Meditating: Why do we think we know more than God and why do we dare to question God?

Prayer: Your creation, Lord, proclaims your greatness, your creation made by your hands helps us understand your love and perfect will. We thank you. Amen.

Reflection:

Tuesday, October 16, 2012

Isaiah 53:4-9

Surely he has borne our infirmities and carried our diseases; yet we accounted him stricken, struck down by God, and afflicted. But he was wounded for our transgressions, crushed for our iniquities; upon him was the punishment that made us whole, and by his bruises we are healed. All we like sheep have gone astray; we have all turned to our own way, and the Lord has laid on him the iniquity of us all. He was oppressed, and he was afflicted, yet he did not open his mouth; like a lamb that is led to the slaughter, and like a sheep that before its shearers is silent, so he did not open his mouth. By a perversion of justice he was taken away. Who could have imagined his future? For he was cut off from the land of the living, stricken for the transgression of my people. They made his grave with the wicked and his tomb with the rich, although he had done no violence, and there was no deceit in his mouth.

Pondering and Meditating: We assume that God sent his son, and that somehow we deserve it. In that attitude we become vain, proud and pretentious, which prevents us from being grateful and acting in a congruent manner with the great sacrifice of Jesus Do we understand the justice of God, are we just pleased with receiving everything in a passive way, or just get all we are happy with so passively?

Prayer: We celebrate the presence of God the Father, Jesus and the Holy Spirit every Sunday in our worship services, but, too often, we only come to receive and don't live according to the received blessings; loving and sharing with everyone as Jesus did. Lord, help us to have more fruits worthy of you. In the name of Jesus, we pray. Amen

Reflection:

Wednesday, October 17, 2012

Hebrews 4:1-10

And one does not presume to take this honor, but takes it only when called by God, just as Aaron was. So also Christ did not glorify himself in becoming a high priest, but was appointed by the one who said to him, "You are my Son, today I have begotten you;" as he says also in another place, "You are a priest forever, according to the order of Melchizedek." In the days of his flesh, Jesus offered up prayers and supplications, with loud cries and tears, to the one who was able to save him from death, and he was heard because of his reverent submission. Although he was a Son, he learned obedience through what he suffered; and having been made perfect, he became the source of eternal salvation for all who obey him, having been designated by God a high priest according to the order of Melchizedek.

Pondering and Meditating: Jesus learned obedience through what he suffered. Are we ready to learn to follow the example of Jesus? Do we know that the obedience that God requests from us will help us in this process of building the Kingdom of God?

Prayer: Lord every lesson is difficult when we are not ready, but the lesson of obedience is the most difficult. We love our things, our ideas, our values and we forget what you teach us. Please teach us the lesson of obedience, giving us the opportunity to serve, love and help as Jesus. Amen.

Reflection:

Mark 10:36-38, 40-45

And he said to them, "What is it you want me to do for you?" And they said to him, "Grant us to sit, one at your right hand and one at your left, in your glory." Then Jesus said to them, "The cup that I drink you will drink; and with the baptism with which I am baptized, you will be baptized; but to sit at my right hand or at my left is not mine to grant, but it is for those for whom it has been prepared." When the ten heard this, they began to be angry with James and John. So Jesus called them and said to them, "You know that among the Gentiles those whom they recognize as their rulers lord it over them, and their great ones are tyrants over them. But it is not so among you; but whoever wishes to become great among you must be your servant, and whoever wishes to be first among you must be slave of all. For the Son of Man came not to be served but to serve, and to give his life a ransom for many."

Pondering and Meditating: In this society we are taught that we must fight for everything and to achieve something we have to know how to play the game. Too often, like the sons of Zebedee, we politicize our principles. We believe that to be leaders we need to be in front and we fight and destroy. Like our fellow apostles, we do not know what we ask.

Prayer: We must be clear, "Help us not to play the game." Help us to know how to ask. We get confused so easily. Let the example of your Son Jesus show us the way. Amen.

Reflection:

Friday, October 19, 2012

Psalm 104:1-9

Bless the Lord, O my soul. ,O Lord my God, you are very great. You are clothed with honor and majesty, wrapped in light as with a garment. You stretch out the heavens like a tent, you set the beams of your chambers on the waters, you make the clouds your chariot, you ride on the wings of the wind, you make the winds your messengers, fire and flame your ministers. You set the earth on its foundations, so that it shall never be shaken. You cover it with the deep as with a garment; the waters stood above the mountains. At your rebuke they flee; at the sound of your thunder they take to flight. They rose up to the mountains, ran down to the valleys to the place that you appointed for them. You set a boundary that they may not pass, so that they might not again cover the earth.

Pondering and Meditating: Recognizing that everything around us proclaims the glory of God helps us to be more humble and position ourselves as God's creation. Actually, the challenge is to recognize that we are all brothers and sisters and there is no reason for wars or conflicts. It is a good exercise to sit quietly and enjoy God's creation in all its magnitude.

Prayer: Lord, give us the sensitivity of your presence in everything around us, including what we are not able to value and accept, because we do not understand it and in our ignorance we judge it and condemn it. Free us from those prejudices that enslave us and blind us. In Christ Jesus we pray. Amen.

Reflection:

Psalm 91:9-16

Because you have made the Lord your refuge, the Most High your dwelling-place, no evil shall befall you, no scourge come near your tent. For he will command his angels concerning you to guard you in all your ways. On their hands they will bear you up, so that you will not dash your foot against a stone. You will tread on the lion and the adder, the young lion and the serpent you will trample under foot. Those who love me, I will deliver; I will protect those who know my name. When they call to me, I will answer them; I will be with them in trouble, I will rescue them and honor them. With long life I will satisfy them, and show them my salvation.

Pondering and Meditating: What fascinates me with children is that they are able to fully trust what we say. Of course, they have no reason to distrust. If we have trusted in God's protection, nothing will be wrong. God's angels are watching over us by God's direct orders. Do we have a faith that is so profound and so simple, that of a child, or do we get consumed in the anguish of doubt and indecision?

Prayer: Blessed God, thank you for your care, protection and love. You even protect us from ourselves. Help us with our faith and increase it. Amen.

Reflection:

Sunday, October 21, 2012

Laity Sunday
Psalm 104:24, 35c

O Lord, how manifold are your works! In wisdom you have made them all; the earth is full of your creatures. Praise the Lord!

Pondering and Meditating: Praising God is something we must do everyday and at all times. Do we praise God no matter what the circumstances we find ourselves in? When we are sad, disappointed, angry, fighting, playing the game, then, definitely, we are not able to praise God. Too often, we get too busy with everything and we do not have time in our life to be in contact with our Creator.

Prayer: God, help us to get rid of everything that prevents us from praising you every day, from those things that disable us from recognizing your protection and care. I acknowledge that I worry so much that it blocks me from enjoying your presence with my whole being. Lord, thank you for everything. In Jesus Christ, Amen.

Reflection:

Monday, October 22, 2012

Job 42:1-2, 10-16

Then Job answered the Lord: "I know that you can do all things, and that no purpose of yours can be thwarted. And the Lord restored the fortunes of Job when he had prayed for his friends; and the Lord gave Job twice as much as he had before. Then there came to him all his brothers and sisters and all who had known him before, and they ate bread with him in his house; they showed him sympathy and comforted him for all the evil that the Lord had brought upon him; and each of them gave him a piece of money and a gold ring. The Lord blessed the latter days of Job more than his beginning; and he had fourteen thousand sheep, six thousand camels, a thousand yoke of oxen, and a thousand donkeys. He also had seven sons and three daughters. He named the first Jemimah, the second Keziah, and the third Keren-happuch. In all the land there were no women so beautiful as Job's daughters; and their father gave them an inheritance along with their brothers. After this Job lived for one hundred and forty years, and saw his children, and his children's children, four generations.

Pondering and Meditating: The process of recognizing and repenting is a great example given by Job. Do we dare to listen to the voice of God through everyone and everything around us?

Prayer: God, clean our inner being of those things that prevent us from listening to your voice. Lord, we need wisdom and knowledge to walk in your will. Amen.

Reflection:

Tuesday, October 23, 2012

Jeremiah 31:7-9

For thus says the Lord: Sing aloud with gladness for Jacob, and raise shouts for the chief of the nations; proclaim, give praise, and say, "Save, O Lord, your people, the remnant of Israel." See, I am going to bring them from the Land of the north, and gather them from the farthest parts of the earth, among them the blind and the lame, those with child and those in labor, together; a great company, they shall return here. With weeping they shall come, and with consolations I will lead them back, I will let them walk by brooks of water, in a straight path in which they shall not stumble; for I have become a father to Israel, and Ephraim is my firstborn.

Pondering and Meditating: When I came to this country 14 years ago, I learned that God's creation is so diverse and the ways of living are so different, and because of this many people cry and suffer. Then I realized the promise of consolation from God. He listens to his people who suffer, moan, wail and yearn for justice. Are we, as people of God and disciples of Jesus able to hear their cries? Of course, the temptation we have is that God hears our moans and suffering and will help us, and then we forget about others who suffer.

Prayer: My God and God of the whole world, do not let us believe that we are the center of the universe and that everything revolves around us. Lead us not into the temptation of thinking that everything you did, you did for us alone and just forget about those around us. Help us to be sensitive and also help those who suffer in your name. Amen.

Reflection:

Wednesday, October 24, 2012

Hebrews 7:23-28

Furthermore, the former priests were many in number, because they were prevented by death from continuing in office; but he holds his priesthood permanently, because he continues forever. Consequently he is able for all time to save those who approach God through him, since he always lives to make intercession for them. For it was fitting that we should have such a high priest, holy, blameless, undefiled, separated from sinners, and exalted above the heavens. Unlike the other high priests, he has no need to offer sacrifices day after day, first for his own sins, and then for those of the people; this he did once for all when he offered himself. For the Law appoints as high priests those who are subject to weakness, but the word of the oath, which came later than the law, appoints a Son who has been made perfect forever.

Pondering and Meditating: I always joke in the congregation, saying that nobody is perfect, and therefore all are welcome. What happens when we really believe that we are perfect and we dare to judge, condemn and reject anyone who is different from us or thinks differently? Do we really accept that the only perfect one is Christ and no one else?

Prayer: We rejoice in the perfection of your Son, Jesus, because thanks to him, we can come before you; since in his perfection Jesus was an acceptable sacrifice to you. In Christ Jesus we pray. Amen.

Reflection:

Mark 10:46-52

They came to Jericho. As he and his disciples and a large crowd were leaving Jericho, Bartimaeus son of Timaeus, a blind beggar, was sitting by the roadside. When he heard that it was Jesus of Nazareth, he began to shout out and say, "Jesus, Son of David, have mercy on me!" Many sternly ordered him to be quiet, but he cried out even more loudly, "Son of David, have mercy on me!" Jesus stood still and said, "Call him here." And they called the blind man, saying to him, "Take heart; get up, he is calling you." So throwing off his cloak, he sprang up and came to Jesus. Then Jesus said to him, "What do you want me to do for you?" The blind man said to him, "My teacher, let me see again." Jesus said to him, "Go; your faith has made you well." Immediately he regained his sight and followed him on the way.

Pondering and Meditating: The blind man did not hesitate to leave his cloak and go to Jesus when he was called. He knew what he wanted. What things keep us from obeying the call of God? What are we unable to leave because we are used to or enslaved by those things? When God asks us what do we need, are we speechless because we do not know what we need? We know what we want, but that is not the same?

Prayer: Lord, when you have heard us and called us by name, and we get caught up in our lives, our fears and passions. We are unable to move. Please help us have the courage to get away from what hinders us in answering your call. Give us the clarity to understand what we need, and not what we want. In Christ Jesus we pray. Amen.

Reflection:

Friday, October 26, 2012

Psalm 34:1-8

(Of David, when he feigned madness before Abimelech, so that he drove him out, and he went away.)I will bless the Lord at all times; his praise shall continually be in my mouth. My soul makes its boast in the Lord; let the humble hear and be glad. O magnify the Lord with me, and let us exalt his name together. I sought the Lord, and he answered me, and delivered me from all my fears. Look to him, and be radiant; so your faces shall never be ashamed. This poor soul cried, and was heard by the Lord, and was saved from every trouble. The angel of the Lord encamps around those who fear him, and delivers them. O taste and see that the Lord is good; happy are those who take refuge in him.

Pondering and Meditating: David praises God after being chased. When we are persecuted or driven by our position or way of thinking? How do we react?

Prayer: Lord, we praise you because your presence is with us. You are so good that at any moment, when we walk together, you help us and give us shelter in difficult situations. In Christ Jesus we pray. Amen.

Reflection:

Psalm 126

When the Lord restored the fortunes of Zion, we were like those who dream. Then our mouth was filled with laughter, and our tongue with shouts of joy; then it was said among the nations, "The Lord has done great things for them." The Lord has done great things for us, and we rejoiced. Restore our fortunes, O Lord, like the watercourses in the Negeb. May those who sow in tears reap with shouts of joy. Those who go out weeping, bearing the seed for sowing, shall come home with shouts of joy, carrying their sheaves.

Pondering and Meditating: I remember when I was young and we were invited to preach or share the Gospel with someone else, and I always argued that it was not my responsibility, but the pastor's. Now that I am pastor and people come with the same argument, I say what I learned in those years, that the work of sowing and sharing the good news of the Kingdom of God here and now, is for all those of us who say we are disciples of Jesus..

Prayer: Lord, to plant with joy and weeping is an experience we all need. We want to share the Good News. May your spirit help us grow. In Christ Jesus we pray. Amen

Reflection:

Sunday, October 28, 2012

Psalm 34:19-22

Many are the afflictions of the righteous, but the Lord rescues them from them all. He keeps all their bones; not one of them will be broken. Evil brings death to the wicked, and those who hate the righteous will be condemned. The Lord redeems the life of his servants; none of those who take refuge in him will be condemned.

Pondering and Meditating: Are you doing what is right or wrong? According to David, the consequences are clear. Are we righteous according to the ethical values of the Kingdom of God, or our own cultural values? Are we falling to the temptation to evade the consequences of being fair because we do not like to suffer?

Prayer: Lord, the way of righteousness is narrow, but that's where we will walk. We are not asking to receive justice, but we do ask to live as Christ, as you care for us. In Christ Jesus we pray. Amen.

Reflection:

NOVEMBER

Bishop Sally Dyck

Recurring themes appear in this month's lectionary texts as the Christian year comes to an end.

Those considered outsiders – primarily women and specifically foreign women – faithfully respond to God and enter the story of our salvation. Ruth is a foreigner who attaches herself to her mother-in-law and by doing so, gives life to the two of them, but also to the future Messiah. The widow of Zarephath is an outsider by race, culture and gender and she doesn't even rate a name. Yet she is the one who cares for Elijah and by doing so experiences the abundance of God. Another nameless woman at the Temple gives her all and Jesus recognizes her generosity. Hannah is one of the women in the Scriptures who is unable to bear a child and so, although she is an Israelite, she too is an outsider until her prayer and promise are fulfilled.

Another theme in these passages is the freedom our salvation brings us. We are free from fear and free of all barriers to God. Therefore, we can have a close and personal relationship with God through Jesus Christ in our worship. The question that keeps getting raised is whether we keep the path to God barrier-free for others.

The apocalyptic passages from Daniel and Revelation can seem mysterious and other worldly but when we understand them in the context of chaotic and troubled times, they resonate with us.

David (in 2 Samuel 23:1-5) and Hannah's songs as well as the Psalms, remind us that without justice for the poor and needy, there is no true worship because God is the God of justice as well as the God who comforts us.

Ruth 1:1-2b

In the days when the judges ruled, there was a famine in the land, and a certain man of Bethlehem in Judah went to live in the country of Moab, he and his wife and two sons. They went into the country of Moab and remained there.

Pondering and Meditating: There was no bread in the "house of bread," the literal name for Bethlehem. What does it mean when there's no bread in the bakery? People are spiritually famished in our communities. Is the church like a bakery without bread at times? How do we make sure that people can find bread – that which spiritually satisfies – in our house of bread?

Prayer: O Bread of Life, teach us to be a spiritual bakery for our community, offering sustenance that "fills the hungry with good things." Amen.

Reflection:

Tuesday, October 30, 2012

Deuteronomy 6:4-5, 8-9

Hear, O Israel: The Lord is our God, the Lord alone. You shall love the Lord your God with all your heart, and with all your soul, and with all your might…Bind (these words) as a sign on your hand, fix them as an emblem on your forehead, and write them on the doorposts of your house and on your gates.

Pondering and Meditating: The people were to bind the commandment to love God with their heart, soul and might to their hands, foreheads and doorposts. In the midst of the thousands of messages that we receive each day, how are we reminded everyday and throughout the day of the commandment to love God?

Prayer: Open our eyes to see you in all creation, people and situations in our lives throughout the day so that we may always know your presence and hear the call to love you. Give us spiritual creativity to see and to place signs and symbols in our lives that turn our hearts to you. Amen.

Reflection:

Deuteronomy 6:6-7

Keep these words that I am commanding you today in your heart. Recite them to your children and talk about them when you are at home and when you are away, when you lie down and when you rise.

Pondering and Meditating: The commandment to love God with one's whole heart, soul and might wasn't to be kept to oneself, but to commend to others, particularly the next generation. Reminders of God's presence in our lives are meant to do more than inspire or encourage our own faith but to teach and guide others' faith. How do you commend the faith that is within you to the next generation? In your family? In your faith community?

Prayer: O loving God, who first loved us, remind, encourage and teach us to commend the faith that is within us to the next generation. May our faith be as natural as breathing and our sharing of it as natural as relating the news of our day. Amen.

Reflection:

Hebrews 9:11-14

But when Christ came as a high priest of the good things that have come, then through the greater and perfect tent (not made with hands, that is, not of this creation), he entered once for all into the Holy Place, not with the blood of goats and calves, but with his own blood, thus obtaining eternal redemption. For if the blood of goats and bulls, with the sprinkling of the ashes of a heifer, sanctifies those who have been defiled so that their flesh is purified, how much more will the blood of Christ, who through the eternal Spirit offered himself without blemish to God, purify our conscience from dead works to worship the living God!

Pondering and Meditating: The cross cleared the way for us so that we can freely and fully worship God, assured of God's love. Yet we continue to put barriers between us and God; and worse, between others and God. What attitudes, practices or behaviors do we place between ourselves and God or between God and others?

Prayer: Like a divine bulldozer, you have removed all the obstacles, hurdles and barriers between us and you, O God. Help us to live freely and fully in your grace so that we will remove obstacles, hurdles and barriers for others who long for your redeeming grace. Amen.

Reflection:

Friday, November 2, 2012

Mark 12:28-32, 33b-34

One of the scribes came near and heard them disputing with one another, and seeing that he answered them well, he asked him, "Which commandment is the first of all?" Jesus answered, "The first is, 'Hear, O Israel: the Lord our God, the Lord is one; you shall love the Lord your God with all your heart, and with all your soul, and with all your mind, and with all your strength.' The second is this, 'You shall love your neighbor as yourself.' There is no other commandment greater than these." Then the scribe said to him, "You are right, Teacher; you have truly said that 'he is one, and besides him there is no other'; and 'to love him with all the heart, and with all the understanding, and with all the strength, and to love one's neighbor as oneself,' – this is much more important than all whole burnt offerings and sacrifices." When Jesus saw that he answered wisely, he said to him, "You are not far from the Kingdom of God." After that no one dared to ask him any question.

Pondering and Meditating: The scribe "gets it." Love for God and for one's neighbor is the essence of true religion. What gets in the way of loving God and neighbor and causes us to wander far from the Kingdom of God? How have you learned to love your neighbors – the ones who are hard to love?

Prayer: O God of love, help us to love you more dearly by loving our neighbor in word and action. Let us always err on the side of love and grace, even when we're uncertain about how to respond to others we don't understand, know or naturally love. Fill us with your love that we may love you and our neighbor. Amen.

Reflection:

Psalm 146:1-2

Praise the Lord! Praise the Lord, O my soul! I will praise the Lord as long as I live; I will sing praises to my God all my life long.

Pondering and Meditating: "I will sing praises to my God all my life long." Really? When nothing seems to be going my way, in times of doubt and suffering, in times of destitution and affluence, in all things, will I really sing praises to God? When do I fail to "sing praises to my God?" Is it possible that when I'm least likely to sing praises that I need to sing praises until I experience gratitude and then because I am grateful, I will sing praises?

Prayer: O God, help me to start each day with praises in my heart and on my lips so that whether I am happy or sad, rich or poor, struggling or enjoying life, having a good or bad day, I will praise you all my life long, day in and day out. Amen.

Reflection:

Sunday, November 4, 2012

Psalm 119:1-5

Happy are those whose way is blameless, who walk in the law of the Lord. Happy are those who keep his decrees, who seek him with their whole heart, who also do no wrong, but walk in his ways. You have commanded your precepts to be kept diligently. O that my ways may be steadfast in keeping your statutes!

Pondering and Meditating: When we think of the law as a duty and rules, we miss the spirit of this psalm. The law was the way of the Lord, and we are called to walk the way of God. What keeps you on course in your walk with God? What signposts guide you? What detours do you keep taking?

Prayer: You are the way but also the signpost and the companion along the way. Guide me through the detours of life when I veer from your direction and guidance. Even then, help me to grow in compassion and grace toward others as a result of the detours I have taken. Amen.

Reflection:

Ruth 3:1-2, 4-5, 13, 17

Naomi her mother-in-law said to her, "My daughter, I need to seek some security for you, so that it may be well with you. Now here is our kinsman Boaz, with whose young women you have been working. See, he is winnowing barley tonight at the threshing floor… When he lies down, observe the place where he lies; then, go and uncover his feet and lie down; and he will tell you what to do." She said to her, "All that you tell me I will do … " So Boaz took Ruth and she became his wife. When they came together, the Lord made her conceive, and she bore a son … The women of the neighborhood gave him a name, saying, "A son has been born to Naomi." They named him Obed; he became the father of Jesse, the father of David.

Pondering and Meditating: As a foreigner, Ruth took her place in our salvation history because she listened to the wisdom of her mother-in-law and also took initiative herself. When we feel "out of it," as individuals or a church, who do we listen to who will empower and direct us? How do we risk taking the initiative to make a new life, go a new direction, and find a new way?

Prayer: O God of power and might, help us to listen to you, to those around us, and resolve to risk and thereby find ourselves empowered and strengthened to do amazing, surprising and unexpected things. Free us from victimhood as individuals and as faith communities so that we can be empowered to bring forth new life in your name. Amen.

Reflection:

Tuesday, November 6, 2012

1 Kings 17:8-11, 15-16

Then the word of the Lord came to him, saying, "Go now to Zarephath, which belongs to Sidon, and live there; for I have commanded a widow there to feed you." So he set out and went to Zarephath. When he came to the gate of the town, a widow was there gathering sticks; he called to her and said, "Bring me a little water in a vessel, so that I may drink." As she was going to bring it, he called to her and said, "Bring me a morsel of bread in your hand. ..." She went and did as Elijah said, so that she as well as he and her household ate for many days. The jar of meal was not emptied, neither did the jug of oil fail, according to the word of the Lord that he spoke by Elijah.

Pondering and Meditating: Centuries later Jesus asked, "Were there no widows in Israel who would care for Elijah?" Once again, an outsider to Judaism steps into our salvation history by listening and trusting. Who are those outside the walls of the church who are listening and trusting God for God's providence and abundance in their lives? What could we learn from them?

Prayer: As insiders of the faith, help us to see you working, O God, in the lives of "outsiders," people we wouldn't immediately regard as your servants. Give us humble hearts to accept from them what they have to offer us. Amen.

Reflection:

1 Kings 17:12-16

But (the widow of Zarephath) said (to Elijah), "As the Lord your God lives, I have nothing baked, only a handful of meal in a jar, and a little oil in a jug; I am now gathering a couple of sticks, so that I may go home and prepare it for myself and my son, that we may eat it, and die." Elijah said to her, "Do not be afraid; go and do as you have said; but first make me a little cake of it and bring it to me, and afterwards make something for yourself and your son. For thus says the Lord the God of Israel: The jar of meal will not be emptied and the jug of oil will not fail until the day that the Lord sends rain on the earth." She went and did as Elijah said, so that she as well as he and her household ate for many days. The jar of meal was not emptied, neither did the jug of oil fail, according to the word of the Lord that he spoke by Elijah.

Pondering and Meditation: The widow trusted the prophet's word not to fear and she gave the last supper that she and her son would have eaten to him but her resources never ran out because she trusted in God's abundance. Do we fear that the resources needed in life to care for our neighbors, to reach out to our communities, and to be fruitful in sharing God's love will run out?

Prayer: Abundant God, help us not to fear when our resources of time, strength and love seem to run low and scarce. Fill the jars of our hearts and the jugs of our energy so that we may keep serving you and yours. Amen.

Reflection:

Thursday, November 8, 2012

Hebrews 9:24-28

For Christ did not enter a sanctuary made by human hands, a mere copy of the true one, but he entered into heaven itself, now to appear in the presence of God on our behalf. Nor was it to offer himself again and again, as the high priest enters the Holy Place year after year with blood that is not his own; for then he would have had to suffer again and again since the foundation of the world. But as it is, he has appeared once for all at the end of the age to remove sin by the sacrifice of himself. And just as it is appointed for mortals to die once, and after that the judgment, so Christ, having been offered once to bear the sins of many, will appear a second time, not to deal with sin, but to save those who are eagerly waiting for him.

Pondering and Meditating: "No fear!" a Nike ad once proclaimed. Through the cross, we need not fear, worry or become preoccupied with our own salvation. We are free to serve and fully give ourselves away. What fear, needless worry and distracting preoccupation keeps you, or your church, from serving and fully giving yourself or your church away?

Prayer: O God, throughout our salvation history, your word to us through angels and messengers of all kinds has been to have "no fear!" Help us to live in faith, not fear; in trust, not worry; in rapt attention, not distracted by our preoccupations. Amen.

Reflection:

Friday, November 9, 2012

Mark 12:41-44

(Jesus) sat down opposite the treasury, and watched the crowd putting money into the treasury. Many rich people put in large sums. A poor widow came and put in two small copper coins, which are worth a penny. Then he called his disciples and said to them, "Truly I tell you, this poor widow has put in more than all those who are contributing to the treasury. For all of them have contributed out of their abundance; but she out of her poverty has put in everything she had, all she had to live on."

Pondering and Meditating: A child was asked what he learned in Sunday School. He said, "You can give a coin from your mother's purse or you can give everything that you have." Jesus watched people giving various amounts with various levels of commitment; a sliding scale of generosity. Where are you on the sliding scale of generosity?

Prayer: Abundant God, you give to us freely and fully. Help us to be generous in our giving to others who lack for basic needs, who need the hope of our contributions to rebuild destroyed communities, and who long for health and healing that we can provide. Whatever our means, give us generous hearts. Amen.

Reflection:

Saturday, November 10, 2012

Psalm 127:1-5

Unless the Lord builds the house, those who build it labor in vain. Unless the Lord guards the city, the guard keeps watch in vain. It is in vain that you rise up early and go late to rest, eating the bread of anxious toil; for he gives sleep to his beloved. Sons are indeed a heritage from the Lord, the fruit of the womb a reward. Like arrows in the hand of a warrior are the sons of one's youth. Happy is the man who has his quiver full of them. He shall not be put to shame when he speaks with his enemies in the gate.

Pondering and Meditating: "Life goes better with a plan," says the poster on the wall of a fitness center. Mission statements, goals and strategies are important in being faithful and fruitful in our discipleship. Yet unless God is the beginning and the end of the mission statement, the One behind the goals, and the Designer of the strategies, it will be in vain. How do we make sure our mission, goals and strategies as individuals and a church are built and watched over by God?

Prayer: Giver of all that we need to be faithful and fruitful in your work, be our inspiration, direction and guidance so that we may accomplish your will on earth as it is in heaven. Amen.

Reflection:

Sunday, November 11, 2012

Psalm 42:1-3, 11

As a deer longs for flowing streams, so my soul longs for you, O God. My soul thirsts for God, for the living God. When shall I come and behold the face of God? My tears have been my food day and night, while people say to me continually, "Where is your God?" Why are you cast down, O my soul, and why are you disquieted within me? Hope in God; for I shall again praise him, my help and my God.

Pondering and Meditating: More than anything else, we long for a personal experience of the Divine like a deer who goes from stream to stream in search of water. Where do people search for meaning and love in this culture? How do we offer streams of life-giving water in the deserts of our culture and in our lives?

Prayer: O God, you are the living water that gives us hope and help in our daily lives. When our souls are cast down, help us to drink deeply from the well of your love and grace so that we may praise you. Amen.

Reflection:

Monday, November 12, 2012

1 Samuel 1:4-5, 10-11, 17-18

On the day when Elkanah sacrificed, he would give portions to his wife Peninnah and to all her sons and daughters; but to Hannah he gave a double portion, because he loved her, though the Lord had closed her womb. … She was deeply distressed and prayed to the Lord, and wept bitterly. She made this vow: "O Lord of hosts, if only you will look on the misery of your servant, and remember me, and not forget your servant, but will give to your servant a male child, then I will set him before you as a nazirite until the day of his death. He shall drink neither wine nor intoxicants, and no razor shall touch his head. …" Then Eli answered, "Go in peace; the God of Israel grant the petition you have made to him." And she said, "Let your servant find favor in your sight."

Pondering and Meditating: Hannah wouldn't have been someone in her day and culture that would have exemplified favor in God's sight in many peoples' minds since she had not borne a child for her husband. Yet she dared to ask for God's favor. What does it mean to find favor in the sight of God? What do you dare to ask from God?

Prayer: O God, who favors all your children, help us to see how you have remembered and favored us with your blessing. And then, like Hannah, help us to give thanks to you for your many blessings and favors. Amen.

Reflection:

1 Samuel 1: 18b-20

Then (Hannah) went to her quarters, ate and drank with her husband, and her countenance was sad no longer. They rose early in the morning and worshiped before the Lord; then they went back to their house at Ramah. Elkanah knew his wife Hannah, and the Lord remembered her. In due time Hannah conceived and bore a son. She named him Samuel, for she said, "I have asked him of the Lord."

Pondering and Meditating: Through Hannah's prayer and commitment to God, she received and then offered her firstborn child back to God. What's the greatest gift you have ever given God? Or that God is asking of you? What's the greatest gift your church could give God?

Prayer: O God, you gave your Son as the greatest gift to us and we thank you for Jesus, the giver of our life and salvation. Give us courage to ask of you what we need to faithfully follow you and to bring help and hope to the world as Hannah did. Amen.

Reflection:

Wednesday, November 14, 2012

1 Samuel 2:1-2, 7-10

Hannah prayed and said, "My heart exults in the Lord; my strength is exalted in my God. My mouth derides my enemies, because I rejoice in my victory. There is no Holy One like the Lord, no one besides you; there is no Rock like our God. ...The Lord makes poor and makes rich; he brings low, he also exalts. He raises up the poor from the dust; he lifts the needy from the ash heap, to make them sit with princes and inherit a seat of honor. For the pillars of the earth are the Lord's, and on them he has set the world. He will guard the feet of his faithful ones, but the wicked shall be cut off in darkness; for not by might does one prevail. The Lord! His adversaries shall be shattered; the Most High will thunder in heaven. The Lord will judge the ends of the earth; he will give strength to his king, and exalt the power of his anointed."

Pondering and Meditating: Hannah's song gives thanks to God not just for her own victory, but because God repeatedly lifts up the laborers, those who are hungry, the barren, those who are dead, the poor and needy. Hannah identifies with these and gives thanks. How does our relative affluence and influence keep us from identifying with the neediest and therefore keep us from singing praises to God?

Prayer: O God who cares for the laborers, the hungry, the barren, those who are lifeless, poor and needy. Help us to identify with these, your loved ones. Give us eyes to see them in our daily lives and hearts to help. In Jesus' name we pray, Amen.

Reflection:

Daniel 12:1-3

At that time Michael, the great prince, the protector of your people, shall arise. There shall be a time of anguish, such as has never occurred since nations first came into existence. But at that time your people shall be delivered, everyone who is found written in the book. Many of those who sleep in the dust of the earth shall awake, some to everlasting life, and some to shame and everlasting contempt. Those who are wise shall shine like the brightness of the sky, and those who lead many to righteousness, like the stars forever and ever.

Pondering and Meditating: The angel, Michael, is a champion for the people. Angels aren't just supernatural forces but people in our midst who are wise and have lived well, guiding us with their wisdom and counsel. Who are the saints or angels in your life? In the community of faith where you attend?

Prayer: Thank you, O God, for the angels you send us who have given us wisdom to live and serve. Help us to recognize the many ways that your angels have dwelt among us and guided us, never leaving us alone. Amen.

Reflection:

Friday, November 16, 2012

Hebrews 10:23-25

Let us hold fast to the confession of our hope without wavering, for he who has promised is faithful. And let us consider how to provoke one another to love and good deeds, not neglecting to meet together, as is the habit of some, but encouraging one another, and all the more as you see the Day approaching.

Pondering and Meditation: We are empowered and encouraged to be inventive, innovative entrepreneurs of doing good for others. What would be an inventive and innovative act of kindness and goodness that you and your church are called to do to let your community know of your care for them?

Prayer: Inspire us to be inventive and innovative in our acts of kindness and goodness toward others – those we know and those we don't know. Help us to provoke one another to love and do good deeds, quick to help and to give hope. Amen.

Reflection:

Mark 13:5-8

Then Jesus began to say to them, "Beware that no one leads you astray. Many will come in my name and say, "I am he!' and they will lead many astray. When you hear of wars and rumors of wars, do not be alarmed; this must take place, but the end is still to come. For nation will rise against nation, and kingdom against kingdom; there will be earthquakes in various places; there will be famines. This is but the beginning of the birth pangs.

Pondering and Meditating: In a rapidly changing, chaotic world, it's easy to become like Chicken Little, fearful that the sky is falling around us. She led barnyard animals to their death through her fear, except for Henny Penny who heard the cock crow, headed back to the hen house to do her faithful duty and was saved. How have you and your church been like Chicken Little in the last few years? Who has helped you be more like Henny Penny?

Prayer: When there seems to be nothing but alarming change and catastrophe around us, O God, help us to keep faithfully at our task of being your disciples and making disciples. Let the confidence that we have in being your children, make us more like Henny Penny than Chicken Little. Amen.

Reflection:

Sunday, November 18, 2012

Psalm 16: 5, 8-11

The Lord is my chosen portion and my cup; you hold my lot. … I keep the Lord always before me; because he is at my right hand, I shall not be moved. Therefore my heart is glad, and my soul rejoices; my body also rests secure. For you do not give me up to Sheol, or let your faithful one see the Pit. You show me the path of life. In your presence there is fullness of joy; in your right hand are pleasures forevermore.

Pondering and Meditating: A portion sounds like a piece or part of the whole. Yet in Hebrew portion means our inheritance. All that is God's is ours; all that God gives us is what we need. There is no piece or part to God's grace; only the whole of it. What are ways that you find yourself feeling like you just got a piece or part of God's grace instead of the whole grace upon grace? How does your faith community seek to give grace upon grace to others?

Prayer: Gracious God, the whole of your grace surrounds and sustains us, grace upon grace. Help us to act out of abundance in our love, graciousness and compassion instead of scarcity. Amen.

Reflection:

2 Samuel 23:1a, 2-5

Now these are the last words of David. … The spirit of the Lord speaks through me, his word is upon my tongue. The God of Israel has spoken, the Rock of Israel has said to me: One who rules over people justly, ruling in the fear of God, is like the light of morning, like the sun rising on a cloudless morning, gleaming from the rain on the grassy land. Is not my house like this with God? For he has made with me an everlasting covenant, ordered in all things and secure. Will he not cause to prosper all my help and my desire?

Pondering and Meditating: These were the last words of David. They reveal what he aspired to in his living and leading. What strikes you about these words? Who do you think they were meant for? What would be the last words you would say that reveal what you aspire to in life, leading and loving God and others?

Prayer: As we live each day of our lives, O God, help us to live out what we aspire to in our living, leading and loving. May there be congruence between what we say and how we live. Amen.

Reflection:

Tuesday, November 20, 2012

Daniel 7:9-10

As I watched, thrones were set in place, and an Ancient One took his throne, his clothing was white as snow, and the hair of his head like pure wool; his throne was fiery flames, and its wheels were burning fire. A stream of fire issued and flowed out from his presence. A thousand thousands served him, and ten thousand times ten thousand stood attending him. The court sat in judgment, and the books were opened.

Pondering and Meditating: These verses provide an image to remind people in the midst of troubled times that God is still in charge. No matter how chaotic the powerful political, economic, social, and even religious institutions and organizations may be, God still reigns. How do we know and trust in that promise during the political, economic, social and religious turmoil we find ourselves in today? What images would you use?

Prayer: Almighty God, though the earth quakes and the seas roar in our lives, remind us of your rock-solid presence and support. Help us to trust that no matter what political, economic, social or religious turmoil threatens us, you are our support and strength. Amen.

Reflection:

Daniel 7:13-14

As I watched in the night visions, I saw one like a human being coming with the clouds of heaven. And he came to the Ancient One and was presented before him. To him was given dominion and glory and kingship, that all peoples, nations, and languages should serve him. His dominion is an everlasting dominion that shall not pass away, and his kingship is one that shall never be destroyed.

Pondering and Meditating: God's grace is an invitation to all people – all nations and languages, ethnicities and races. It's an inclusive grace that knows no boundaries but invites all to come and dwell in the presence of God. Why do we keep trying to limit who is invited and called to dwell in the Kingdom of God? Who is God calling us to include in God's Kingdom?

Prayer: Open our hearts to all people, nations and languages, those we know and understand as well as those we don't. Keep the limitations of our hearts and minds from limiting others' access and relationship to you. May your glory and power reign forever, beginning with us, now and forever. Amen.

Reflection:

Revelation 1:4-8

John to the seven churches that are in Asia: Grace to you and peace from him who is and who was and who is to come, and from the seven spirits who are before his throne, and from Jesus Christ, the faithful witness, the firstborn of the dead, and the ruler of the kings of the earth. To him who loves us and freed us from our sins by his blood, and made us to be a kingdom, priests serving his God and Father, to him be glory and dominion forever and ever. Amen. Look! He is coming with the clouds; every eye will see him, even those who pierced him; and on his account all the tribes of the earth will wail. So it is to be. Amen. "I am the Alpha and the Omega," says the Lord God, who is and who was and who is to come, the Almighty.

Pondering and Meditating: It's the in-between times that require faith. We can see God in yesterday, we hope for God in tomorrow, but where is God today, now, in the in-between times; right here, right now? How do we trust in the present moment without the benefit of 20/20 hindsight or the not-yet experience of God's presence in the future?

Prayer: God of yesterday, today and forever, help us to live fully today by letting go of yesterday and not fearing tomorrow. Give us what we need for each moment of every day to experience you. Amen.

Reflection:

John 18:33-37

Then Pilate entered the headquarters again, summoned Jesus, and asked him, "Are you the King of the Jews?" Jesus answered, "Do you ask this on your own, or did others tell you about me?" Pilate replied, "I am not a Jew, am I? Your own nation and the chief priests have handed you over to me. What have you done?" Jesus answered, "My kingdom is not from this world. If my kingdom were from this world, my followers would be fighting to keep me from being handed over to the Jews. But as it is, my kingdom is not from here." Pilate asked him, "So you are a king?" Jesus answered, "You say that I am a king. For this I was born, and for this I came into the world, to testify to the truth. Everyone who belongs to the truth listens to my voice."

Pondering and Meditating: Pilate's response to Jesus was to ask, "What is truth?" In any given moment of our lives, we don't know the whole truth about what others are thinking and doing, just as Pilate didn't know. Yet we know that God has given us the truth we need to follow Jesus. What uncertainties do you have about the truth of following Jesus? What gives you faith to stand firm and to trust in what God has for you?

Prayer: O God of truth, speak to our hearts and minds so that we may live out your truth in the world; a truth that is often counter to the conventional wisdom of our world. Amen.

Reflection:

Saturday, November 24, 2012

Psalm 132:1-5, 14-18

O Lord, remember in David's favor all the hardships he endured; how he swore to the Lord and vowed to the Mighty One of Jacob, "I will not enter my house or get into my bed; I will not give sleep to my eyes or slumber to my eyelids, until I find a place for the Lord, a dwelling place for the Mighty One of Jacob." … (Says the Lord), "This is my resting place forever; here I will reside, for I have desired it. I will abundantly bless its provisions; I will satisfy its poor with bread. Its priests I will clothe with salvation, and its faithful will shout for joy. There I will cause a horn to sprout up for David; I have prepared a lamp for my anointed one. His enemies I will clothe with disgrace, but on him, his crown will gleam."

Pondering and Meditating: King David's driving force at the end of his life was to provide a resting place or a place of worship for God. How much do we long to provide a place for God to abide, especially a place of worship that is also a place of justice for the poor? What would make our place of worship a place of justice for the poor?

Prayer: O God of justice and mercy, give us the desire that King David had to make a place of worship for you in our lives that is also a place of justice for those in need. Consecrate our house of worship as a house of justice. Amen.

Reflection:

Psalm 93:1-5

The Lord is king, he is robed in majesty; the Lord is robed, he is girded with strength. He has established the world; it shall never be moved; your throne is established from of old; you are from everlasting. The floods have lifted up, O Lord, the floods have lifted up their voice; the floods lift up their roaring. More majestic than the thunders of mighty waters, more majestic than the waves of the sea, majestic on high is the Lord! Your decrees are very sure; holiness befits your house, O Lord, forevermore.

Pondering and Meditating: The floods represent overwhelming chaos, but God is stronger and mightier than the mightiest of chaotic waters. What represents the chaotic waters or floods in your life? In your community of faith? How do you know that God's holiness continues to abide in the midst of the chaos?

Prayer: O God, who stills the storms and the seas, calm the chaos in our hearts so that we may forever give witness to your mighty power and love. Help us to live like people who know and believe that you are a never-ending source of strength now and forever. Amen.

Reflection:

DECEMBER 2012

Rev. Sherrin Marshall

This is Advent. We are waiting. Waiting is difficult for everyone, whether we are waiting to be old enough for a learner's permit to drive, for medical tests that may be life-changing or for a new baby to be born. Every now and then we may feel we've been overlooked as others are summoned before us. In our humanness, we are more eager to arrive than to wait. Regardless of how many times in our lives we have anticipated the birth and coming again of the infant Jesus and the Savior Christ, something about this time of year is both new and renewing – if only we can let it come to us.

Our readings begin with the expected promise – the Lord's assurance to his people, that they have not been forgotten, that the One who is to come will celebrate the Jubilee, bringing righteousness. It is no longer business as usual, but the call to be about God's holy business, called, as Paul's letter to the church at Thessalonica says, to "strengthen our hearts in holiness that we may be blameless before our God at the coming of our Lord Jesus Christ with all his Saints."

Show us how we are to do that, Lord, with the myriad concerns and responsibilities in our lives, engrossed in self-absorption and minutia. You summon us to stop, reflect, pray, to hear your voice in stillness, to find Christ at the Mall, in the Christmas preparations, in the sharing of food with the hungry and the homeless. We are called to seek out the saints everywhere, and most of all, called to wait upon the Lord, as Mary did, awaiting the birth.

Christmas will come with joy and gladness, if we remember the babe born small and helpless, far from home. Christmas will not end for us on December 25, but remain God's gift of love and grace, with us forever.

Psalm 25:5

Lead me in your truth and teach me, for you are the God of my salvation; for you I wait all day long.

Pondering and Meditating: We are often unaware of holy waiting, waiting that affirms and demonstrates our reliance on the Lord above all. What are you waiting for as the holiday season is upon us and the year draws to an end? How can we choose, as followers of the God of salvation, that which will make us more aware that the God for whom we wait is present even now, in this moment? How can we be more open to the indwelling God?

Prayer: O Lord, still our anxious hearts; calm our souls; give us wisdom to know your teachings and truth, that we may find our center in you. Give us, we pray, the awareness to live into holy waiting. Amen.

Reflection:

Tuesday, November 27, 2012

Luke 21: 25-28

There will be signs in the sun, the moon, and the stars, and on the earth distress among nations confused by the roaring of the sea and the waves. People will faint from fear and foreboding of what is coming upon the world, for the powers of the heavens will be shaken. Then they will see 'the Son of Man coming in a cloud' with power and great glory. Now when these things begin to take place, stand up and raise your heads, because your redemption is drawing near.

Pondering and Meditating: When the Son of Man returns with power and great glory, the message to us is clear: we are not to fall flat on our faces and grovel in the dust. Rather, we are called to stand and raise our heads, for God has come to save us. What in your life makes you feel like fainting from fear rather than standing tall?

Prayer: Dear Lord, help us to believe that your love for us is boundless and that we can stand in your sight, because you stand with us and hold us fast. Amen.

Reflection:

Wednesday, November 28, 2012

1 Thessalonians 3:11-13

Now may our God and Father himself and our Lord Jesus direct our way to you. And may the Lord make you increase and abound in love for one and all, just as we abound in love for you. And may he so strengthen your hearts in holiness that you may be blameless before our God and Father at the coming of our Lord Jesus with all his saints.

Pondering and Meditating: Lord, help us, your people, find our way to you. You call us, but we sometimes turn away or even turn our backs. What keeps you from finding your way to God? Think about a time you unexpectedly found God waiting for you. Reflect, also, on the times you turned away.

Prayer: Lord, shed your mercy upon us as we seek to know you more fully and love you more deeply, for when we seek to love you and love one another, we will recognize you as Lord of our lives. God of challenge and grace, lead us beyond our comfort zones to better embrace you and your love for all your children. Amen.

Reflection:

Thursday, November 29, 2012

1 Thessalonians 3:9

How can we thank God enough for you in return for all the joy that we feel before our God because of you?

Pondering and Meditating: Is Thanksgiving just another day for us, or do we build thankfulness into our daily lives? What acts of thanksgiving is God calling you to today? Paul thanks God for the Thessalonians and their help to him, and he says he can never thank God enough. Do we remember to thank God for the goodness of others?

Prayer: Our gratitude toward God is evidenced by actions, often unexpected, that bring thanksgiving and joy to our hearts. Lord, grant us grace to give thanks with our lips and in our hearts, as we thank you and our brothers and sisters for the blessings they bring to us. Amen.

Reflection:

Friday, November 30, 2012

Jeremiah 33: 14-15

The days are surely coming, says the Lord, when I will fulfill the promise I made to the house of Israel and the house of Judah. In those days and at that time I will cause a righteous Branch to spring up for David, and he shall execute justice and righteousness in the land.

Pondering and Meditating: Jeremiah lived and wrote in a grim time, and he has repeatedly prophesied doom and judgment to the people of Israel. But here, he promises and testifies that a "righteous Branch will spring up for David." How often do we conclude that there is no life to be had, when something appears to be dead? Does this sometimes make it impossible for new life to come and be born again? How do you feel when you come to that conclusion – discouraged? Sad? Hopeless?

Prayer: God of surprising hope and extraordinary miracles, help us to see and know that though your saving acts are not apparent to us, you are at work always and everywhere, in our lives and in our world. Amen.

Reflection:

Saturday, December 1, 2012

Psalm 25:7

Do not remember the sins of my youth or my transgressions; according to your steadfast love remember me, for your goodness' sake, O Lord!

Pondering and Meditating: We each bear burdens over errors of omission and commission, the times we participated in wrongdoing and the times we stood by and watched. These sins and transgressions can paralyze us. Has there been a time in your life when you desperately needed pardon from God, but did not know how to ask? Has there been a time when pardon was granted, and then wasted or ignored?

Prayer: Loving Lord, just as you pardon us through your steadfast love which is unfailing, help us to pardon ourselves. Set us free, Lord, to carry your good news to all. Amen.

Reflection:

Luke 21:29-36

Then he told them a parable: "Look at the fig tree and all the trees; as soon as they sprout leaves you can see for yourselves and know that summer is already near. So also, when you see these things taking place, you know that the kingdom of God is near. Truly I tell you, this generation will not pass away until all things have taken place. Heaven and earth will pass away, but my words will not pass away. Be on guard so that your hearts are not weighed down with dissipation and drunkenness and the worries of this life, and that day catch you unexpectedly, like a trap. For it will come upon all who live on the face of the whole earth. Be alert at all times, praying that you may have the strength to escape all these things that will take place, and to stand before the Son of Man."

Pondering and Meditating: Jesus shares a parable that is filled with signs: trees, sprouting leaves, weights upon our hearts, being caught in a trap of our own making. Can we experience signs of new life and growth even as we approach winter? How do you identify these signs, and what helps you become aware that the kingdom of God is drawing near? What causes us to miss these signs and take the "wrong turn?"

Prayer: O Lord, you are the God of surprises and eternal hope. Make our hearts light, we pray, and not weighed down. Wake us from our slumber and may we be alert even for your coming again in glory. Amen.

Reflection:

Monday, December 3, 2012

Luke 1:72-75

Thus he has shown the mercy promised to our ancestors, and has remembered his holy covenant, the oath that he swore to our ancestor Abraham, to grant us "that we, being rescued from the hands of our enemies, might serve him without fear, in holiness and righteousness before him all our days."

Pondering and Meditating: What meaning does the word "covenant" have for us today? How do you reconcile that word with the grace that God offers generously and unrelentingly to us, for God offered this love to our ancestors long ago? Have you ever felt yourself to be rescued by God from an enemy? How did you know that? In what way did you respond?

Prayer: Lord of boundless love and salvation, we praise you for your oath and covenant, blessing your holy name for delivering your people from every enemy that confronts us. God of love, we cannot thank you enough for your gifts of faithfulness, salvation and peace. May our hearts and tongues give voice for all you have done and still do for us, now and forever. Amen.

Reflection:

Tuesday, December 4, 2012

Luke 1:76-79

And you, child, will be called the prophet of the Most High; for you will go before the Lord to prepare his ways, to give knowledge of salvation to his people by the forgiveness of their sins. By the tender mercy of our God, the dawn from on high will break upon us, to give light to those who sit in darkness and in the shadow of death, to guide our feet in the way of peace.

Pondering and Meditating: We hear in this passage Zechariah's prophecy of great things to come. John the Baptist is a tiny baby when his father shares this testimony; John is the one who will go before the Lord. We are always called to walk with Jesus, to kneel in faith, to believe in hope, to pray for the coming of the Savior. And yet, we know we can find ourselves sitting in darkness and in the shadow of death. This prophecy came at a time when the temple in Jerusalem had been destroyed and the good news about Jesus was spreading beyond the borders of Palestine. What can we learn about light in darkness and the way of peace from that time and place?

Prayer: Powerful God of plenty and peace, your wish for us is salvation and hope. Fill our hearts with faith and joy as we await the one who was, and is, and is to come, Jesus the Christ. Amen.

Reflection:

Philippians 1:3-5

I thank my God every time I remember you, constantly praying with joy in every one of my prayers for all of you, because of your sharing in the gospel from the first day until now.

Pondering and Meditating: There are tangible ways that God challenges us to share in the Gospel – prayer, witness, testifying, preaching and teaching. What are some of the ways you have been blessed when you have shared the Gospel with someone else? Is there someone for whom you thank God because that person shared the Gospel with you?

Prayer: Holy Lord, you bring your blessing to us as we share your message. We pray that you give us humility and a heart to serve you as we open the Gospel message at all times and in all places – as St. Francis said, if necessary, using words. Amen.

Reflection:

Thursday, December 6, 2012

Malachi 3:1-3

See, I am sending my messenger to prepare the way before me, and the Lord whom you seek will suddenly come to his temple. The messenger of the covenant in whom you delight – indeed, he is coming, says the Lord of hosts. But who can endure the day of his coming, and who can stand when he appears? For he is like a refiner's fire and like fullers' soap; he will sit as a refiner and purifier of silver, and he will purify the descendants of Levi and refine them like gold and silver, until they present offerings to the Lord in righteousness.

Pondering and Meditating: The day of the coming of the Lord is both a fearful time and a joyous time. We are more inclined to focus on the joy and try and forget about any fear we might have. Malachi prophesies that God will bleach out the stains and evil sin, much as a garment would be cleaned. And once we are cleaned, we are purified. How do you acknowledge fear that you might feel with the coming again of the Lord? How do you affirm joy – for the joy that will come is the joy of our salvation?

Prayer: Lord God, you love us enough to send Emmanuel, God-with-us, to bring us from death to life. You love us enough that you come to destroy the evil within us. Thank you, dear Lord, for caring for both of these needs. Amen.

Reflection:

Luke 3:1-2

In the fifteenth year of the reign of Emperor Tiberius, when Pontius Pilate was governor of Judea, and Herod was ruler of Galilee, and his brother Philip ruler of the region of Ituraea and Traconitis, and Lysanias ruler of Abilene, during the high priesthood of Annas and Caiaphas, the word of God came to John son of Zechariah in the wilderness.

Pondering and Meditating: Luke is interested in the historical framework of the time in which Jesus' life and the beginning of the Gospel are situated. Why do you think Luke goes into all these details? How many of them do we ever hear in church? Which of the names that we see here and read are most important to you personally, and why? Do you think we need to know these things to share the Gospel message?

Prayer: Lord, we praise you for your servant Luke and for his emphasis at the end of this long sentence on the fact that "the word of God came to John son of Zechariah in the wilderness." Every name is important in the story told; similarly, each of us is important to you, God. We hear the names of those who promoted evil, and those who brought good, and pray we may be numbered among those who know and share your word, though we may from time to time find ourselves in the wilderness. Amen.

Reflection:

Philippians 1:9-11

And this is my prayer, that your love may overflow more and more with knowledge and full insight to help you to determine what is best, so that in the day of Christ you may be pure and blameless, having produced the harvest of righteousness that comes through Jesus Christ for the glory and praise of God.

Pondering and Meditating: Paul prays for the church at Philippi so that their love may overflow more and more to help them determine what is best. What would it mean to you in your own life if your love were to overflow more and more? Who could be impacted, and how? Becoming pure and blameless is a challenge to all of us, but allowing our love to overflow more and more is something we can do. How can you help to make this happen?

Prayer: God of love beyond measure, you give us the desire to do all that we can, and then give us the strength and power to go beyond what we think we can do, to know boundless love for ourselves. May your overflowing love stir up in us such gratitude that we long only to know you more fully, and give of ourselves more generously. Amen.

Reflection:

Philippians 1: 7-8

It is right for me to think this way about all of you, because you hold me in your heart, for all of you share in God's grace with me, both in my imprisonment and in the defense and confirmation of the gospel. For God is my witness, how I long for all of you with the compassion of Christ Jesus.

Pondering and Meditating: Paul says that the saints in Christ Jesus who are in Philippi "share in his imprisonment and in the defense and confirmation of the Gospel." When we work together for the sake of the Gospel, we share with those everywhere who have a share in the work of the good news. We are supported by one another. Paul was literally in prison at the time; are there ways we can support other believers who may be in prison in one way or another, spiritually or physically, by working together?

Prayer: Lord of life, bless our call to defend and stand fast for the good news of Jesus Christ, for you truly have given us the grace to surmount and demolish every wall that divides and holds us captive. Amen.

Reflection:

Monday, December 10, 2012

Zephaniah 3:16-18

On that day it shall be said to Jerusalem: Do not fear, O Zion; do not let your hands grow weak. The Lord , your God, is in your midst, a warrior who gives victory; he will rejoice over you with gladness; he will renew you in his love; he will exult over you with loud singing as on a day of festival. I will remove disaster from you, so that you will not bear reproach for it.

Pondering and Meditating: The words, "fear not," are often found in Scripture in one text or another. Especially in this Advent season as we prepare for the coming of Christ, we remember that God is in our midst, is with us, and rejoices to be with us. This day is one where God rejoices over us with gladness and singing. Is it easier to believe that God comes only to judge us? Do you have difficulty letting go of fear as we are called to believe that God loves and rejoices with us? What would it be like if we rejoiced with and for God, just as God rejoices with and for us?

Prayer: Help us, Lord of song and rejoicing, to life up our hands and trust that they will not grow weak. May we draw our strength from you as you offer rapturous joy and restoration? Amen.

Reflection:

Tuesday, December 11, 2012

Luke 2: 15-16

As the people were filled with expectation, and all were questioning in their hearts concerning John, whether he might be the Messiah, John answered all of them by saying, "I baptize you with water; but one who is more powerful than I is coming; I am not worthy to untie the thong of his sandals. He will baptize you with the Holy Spirit and fire."

Pondering and Meditating: John tells the people, and us, of the One who is to come. We, too, are filled with anticipation during this holy season – waiting for the Messiah once again. At the same time, we question in our hearts, wondering at the years that have passed, the time that has elapsed, between then and now, living as we do between the "already" and the "not yet." Have you ever felt that you were "baptized with the Holy Spirit and fire?" How did you recognize that feeling, and what actions did you take in response to it?

Prayer: Lord Jesus, enable us to be a people whose hearts are set on fire and who long for you with every ounce of our being. And help us, Lord, to remember that expectation and questioning can join together in every longing heart. Amen.

Reflection:

Wednesday, December 12, 2012

Zephaniah 3:19-20

I will deal with all your oppressors at that time. And I will save the lame and gather the outcast, and I will change their shame into praise and renown in all the earth. At that time I will bring you home, at the time when I gather you; for I will make you renowned and praised among all the peoples of the earth, when I restore your fortunes before your eyes, says the Lord.

Pondering and Meditating: It is very powerful to believe that the Lord will deal with all that oppresses us, all our oppressors. And it is powerful to consider that God will gather all God's people, the strong and the weak, into his flock, and bring every single one home. What might it be like for us if we could sense God's purpose and way in dealing with all our oppressors in any shape and form? What would it be like to come home to God – gathered in – all of us, brothers and sisters? When in your life have you been able to believe in that vision, and how does that bring God's kingdom closer to you?

Prayer: O Lord, bring us together and gather us in that we might know that day of praise and renown. Our hearts cry out for you, O living God. Amen.

Reflection:

Thursday, December 13, 2012

Isaiah 12:1-3

You will say in that day: I will give thanks to you, O Lord, for though you were angry with me, your anger turned away, and you comforted me. Surely God is my salvation; I will trust, and will not be afraid, for the Lord God is my strength and my might; he has become my salvation. With joy you will draw water from the waters of salvation.

Pondering and Meditating: Isaiah lived in a time that is similar to ours in some ways: it was a time of uncertainty, fear of foreign invasion and crises. The people of Judah and Jerusalem to whom Isaiah spoke were frightened. How can we confront fear and uncertainty, whether in our country, our economy or our personal lives, and say, "I will trust?" When in your life were you able to do that, and what did you learn from that experience?

Prayer: Precious Lord, be our shield and our strength. Give us wisdom to know the joy of your salvation in good times and bad. Amen.

Reflections:

Friday, December 14, 2012

Luke 3:10-14

And the crowds asked [John], "What then should we do? In reply he said to them, "Whoever has two coats must share with anyone who has none; and whoever has food must do likewise." Even tax collectors came to be baptized, and they asked him, "Teacher, what should we do?" He said to them, "Collect no more than the amount prescribed for you." Soldiers also asked him, "And we, what should we do?" He said to them, "Do not extort money from anyone by threats or false accusation, and be satisfied with your wages."

Pondering and Meditating: John is being very specific and clear in his instructions to those listening to him – the crowd, tax collectors, soldiers – essentially, anyone who showed up. John tells them, and us, to share what we have, to be fair in our dealings, and to be satisfied with what we earn. Sometimes we make the Gospel very complicated, but John reminds us that each of us has the opportunity to live this way. Based on who John was talking to, it is a powerful message that any and all, each of us, everyone, can live in such a way to bear fruit.

Prayer: Lord, give us grace to welcome all and judge none, in the name of Christ Jesus, for Jesus taught that all may enter into the Kingdom of God. Amen.

Reflection:

Saturday, December 15, 2012

Philippians 4:4-5

Rejoice in the Lord always; again I will say, Rejoice. Let your gentleness be known to everyone. The Lord is near.

Pondering and Meditating: This passage is one that is well known, but Paul's words to the church at Philippi ring fresh in our ears and hearts. The theme is to "rejoice," always, that is, at all times and in all circumstances. For us, this means that we can rejoice in the Lord, no matter what is going on in our lives. Sometimes we confuse "joy" with being "happy." How can we grasp that we can have joy in the Lord even if we are not happy at a particular moment or in a special circumstance? When the Lord is near, what difference does it make in our lives?

Prayer: O God, to find joy in you is to find hidden strength in ourselves. Give us a gentle heart to be aware of your presence, regardless of pain or suffering. Amen.

Reflection:

Philippians 4:6-9

Do not worry about anything, but in everything by prayer and supplication with thanksgiving let your requests be made known to God. And the peace of God, which surpasses all understanding, will guard your hearts and your minds in Christ Jesus. Finally, beloved, whatever is true, whatever is honorable, whatever is just, whatever is pure, whatever is pleasing, whatever is commendable, if there is any excellence and if there is anything worthy of praise, think about these things. Keep on doing the things that you have learned and received and heard and seen in me, and the God of peace will be with you.

Pondering and Meditating: Sometimes we find ourselves saying or thinking, "God only knows." Paul's statement of faith is that God indeed does know, because the Lord is close to us, even present with us. God knows what we are about and what we need. When we pray and thank God, we find that God empowers and transforms us. How can this help us focus on that which is true, honorable, just, pure, pleasing, and commendable, rather than becoming distraught with our worries?

Prayer: Loving God, we know we can cast our cares upon you and you strengthen us. We experience your peace, which we long for in a life that can be filled with anxieties and stress. When your peace comes to us, we do indeed thank you, Lord, for your manifold goodness. Amen.

Reflection:

Micah 5:4-5a

And he shall stand and feed his flock in the strength of the Lord in the majesty of the name of the Lord, his God. And they shall live secure, for now he shall be great to the ends of the earth; and he shall be the one of peace.

Pondering and Meditating: What would it mean for you, in this moment of your life, to be fed by the Lord as part of God's flock and to live secure? In what ways can we be blessed to feed one another, so that we show to all that we know what it means for the Lord to help us live secure?

Prayer: Grant, O God, that we might see and believe the ways in which you shelter and feed us, as we bless your Holy Name, and know that you are with us. Amen.

Reflection:

Tuesday, December 18, 2012

Micah 5:2

But you, O Bethlehem of Ephrathah, who are one of the little clans of Judah, from you shall come forth for me one who is to rule in Israel, whose origin is from of old, from ancient days.

Pondering and Meditating: Why is it so difficult for us to believe that a great ruler will arise from something, anything that appears small and insignificant? How does this assumption impact our own lives and the times that we feel ourselves to be small and insignificant?

Prayer: As we fix our eyes on you, O God of the great and the miniscule, leviathan and snail, allow us to apprehend in our hearts that your ways are not our ways – and that you can raise our Messiah from a small clan to be Lord of all. Change our hearts, O Lord. Amen.

Reflection:

Wednesday, December 19, 2012

Hebrews 10:10

And it is by God's will that we have been sanctified through the offering of the body of Jesus Christ once for all.

Pondering and Meditating: Paul reminds us that God ordained we would be sanctified, made holy and blessed, for all time and for all people, through the offering of the body of Jesus Christ. Christ gave himself for us, so that God's will might be manifested and brought to fruition. What do the words "once for all" mean to you personally, and to us as a faith community?

Prayer: It is impossible for us to understand how you, Creator God and our Savior Christ so love us that we receive this great gift of sanctification. May we respond by sharing as much as one iota, perhaps the size of a mustard seed, of the dedication and self-giving love that has been poured upon us, believing, as we do, in that coming day when our whole selves might be offered in the name of our Savior. Amen.

Reflection:

Thursday, December 20, 2012

Luke 1: 46-49

And Mary said, "My soul magnifies the Lord and my spirit rejoices in God my Savior, for he has looked with favor on the lowliness of his servant. Surely, from now on all generations will call me blessed; for the Mighty One has done great things for me, and holy is his name.

Pondering and Meditating: Mary states that all generations will call her blessed; and we are to share that blessing in order to bless others. How often, Lord do we find ourselves hoarding the blessings you have given us?

Prayer: Lord, we your servants call you blessed, praying to be ever mindful of the great things you have done through us, from generation to generation, for we, too, would magnify your name now and forevermore. Amen.

Reflection:

Friday, December 21, 2012

Luke 1: 51

He has shown strength with his arm; he has scattered the proud in the thoughts of their hearts.

Pondering and Meditating: Mary was an ordinary woman who was chosen by God to do extraordinary things – and yet God gave her the choice of whether or not to embrace her call from God. God calls us as well to surrender our pride, and to trust in God's strength. What would happen in your life if you could sing out as Mary does your faith in God's strength and support of those who humble themselves?

Prayer: Lord give us voice to sing your redemption song and to live it out, with word and deed. Amen.

Reflection:

Saturday, December 22, 2012

Luke 1: 50

His mercy is for those who fear him from generation to generation.

Pondering and Meditating: Mary says that God's mercy is for those who fear him throughout time and place. Has fear ever kept you from encountering God's mercy? Did anything happen to allay your fear? What can we do to help us draw near to a God who is both powerful and fearful as well as merciful?

Prayer: Lord, allow us the privilege of teaching those generations who will follow us, just as those who came before taught us to walk in your pathways, guided by your light and your mercy. Amen.

Reflection:

Sunday, December 23, 2012

Hebrews 10:5-6

Consequently, when Christ came into the world, he said, "Sacrifices and offerings you have not desired, but a body you have prepared for me; in burnt offerings and sin offerings you have taken no pleasure.

Pondering and Meditating: As we approach Christmas, how can we reflect on the true and obedient sacrifice that Christ made for us? What does it mean to us to think during the week before Christmas of the reality of Jesus entering, and later, leaving this world in bodily form?

Prayer: Through the incarnation of Jesus, dear Lord, you gave us your Son, a messiah who would be committed to obedience to your will. This week and always, we pray that we may be, ourselves, living into our own commitment to do and live as the Lord desires. Amen.

Reflection:

Monday, December 24, 2012

Luke 2:8-12

In that region there were shepherds living in the fields, keeping watch over their flock by night. Then an angel of the Lord stood before them, and the glory of the Lord shone around them, and they were terrified. But the angel said to them, "Do not be afraid; for see – I am bringing you good news of great joy for all the people; to you is born this day in the city of David a Savior, who is the Messiah, the Lord. This will be a sign for you: you will find a child wrapped in bands of cloth and lying in a manger."

Pondering and Meditating: No matter how many times we have heard these words, there is the prospect of renewed power, purpose and reassurance as we hear them once again. To us, to you, to me, Christ Messiah is born anew. How does God long for these words to be engraved on your heart this evening?

Prayer: Dear Lord, we hope and pray to know your glory more fully and deeply. May we praise you and give thanks for the Messiah, God-With-Us, revealed through your holy Word. Hallelujah! Amen.

Reflection:

Isaiah 62:10-12

Go through, go through the gates, prepare the way for the people; build up, build up the highway, clear it of stones, lift up an ensign over the peoples. The Lord has proclaimed to the end of the earth: Say to daughter Zion, "See your salvation comes; his reward is with him, and his recompense before him." They shall be called, "The Holy People, the Redeemed of the Lord"; and you shall be called, "Sought Out, A City Not Forsaken."

Pondering and Meditating: Sometimes on Christmas Day, it seems as if the presents are unwrapped all too quickly, the dinner consumed, and the celebration comes to an end – perhaps because we are simply worn out. How does God summon you this day to prepare a way for God's holy people, reenergized, to build up a highway that is clear of stones and every obstacle?

Prayer: Salvation has come – Christ Jesus is born! Precious Lord, thank for the call to prepare your way, that we might know the joy of your salvation and be forever redeemed through our Savior, Jesus Christ. Amen.

Reflection:

Psalm 148:11-14

Kings of the earth and all peoples, princes and all rulers of the earth! Young men and women alike, old and young together! Let them praise the name of the Lord for his name alone is exalted; his glory is above earth and heaven. He has raised up a horn for his people, praise for all his faithful, for the people of Israel who are close to him. Praise the Lord!

Pondering and Meditating: Psalm 148 proclaims to one and all "Praise the Lord!" It even comes with an exclamation point: Praise the Lord! How can each of us exclaim that the birth of the Messiah is to all God's people a source of hope and joy, even in the midst of life's trouble and problems? What does it mean to show how God's work in all creation has brought salvation to all people for all time?

Prayer: O God, let our praises sound to the heavens; let us not be silenced; for you, O Lord, bless us forever through your manifold works! Praise the Lord! Amen.

Reflection:

Thursday, December 27, 2012

Colossians 3:12

As God's chosen ones, holy and beloved, clothe yourselves with compassion, kindness, humility, meekness, and patience.

Pondering and Meditating: Paul's call to us in this week after Christmas is to reflect on the ways in which God has chosen and blessed us – ways to clothe ourselves with compassion, kindness, humility, meekness, and patience. Paul knew what he was talking about. These virtues are often so hard for us to embody during difficult times. Can you think of a time when being kind and humble were difficult, even though you knew God desired it?

Prayer: Almighty and ever living God, who loves and receives each one of us, surround us with the assurance of your holiness, and help us to live out our Christian calling so as to share these virtues with others. In the precious name of the One who came for us, we pray. Amen.

Reflection:

Colossians 3:13

Bear with one another and, if anyone has a complaint against another, forgive each other; just as the Lord has forgiven you, so you also must forgive.

Pondering and Meditating: Even as we read these words, we know how challenging it can be to "bear with one another," and "forgive, just as the Lord has forgiven." Can you think of a time you found yourself unable to forgive another? What made it difficult to forgive? As you reflect on it now, how did God's forgiveness help you forgive another?

Prayer: Lord, we find it easier to grumble and voice our complaints than to forgive. If we are honest, we know that we have ourselves been forgiven more times than we know or acknowledge. Grant us grace, blessed Lord, help us, dear Jesus, since forgiveness is a treasure to be cherished and a solace to us always. Amen.

Reflection:

Luke 2: 41-43

Now every year his parents went to Jerusalem for the festival of the Passover. And when he was twelve years old, they went up as usual for the festival. When the festival was ended and they started to return, the boy Jesus stayed behind in Jerusalem, but his parents did not know it.

Pondering and Meditating: Children grow up fast, don't they? Less than a week ago we were sharing the great good news of the birth of Jesus, and here Scripture tells us that Jesus is a boy of twelve-years-old. It may not take place this quickly with our own children and those in the church, but children grow up fast. Think of young people you have watched change from baby to toddler to child to teenager. Youth today are challenged to assume new roles very rapidly. Can you sympathize with Jesus' parents in this situation?

Prayer: Lord, comfort us in the knowledge that just as Jesus followed the path you set for him, so, too, must our children and youth. Help us accept the times that our children and youth are called to go a different way than we would like, and grant us peace for we know you are with them. Amen.

Reflection:

Sunday, December 30, 2012

Luke 2:49-52

He said to them, "Why were you searching for me? Did you not know that I must be in my Father's house?" But they did not understand what he said to them. Then he went down with them and came to Nazareth, and was obedient to them. His mother treasured all these things in her heart. And Jesus increased in wisdom and in years, and in divine and human favor.

Pondering and Meditating: We stand on the verge of a new year, and can never know for sure what that year will bring. Similarly, we cannot grasp what Jesus will make plain to us in times to come. There can be a place inside of us that causes us to question why we are searching, and for what. Sometimes, accepting that God holds the future for us, and each of us rests in the palm of God's hand, brings us the gift of being more able to treasure every moment, as Mary treasured all these things in her heart.

Prayer: Lord, each day is a gift from you, Creator, Redeemer, and Spirit. As we stand between past and future, make us mindful of this great gift of life and love. Bless our questioning and our treasuring. Amen.

Reflection:

JANUARY 2013

BISHOP PAUL L. LEELAND

Epiphany is the liturgical season within the Christian Church reminding us of the manifestation of God in the world. We shift from a day to day view of our lives and begin to embrace an awareness of God's personal intervention in the world through Jesus Christ. We now see how the Presence of God illuminates our darkened world by means of the incarnation of Jesus, who is the visible image of the invisible God, the one who said, "I am the light of the world." As we follow this Light we are reminded we are the children of light.

During this season of Epiphany, we celebrate three manifestations of God in Christ: the visit of the Magi, the baptism of Jesus in the Jordan, and the miracle at the wedding of Cana. Each of these events reminds us God is present, revealing the Divine Love at work everywhere. God has come to us in mystery and wonder creating deep reverence. "This, this is Christ the King, whom shepherds guard and angels sing."

The Scripture we read during this time of Epiphany both prepares us for worship and points to Incarnation, Christ Jesus manifested in the flesh, proclaimed to others, and exalted in glory. May the light of God's Spirit kindle a desire within us for God's kingdom, now at hand.

Let us pray that each day of Scripture reading, meditation and worship will guide us to "kneel down and pay him homage. Then opening their treasures they offered him gifts." (Mt. 2:11).

Almighty God, we want to follow Jesus, who came into this world as a light shining in the darkness. Receive our lives as a gift for others. Amen.

Isaiah 60:1-3

Arise, shine; for your light has come, and the glory of the Lord has risen upon you. For darkness shall cover the earth, and thick darkness the peoples; but the Lord will arise upon you, and his glory will appear over you. Nations shall come to your light, and kings to the brightness of your dawn.

Pondering and Meditating: Darkness takes many forms. In what ways do you see the signs of a new light following the announcement of God's presence in the world? What are the indications that God's glory has now appeared over you? Do we embrace the promise that the nations and kings of this world will "come to your light?"

Prayer: Lord of Light, allow us to spend this last day of the year in profound praise and gratitude for the gift of our salvation in Jesus Christ, the Light of the world.

Reflection:

Tuesday, January 1, 2013

Matthew 2:1-2; 10-11

In the time of King Herod, after Jesus was born in Bethlehem of Judea, wise men from the East came to Jerusalem, asking, 'Where is the child who has been born king of the Jews? For we observed his star at its rising, and have come to pay him homage. When they saw that the star had stopped, they were overwhelmed with joy. On entering the house, they saw the child with Mary his mother; and they knelt down and paid him homage. Then, opening their treasure-chests, they offered him gifts of gold, frankincense, and myrrh.

Pondering and Meditating: "Where is the child" Christ in our lives to be seen? What are the indications that we can humble ourselves before Christ as we "kneel down and pay him homage?" Can we open the treasure chests of our lives in gratitude to God for all with which we have been blessed through our salvation?

Prayer: God of Creation and Life, your love is near and your light draws us toward all that is holy and good in the world. "Overwhelm us with joy." Lead us to our true and only king, Jesus Christ, our Lord. Amen.

Reflection:

Wednesday, January 2, 2013

Isaiah 60:4-6

Lift up your eyes and look around; they all gather together, they come to you; your sons shall come from far away, and your daughters shall be carried on their nurses' arms. Then you shall see and be radiant; your heart shall thrill and rejoice, because the abundance of the sea shall be brought to you, the wealth of the nations shall come to you. A multitude of camels shall cover you, the young camels of Midian and Ephah; all those from Sheba shall come. They shall bring gold and frankincense, and shall proclaim the praise of the LORD.

Pondering and Meditating: If we were to "lift our eyes and look around," can we point to the gracious spirit of those who feel deeply the need to express their gifts to God? Can we see the offerings we place before Christ as expressions of our deepest praise?

Prayer: Almighty God revealed in Jesus Christ, help us to lift our eyes and look around at all who come to you, and then we too will "see and be radiant; our hearts will thrill and rejoice." Amen.

Reflection:

Thursday, January 3, 2013

Ephesians 3:1-6

This is the reason that I Paul am a prisoner for Christ Jesus for the sake of you Gentiles— for surely you have already heard of the commission of God's grace that was given to me for you, and how the mystery was made known to me by revelation, as I wrote above in a few words, a reading of which will enable you to perceive my understanding of the mystery of Christ. In former generations this mystery was not made known to humankind, as it has now been revealed to his holy apostles and prophets by the Spirit: that is, the Gentiles have become fellow-heirs, members of the same body, and sharers in the promise in Christ Jesus through the gospel.

Pondering and Meditating: The word, "Gentile" was used to identify all who were outside the faith. Are we aware that a new revelation has been given through the Apostle Paul that all people may be considered "fellow-heirs, become members of the same body, and share in the promises given in Christ Jesus through the Gospel?" If we were to take this word seriously, what would we have to change about the way we think of those outside the faith? How would we act differently?

Prayer: God of Mystery, God of Love, stir within our hearts a love for all people. Allow us to carry this "mystery which earlier was not made known to humankind" but is now clear because of the Light given through the birth of Jesus to our world that all may receive your divine inheritance, now and in the world to come. Amen.

Reflection:

Friday, January 4, 2013

Ephesians 3:7-9

Of this gospel I have become a servant according to the gift of God's grace that was given to me by the working of his power. Although I am the very least of all the saints, this grace was given to me to bring to the Gentiles the news of the boundless riches of Christ, and to make everyone see what is the plan of the mystery hidden for ages in God who created all things.

Pondering and Meditating: It is not always "what" God wants us to do, but more often it is the "way" God wants us to be. How can we become the "servants of God's grace" in a world that has been covered by darkness? Although we "are the very least" to speak for God, can we acknowledge "the working of his power" in us as we share this Gospel?

Prayer: Creator of all things, place your Holy Spirit within us to shape our invitation and love toward others in such a way that all may experience God's welcoming, loving and protective grace. May each person within our lives recognize in us the "boundless riches of Christ, and to make everyone see what is the plan of the mystery hidden for ages in God who created all things." Amen.

Reflection:

Psalm 72:1-7

Give the king your justice, O God, and your righteousness to a king's son. May he judge your people with righteousness, and your poor with justice? May the mountains yield prosperity for the people, and the hills, in righteousness. May he defend the cause of the poor of the people, give deliverance to the needy, and crush the oppressor. May he live while the sun endures, and as long as the moon, throughout all generations. May he be like rain that falls on the mown grass, like showers that water the earth. In his days may righteousness flourish and peace abound, until the moon is no more.

Pondering and Meditating: When the Magi asked, "Where is the child who has been born king?" and then acknowledged this king as they "knelt down and paid him homage," can we hear the praise of the King in this Psalm? How does serving the King who "defends the cause of the poor and the needy" shape our relationship with those who long to see the "days when righteousness will flourish and peace abound?" Is this the King Jesus to whom we give our praise?

Prayer: God of Justice and Rightness, allow your peace to abound. Nourish us like the showers that water the earth with your loving presence and the assurance of your love. We are humbled that you became poor so we might become rich in order to be a blessing to others who long for your deliverance, defense and peace. Amen.

Reflection:

Matthew 2:3-4; 7-9

When King Herod heard this, he was frightened, and all Jerusalem with him; and calling together all the chief priests and scribes of the people, he inquired of them where the Messiah was to be born. … Then Herod secretly called for the wise men and learned from them the exact time when the star had appeared. Then he sent them to Bethlehem, saying, 'Go and search diligently for the child; and when you have found him, bring me word so that I may also go and pay him homage.' When they had heard the king, they set out; and there, ahead of them, went the star that they had seen at its rising, until it stopped over the place where the child was.

Pondering and Meditating: Does it frighten us to know that God asks for our loyalty to be given to him alone? Are we hesitant to seek Jesus and give him our loyalty when the rulers of this world, as a result, become "frightened?" Is it possible for us to "search diligently for Jesus" as our first priority?

Prayer: Unite our hearts to those of the Magi, O Lord, who came before the Child King bearing gifts. Hear our prayer for all leaders throughout our world that Christ will enlighten their understanding and hearts so that every nation will walk by the light of Christ. Amen.

Reflection:

Monday, January 7, 2013

Luke 3:15-17

As the people were filled with expectation, and all were questioning in their hearts concerning John, whether he might be the Messiah, John answered all of them by saying, "I baptize you with water; but one who is more powerful than I is coming; I am not worthy to untie the thong of his sandals. He will baptize you with the Holy Spirit and fire. His winnowing-fork is in his hand, to clear his threshing-floor and to gather the wheat into his granary; but the chaff he will burn with unquenchable fire."

Pondering and Meditating: The beginning of Jesus' public ministry is "filled with expectation." What are the expectations for your life that you have been pondering since the celebration of Christ's birth? Have you given any thought to how Jesus' baptism was a sign that he is the one who has come to baptize all humanity in the Holy Spirit? Where is the "fire" and passion of our baptism and service to God most recognized by others?

Prayer: Gracious God, you have changed our hearts through the waters of baptism. May our hearts and minds move from fear of death to the glory of resurrection with Christ. Instill in us his desire to do your will and to follow where he leads. Baptize us anew with the Holy Spirit. Amen.

Reflection:

Acts 8:14-17

Now when the apostles at Jerusalem heard that Samaria had accepted the word of God, they sent Peter and John to them. The two went down and prayed for them that they might receive the Holy Spirit (for as yet the Spirit had not comeupon any of them; they had only been baptized in the name of the Lord Jesus). Then Peter and Johnlaid their hands on them, and they received the Holy Spirit.

Pondering and Meditating: Often we desire to "call" those who would serve among us. What does it mean to trust our spiritual leaders "to send" those who can best teach and guide our lives together? Are we "only baptized in the name of our Lord Jesus," or have we received the Holy Spirit as well? What does it mean to receive and work out of the passion and fire of the Holy Spirit?

Prayer: Almighty God, we have failed to be an obedient church. Free us for joyful obedience. May we have the same spirit of obedience that was in Christ Jesus our Lord who was obedient even unto death and that we would have the courage to follow wherever he leads us. Grant us your Holy Spirit. Amen.

Reflection:

Isaiah 43:1-4

But now thus says the LORD, he who created you, O Jacob,   he who formed you, O Israel: Do not fear, for I have redeemed you; I have called you by name, you are mine. When you pass through the waters, I will be with you; and through the rivers, they shall not overwhelm you; when you walk through fire you shall not be burned, and the flame shall not consume you. For I am the LORD your God, the Holy One of Israel, your Savior. I give Egypt as your ransom, Ethiopia and Seba in exchange for you. Because you are precious in my sight, and honored, and I love you, I give people in return for you, nations in exchange for your life.

Pondering and Meditating: Does our baptism remind us that it is God "who has created us and formed us?" When God calls us by name does it reduce our fear? What would it take to know that we "are precious in his sight?" here is nothing God would not "exchange for your life."

Prayer: Lord of Life, protect us as we "pass through the waters" that threaten to "overwhelm" us this week. Restore all people in your image, who is Jesus Christ, your Son and our Lord. May every person come to the knowledge that they have been created and formed by you to be a blessing to others. I love you, Lord. Amen.

Reflection:

Thursday, January 10, 2013

Psalm 29:1-2,11b

Ascribe to the LORD, O heavenly beings, ascribe to the LORD glory and strength. Ascribe to the LORD the glory of his name; worship the LORD in holy splendor. May the LORD bless his people with peace!

Pondering and Meditating: There is a clear connection between our "peace" and our ability to "ascribe to the Lord the glory of his name." How is our worship defined when we acknowledge the "glory and strength" of God's presence? Can we acknowledge how the Lord God blesses us with peace?

Prayer: We praise you, O God, for releasing your Spirit into the world and allowing us to become your servants. May our baptism free us to model the life of Jesus and humbly approach you as the child "in whom you are well pleased." We ascribe all glory and strength to you. We worship you "in holy splendor." Amen.

Reflection:

Friday, January 11, 2013

Isaiah 43:5-7

Do not fear, for I am with you; I will bring your offspring from the east, and from the west I will gather you; I will say to the north, 'Give them up', and to the south, 'Do not withhold; bring my sons from far away and my daughters from the end of the earth— everyone who is called by my name, whom I created for my glory, whom I formed and made.'

Pondering and Meditating: There is no place on earth that will not know of God's love for you, "from the east and from the west, the north and the south." If God is so clear in offering this profound love and desire for us, what is it we fear? Do we know we are his "sons" and "daughters?" This is the mystery of our baptism and the mystery of God's mercy. Do you not know that once we were "no people," but through our baptism in Jesus Christ, we are the people of God, the people "who are called by his name?"

Prayer: Inspire us, O Lord, to live the new life you have given us in Jesus Christ that we might be delivered from the power of darkness and transferred to the kingdom of your beloved Son. Amen.

Reflection:

Saturday, January 12, 2013

Luke 3:21-22

Now when all the people were baptized, and when Jesus also had been baptized and was praying, the heaven was opened, and the Holy Spirit descended upon him in bodily form like a dove. And a voice came from heaven, 'You are my Son, the Beloved; with you I am well pleased.'

Pondering and Meditating: When Jesus had been baptized and was praying, "heaven was opened." Can you see the relationship between our baptism and prayer for a new life? Can you see how God would open the heavens to the "beloved" children who desire to be restored to the original plan for which we were created?

Prayer: Loving God, keep us faithful to the gifts of Christmas and Epiphany. May we be immersed in the waters of holiness, and may your Holy Spirit descend upon us in praise and power. Amen.

Reflection:

Luke 3:15-17

As the people were filled with expectation, and all were questioning in their hearts concerning John, whether he might be the Messiah, John answered all of them by saying, 'I baptize you with water; but one who is more powerful than I is coming; I am not worthy to untie the thong of his sandals. He will baptize you with the Holy Spirit and fire. His winnowing-fork is in his hand, to clear his threshing-floor and to gather the wheat into his granary; but the chaff he will burn with unquenchable fire.'

Pondering and Meditating: We recognize our unworthiness before a God of perfect goodness. As we think about God's very real love in our lives, what do we continue "to question in our hearts?" Now that we are baptized what is the journey we are to make? What is your "expectation?"

Prayer: Cleansing God, now that we have died to sin, give us the power to live freely in your spirit. May we live in the newness of life and the glory of your holy name. Richly pour upon us the Holy Spirit so that we might be justified by grace and receive the hope of eternal life. Amen.

Reflection:

Monday, January 14, 2013

Psalm 36: 5-7

Your steadfast love, O Lord, extends to the heavens, your faithfulness to the clouds. Your righteousness is like the mighty mountains; your judgments are like the great deep; you save humans and animals alike, O Lord. How precious is your steadfast love, O God! All people may take refuge in the shadow of your wings.

Pondering and Meditating: God's love, faithfulness, righteousness and judgment toward us is immeasurable. It is "like the great deep," greater than "the mighty mountains," and higher than "the clouds." Whenever we live in this love and truth, we discover the rightness or righteousness of God's desire for us. We come to appreciate how "precious is this love" because it offers us safety and gives protection to save us from the darkness of this world. It is as if we truly discovered the place where we can "find refuge in the shadow of God's wings." Where, at this moment, are we aware of the darkness and hurtfulness that creates deep concern and worry? Is the promise of the one who said, "I am the Light," able to give us refuge in the shelter of his wings?

Prayer: Jesus, Savior of the World, Light and Love, draw near to us and keep us in the shadow of God's wings that we might become the servants of wisdom and truth, giving glory to you, praise your name and offer you all we have. Amen.

Reflection:

Tuesday, January 15, 2013

John 2: 1-5

On the third day there was a wedding in Cana of Galilee, and the mother of Jesus was there. Jesus and his disciples had also been invited to the wedding. When the wine gave out, the mother of Jesus said to him, "They have no wine." And Jesus said to her, "Woman, what concern is that to you and to me? My hour has not yet come." His mother said to the servants, "Do whatever he tells you."

Pondering and Meditating: What is it that attracts us to Jesus? How many times have we felt the desire to be in God's presence and prayed that he might also be invited into our thoughts? As we listen to the voice of love, made humble through the mystery of Christ, we become willing to "do whatever he tells us." The and only the do we live as if we are in the Kingdom of God. Until then, we must confess, his "hour has not yet come."What would we need to do to take Mary's words seriously at this point in our life and "do whatever he tells" us to do? When others fail to respond to Christ, "what concern is that to you?" God seeks only our response, regardless of what others may do. Has Christ's hour come upon your life? Are you still on the way? How far along the way are you?

Prayer: All powerful God, we are renewed by your sacraments. May our thanksgiving for you be shaped by living in faithful service and obedience to your Word. Help us to grow into the likeness of Jesus Christ for the service of others by the power of your word and our obedience to it. Amen.

Reflection:

Isaiah 62: 1-2

For Zion's sake I will not keep silent, and for Jerusalem's sake I will not rest, until her vindication shines out like the dawn, and her salvation like a burning torch. The nations shall see your vindication, and all the kings your glory; and you shall be called by a new name that the mouth of the Lord will give.

Pondering and Meditating: In the most profound moments, when we are aware of God's deep love for us expressed in the Word made Flesh, we imitate God's thoughts; for we "will not keep silent" and we "will not rest" in order to tell how much God has done for us. When we walk in darkness without the benefit of God's light we rapidly move toward destruction. When we yield our lives to God we experience "vindication" and are given a new status in God's eyes. Is it possible that the change that comes to the people of God can cause "the nations and kings" of this world to see the "glory" of God "shine out like the dawn, or like a burning torch?" Is there comfort in knowing that God will not rest until we have been vindicated?

Prayer: Inspire us to live the new life you have given us, O God, as we move from death to life. We pray for the leaders of all nations that they might govern in mercy, seeking to overcome fear and find lasting peace. Amen.

Reflection:

Thursday, January 17, 2013

I Corinthians 12: 1-2, 4-7

Now concerning spiritual gifts, brothers and sisters, I do not want you to be uninformed. You know that when you were pagans, you were enticed and led astray to idols that could not speak. Now there are varieties of gifts, but the same Spirit; and there are varieties of services, but the same Lord; and there are varieties of activities, but it is the same God who activates all of them in everyone. To each is given the manifestation of the Spirit for the common good.

Pondering and Meditating: In this season of Epiphany, the manifestation or coming of the Light, we recognize how easily we "were enticed and led astray." In God's gracious love we have been given a means of overcoming these false paths: "To each is given the manifestation of the Spirit for the common good." This Spirit of God activates "varieties of gifts," and then leads us into "varieties of services."

Prayer: "God the Spirit, guide and guardian, wind-sped flame and hovering dove, breath of life and voice of prophets, sign of blessing, power of love: give to those who lead your people fresh anointing of your grace; send them forth as bold apostles to your church in every place." Amen. (UMH 648).

Reflection:

Friday, January 18, 2013

I Corinthians 12: 8-11

To one is given through the Spirit the utterance of wisdom, and to another the utterance of knowledge according to the same Spirit, to another faith by the same Spirit, to another gifts of healing by the one Spirit, to another the working of miracles, to another prophecy, to another the discernment of spirits, to another various kinds of tongues, to another the interpretation of tongues. All these are activated by one and the same Spirit, who allots to each one individually just as the Spirit chooses.

Pondering and Meditating: There is a balance between our willingness to embrace the gifts of God and the acknowledgment of those gifts by the church. Spiritual gifts are activated and allotted "to each one individually just as the Spirit chooses." Have you received affirmation from others for the way in which you offer wisdom, knowledge or faith? Do you feel attracted to share in healing, miracles, prophecy or discernment? Like all God's gifts, they are poured out into the hands of faith, affirmed by the church and offered for the building up of the Body of Christ.

Prayer: O Lord our God, we acknowledge that we did not choose you but that you have chosen us to be the vessels of your spiritual gifts. Through these gifts allow us to share your light, love and truth in order that you might be manifested in the world. Grant us wisdom to see the demands of love and to make wise decisions on behalf of all who would choose life in you. Amen.

Reflection:

Psalm 36: 7b-10

All people may take refuge in the shadow of your wings. They feast on the abundance of your house, and you give them drink from the river of your delights. For with you is the fountain of life; in your light we see light. O continue your steadfast love to those who know you, and your salvation to the upright of heart!

Pondering and Meditating: Those who have found their home and peace in God's presence have indeed found the "fountain of life." It is only in God's "light we see light." Do the words from Ephesians 5:9, "Light produces every kind of goodness and righteousness and truth," bring the words of the Apostle Paul to mind? It is hard to see the good and right and truth when we are in a dark place. We feel overwhelmed by fear. This is the moment when we need a time away from the parched, empty and barren rewards of this world to be refreshed by the "drink that comes from the river of God's delights and the abundance of his house!"

Prayer: Christ Jesus, you are the Light of the world; the fountain of all truth and the eternal source of our fulfillment. May our life be surrounded and filled with your redeeming grace. Bring light to our darkened understanding allowing us to live according to your love. Bring us, and all our loved ones, from death's darkness into your glorious light. "Continue your steadfast love to all who know you and your salvation to the upright of heart." Hide us and protect us in the shelter of your wings. Amen.

Reflection:

John 2: 6-11

Now standing there were six stone water jars for the Jewish rites of purification, each holding twenty or thirty gallons. Jesus said to them, "Fill the jars with water." And they filled them up to the brim. He said to them, "Now draw some out, and take it to the chief steward." So they took it. When the steward tasted the water that had become wine, and did not know where it came from (though the servants who had drawn the water knew), the steward called the bridegroom and said to him, "Everyone serves the good wine first, and then the inferior wine after the guests have become drunk. But you have kept the good wine until now." Jesus did this, the first of his signs, in Cana of Galilee, and revealed his glory; and his disciples believed him.

Pondering and Meditating: Today we don't give much thought to how God might bypass natural processes and create a miraculous moment. Perhaps the more fundamental question is not whether we believe in miracles, but rather do we believe in a God who can do miraculous things? The emphasis is on God "revealing his glory" and not the "sign." Is God's glory revealed in bringing light into darkness, life out of death, and our personal redemption from a life of sin? When this happens we "believe in him."

Prayer: Almighty God, you are the God in whom we believe. You give life to the dead and call into existence the things that do not exist. We hope against all hope, for with you all things are possible. We believe in Christ. Help our unbelief. Amen.

Reflection:

Nehemiah 8: 5-6; 8

Ezra opened the book in the sight of all the people, for he was standing above all the people; and when he opened it, all the people stood up. Then Ezra blessed the Lord, the great God, and all the people answered, "Amen, Amen," lifting up their hands. Then they bowed their heads and worshiped the Lord with their faces to the ground. So they read from the book, from the law of God, with interpretation. They gave the sense, so that the people understood the reading.

Pondering and Meditating: Our reverence for the Lord is expressed in both hearing the Word of God and in humbling ourselves with "bowed heads as we worship the Lord." Have we given thought to how great the gift of preserved Scripture is for the church? Without the recorded word, faithfully preserved over time and interpreted, the stories would slowly change. Faithful worship allows us to hear the voice of God "so that the people understand the reading." When we worship, we glorify God and affirm God's Lordship over every aspect of our lives. This is expressed in our "Amen. Amen." So be it!

Prayer: God of Grace and God of Power, hear our gratitude for every aspect of our lives with which we are blessed. We praise you for your kindness, love and goodness toward us. We give thanks to you for your steadfast love. How grateful we are that you are our Maker, Defender, Redeemer and Friend. Amen.

Reflection:

Tuesday, January 22, 2013

Psalm 19: 1-7

The heavens are telling the glory of God; and the firmament proclaims his handiwork. Day to day pours forth speech, and night to night declares knowledge. There is no speech, nor are there words; their voice is not heard; yet their voice goes out through all the earth, and their words to the end of the world. In the heavens he has set a tent for the sun, which comes out like a bridegroom from his wedding canopy, and like a strong man runs its course with joy. Its rising is from the end of the heavens, and its circuit to the end of them; and nothing is hid from its heat. The law of the Lord is perfect, reviving the soul; the decrees of the Lord are sure, making wise the simple.

Pondering and Meditating: Anyone who has struggled with long nights of worry and sleeplessness knows the joy of seeing the light of a new day. How thankful we are for "the heavens telling the glory of God." When was the last time you recall experiencing the long hours of a dark and hurtful situation? Was there a moment in which there was a "reviving of the soul?" This is the same joy Christ brings through the light of his resurrection. We know all is indeed in God's hands because we have read his Word, knowing "the law of the Lord is perfect."

Prayer: Lord of Light, illumine our understanding by the light of the Gospel. Pour the light of your will upon our journey. Enlighten our decisions with your love. We devote this day to you and ask only for the wisdom of your Presence to guide us throughout the day. Your will be done. Amen.

Reflection:

Wednesday, January 23, 2013

Psalm 19: 7-10

The law of the Lord is perfect, reviving the soul; the decrees of the Lord are sure, making wise the simple; the precepts of the Lord are right, rejoicing the heart; the commandment of the Lord is clear, enlightening the eyes; the fear of the Lord is pure, enduring forever; the ordinances of the Lord are true and righteous altogether. More to be desired are they than gold, even much fine gold; sweeter also than honey, and drippings of the honeycomb.

Pondering and Meditating: Living in Christ does not excuse us from the law. As the Apostle Paul reminded us, the law has served as "our disciplinarian until Christ came" (Gal 3:23), teaching us right from wrong. Yet Christ has come to fulfill the law. In this way, the simple are made "wise." The law "enlightens the eyes" because it is "true and righteous altogether." In what ways are you meditating on the law?

Prayer: Through Jesus Christ, God's Wisdom and Word, let us pray: Free us from attitudes of lawlessness and bring us into the fullness of your light by means of the Gospel. Draw us out of darkness into your marvelous light. Hear our prayers of gratitude for all clergy who study, preach and teach your word. May they be filled with knowledge and grace to reflect your love, live true to the Light of Christ and guide us in the paths you have ordained for our lives. Amen.

Reflection:

Nehemiah 8:9-10

And Nehemiah, who was the governor, and Ezra the priest and scribe, and the Levites who taught the people said to all the people, "This day is holy to the Lord your God; do not mourn or weep." For all the people wept when they heard the words of the law. Then he said to them, "Go your way, eat the fat and drink sweet wine and send portions of them to those for whom nothing is prepared, for this day is holy to our Lord; and do not be grieved, for the joy of the Lord is your strength."

Pondering and Meditating: Have you ever felt sentimental tears spring forth when recalling old hymns and memories attached to those we loved deeply? We know something of the power of these precious memories when we read how "all the people wept when they heard the words of the law." At what point did you learn that the way of evil leads to suffering, darkness and death? Have you discovered how the way of God leads to light and life, wisdom and joy? When we make this distinction we can share how "the joy of the Lord is our strength."

Prayer: Gracious Lord, Living Christ, we want to come to you for we know your yoke is easy and your burdens are light. Fill us with desire to serve you and grant us grace to live this week in the power of your love. Keep us firmly planted on the path of Christ that we might be made in his image for the sake of others. Make each day "holy to you, our Lord and our God." Amen.

Reflection:

Friday, January 25, 2013

Luke 4: 16b-19, 21

He (Jesus) stood up to read, and the scroll of the prophet Isaiah was given to him. He unrolled the scroll and found the place where it was written: "The Spirit of the Lord is upon me, because he has anointed me to bring good news to the poor. He has sent me to proclaim release to the captives and recovery of sight to the blind, to let the oppressed go free, to proclaim the year of the Lord's favor." Then he began to say to them, "Today this Scripture has been fulfilled in your hearing."

Pondering and Meditating: Captivity, blindness and oppression come in many forms. These words simply capture a life lived devoid of peace, gratitude and joy. When we seek to live in God's Presence, each decision and action is to be held in the light of his approval. At this point it is no longer our thoughts that drive our behavior, but the Christ who dwells within us, transforming and shaping us into his will that will direct our steps. Can you see how this becomes the moment when "today this Scripture is fulfilled?" Can you see how this is the moment when "the Spirit of the Lord is upon" us?

Prayer: Pour forth the gift of your Holy Spirit upon my life, O God, that I might be ablaze with love for you and for my neighbor. Amen.

Reflection:

Luke 4: 14-15

Then Jesus, filled with the power of the Spirit, returned to Galilee, and a report about him spread through all the surrounding country. He began to teach in their synagogues and was praised by everyone.

Pondering and Meditating: Discovering a life "filled with the power of the Spirit" can make it difficult to return to those who knew us before Jesus began to shape our thinking and our lives. We cannot always control the report about us that is "spread through all the surrounding country." In what ways could you speak about your desire to keep yourself faithfully in God's presence? Do you believe God's grace is sufficient for these conversations? Are we able to shift from the sociological and psychological vocabulary that normally shapes our conversations to a biblical vocabulary that is more expressive of God's real presence? The fullness and meaning of life so many seek is only to be found in Christ as we are "filled with the power of the Spirit." This is the abundance of life Jesus promised. It is the only path where we are freed from the false self and discover our true selves, a life that is replenished by an unending source of salvation, Jesus Christ the Light of Life.

Prayer: Almighty God our deliverer, help us to take up our cross and follow him who is the Way, the Truth and the Life, that we might move from death to life. Fill us with the power of the Spirit. Grant us the grace and courage to be obedient to you in all things. Amen.

Reflection:

I Corinthians 12: 24b-27

But God has so arranged the body, giving the greater honor to the inferior member, that there may be no dissension within the body, but the members may have the same care for one another. If one member suffers, all suffer together with it; if one member is honored, all rejoice together with it. Now you are the body of Christ and individually members of it.

Pondering and Meditating: The progression of appearances in the season of Epiphany, the birth of Christ, the sighting of the angels, the visit of the Magi, Jesus' baptism, first miracle and the announcement of his ministry lead us naturally to the purpose of God revealed in Christ Jesus: "For God so loved the world that he gave his only Son, so that everyone who believes in him may not perish but may have eternal life" (John 3:16). For "everyone who believes" God has given his Spirit in order to "arrange the body" that we become "the body of Christ" and at the same time remain "individually members of it." The purpose is two-fold, to proclaim the Light of God that has come into the world, and secondly, to create a place where we "care for one another." God's desire is that we live in this community so the world might understand when we are in Christ Jesus there is "no dissension with the body." In this way we all rejoice together. Is this your experience in your local church?

Prayer: Loving God, we turn to you as the source of our strength. We pray that our local church may flourish in all her activities of preaching, teaching and serving in your name. Graciously hear our prayer through Christ Jesus our Lord. Amen.

Reflection:

FEBRUARY

REV. ROBERT W. BARNES, JR.

What does the Word of God mean to you? As Christians, we know that the Bible is a part of our faith and, as human beings, we know it offers us answers; but how does the Word "work" as a guide for the adventure of life?

Recently, I was thinking about the guides we use when driving and how God guides us in similar ways. My wife loves her new GPS. It does a great job of telling us to turn right in .two miles and then to turn left a mile later. The problem is that it is possible to get where we are going and still be lost because we don't know where we have been.

Maps are much better for understanding the big picture. Recently I had to learn to drive up the east coast, skirting around New York City. Many people (and electronic devices) gave me advice but I wasn't comfortable until at last I could sit down with a map and understand just where the Tapanzee Bridge was and why it matters whether I am on the New Jersey Turnpike or the Garden State Parkway.

Finally, sometimes we just need a voice to speak to us. During our last trip to Vermont I asked my wife to turn off the GPS and just tell me herself where to turn. (It worked out well)

Letting God's Word guide you this month is a lot like these options. Sometimes a single verse will tell you the next step to take. At other times the passage may give you a glimpse of the big picture so that you better understand everything. Finally, if you open yourself to God, the Holy Spirit will sometimes be the voice that directs you when the maps are unclear.

Monday, January 28, 2013

Jeremiah 1:4-5

Now the word of the Lord came to me saying, "Before I formed you in the womb I knew you, and before you were born I consecrated you; I appointed you a prophet to the nations."

Pondering and Meditating: Jeremiah's sense that he was a prophet was based on the belief that God had formed him and called him and that God's knowledge of him began before he was born. What if anything do you believe this passage has to say about when human life begins and ends? Do you believe that God values your life in something like the same way God valued Jeremiah's, even if you are not called to be a prophet? Do you believe that God actually values every human life in such a personal way, or does God only care for some? Do you believe Jesus' words that God sees even a sparrow fall are true? (Matthew 10:29)

Prayer: O God, we cannot stand the thought that our lives are only the products of chemicals and chance; but the belief that what we do has meaning is also staggering. Teach us, Lord, to be able to accept the "weight" of the glory you have endowed us and the "lightness" of knowing that, like the birds of the air, we are always in your hands. Amen.

Reflection:

Jeremiah 1:6-10

Then I said, "Ah, Lord God! Truly I do not know how to speak, for I am only a boy." But the Lord said to me, "Do not say, 'I am only a boy'; for you shall go to all to whom I send you, and you shall speak whatever I command you. Do not be afraid of them, for I am with you to deliver you," says the Lord. Then the Lord put out his hand and touched my mouth; and the Lord said to me, "Now I have put my words in your mouth. See, today I appoint you over nations and over kingdoms, to pluck up and to pull down, to destroy and to overthrow, to build and to plant."

Pondering and Meditating: Not everyone is called to be a prophet, but everyone is called to do something. What do you feel called by God to do? If Jeremiah was tempted to claim that he was too young to be a prophet, are there reasons why you doubt yourself? Do you believe that God truly can work through you to make a difference?

Prayer: O Lord, sometimes it is hard for us to believe in a God we cannot see, but more often it is hard for us to believe that you can work through the person we do see in the mirror. Please help us to believe in you and then help us to learn to believe in the person we can become when we walk with you. This we ask in Jesus' name. Amen.

Reflection:

Wednesday, January 30, 2013

Psalm 71:1-6

In you, O Lord, I take refuge; let me never be put to shame. In your righteousness deliver me and rescue me; incline your ear to me and save me. Be to me a rock of refuge, a strong fortress, to save me, for you are my rock and my fortress. Rescue me, O my God, from the hand of the wicked, from the grasp of the unjust and cruel. For you, O Lord, are my hope, my trust, O Lord, from my youth. Upon you I have leaned from my birth; it was you who took me from my mother's womb. My praise is continually of you.

Pondering and Meditating: Serving God isn't easy. Sometimes it is scary. The writer of Psalm 71 could really be writing for anyone who has ever taken a stand for God when asking for God to deliver and protect him or her. When, if ever, have you been persecuted for righteousness sake? Did you really trust that God was with you? Or did you think that everything rested with you?

Prayer: O God, who shut the mouth of Daniel's lions and raised Jesus from the dead, please teach me to trust you, not only in theory, but in the realities of my life. This I ask in Jesus' name. Amen.

Reflection:

I Corinthians 13:1-7

If I speak in the tongues of mortals and of angels, but do not have love, I am a noisy gong or a clanging cymbal. And if I have prophetic powers, and understand all mysteries and all knowledge, and if I have all faith, so as to remove mountains, but do not have love, I am nothing. If I give away all my possessions, and if I hand over my body so that I may boast, but do not have love, I gain nothing. Love is patient; love is kind; love is not envious or boastful or arrogant or rude. It does not insist on its own way; it is not irritable or resentful; it does not rejoice in wrongdoing, but rejoices in the truth. It bears all things, believes all things, hopes all things, endures all things.

Pondering and Meditating: Learning to follow Christ is a process. First we have to accept the call of Christ to do something. Then we have to learn that nothing that we do has meaning if we fail to love. Have you ever found yourself trying to serve God but forgetting to love? What fruit did your effort bear? What can you do that will help you learn to keep your spiritual focus as a Christ-follower?

Prayer: O God, my self-centeredness can go to the very core of my soul. Even when I give or serve or speak in your name; everything can be about me. Please help me to learn that I am loved with an everlasting love and from that knowledge then learn to properly love first myself, and then others as myself. Amen.

Reflection:

Friday, February 1, 2013

I Corinthians 13:8-13

Love never ends. But as for prophecies, they will come to an end; as for tongues, they will cease; as for knowledge, it will come to an end. For we know only in part, and we prophesy only in part; but when the complete comes, the partial will come to an end. When I was a child, I spoke like a child, I thought like a child, I reasoned like a child; when I became an adult, I put an end to childish ways. For now we see in a mirror, dimly, but then we will see face to face. Now I know only in part; then I will know fully, even as I have been fully known. And now faith, hope, and love abide, these three; and the greatest of these is love.

Pondering and Meditating: Love never ends. It is the greatest of all things that endure forever. So often we miss that truth until we have exhausted every passion of life. When have you experienced the reality of Christ-like love? When have you shared it with others? Is there a situation in your life now in which you are struggling to find a way to live out the reality of God's love?

Prayer: O God, it can be so hard to remember how much more love matters than all the things that thrill and upset us. Teach us, Lord, to see the events that take place in this world and in our lives through the lens of the eternal value of love. This we ask in the name of he who died for us out of love, rose again to give us hope and will return to make all things new. Amen.

Reflection:

Luke 4:21-22, 28-30

Then he began to say to them, "Today this Scripture has been fulfilled in your hearing." All spoke well of him and were amazed at the gracious words that came from his mouth. They said, "Is not this Joseph's son?"... When they heard this, all in the synagogue were filled with rage. They got up, drove him out of the town, and led him to the brow of the hill on which their town was built, so that they might hurl him off the cliff. But he passed through the midst of them and went on his way.

Pondering and Meditating: Jesus is a challenge to us and to the world. We are drawn to his person and find him inspiring; but then we are staggered by the authority of his words and the enormity of the claims about who he is. We want to believe, but believing seems too much and we would cast him from our lives. When have you wrestled with the identity of Jesus? Who do you believe that he is? When has Christ seemed especially close to you?

Prayer: Dear Lord, we believe but doubt; we understand but question. We only know that Christ is our one true hope. Help us to grow in our faith that we might be rooted and grounded in Christ and in our identity in him. This we ask in the name of the One who died for those who rejected him. Amen.

Reflection:

Luke 4:23-27

He said to them, "Doubtless you will quote to me this proverb, "Doctor, cure yourself!' And you will say, "Do here also in your hometown the things that we have heard you did at Capernaum." And he said, "Truly I tell you, no prophet is accepted in the prophet's hometown. But the truth is, there were many widows in Israel in the time of Elijah, when the heaven was shut up three years and six months, and there was a severe famine over all the land; yet Elijah was sent to none of them except to a widow at Zarephath in Sidon. There were also many lepers in Israel in the time of the prophet Elisha, and none of them was cleansed except Naaman the Syrian."

Pondering and Meditating: Belief in Christ matters but sometimes it is hard for us to accept that God loves other people besides us. The Jews in Jesus' hometown grew angry when he reminded them that God sometimes healed people who weren't even Jews. As Christians, we too can struggle to accept the possibility that God loves people who do not know what we know. Do you believe that there is hope for people who never hear the Gospel in this world? What Scriptures inform your faith? What does Jesus' prayer, "Father forgive them, for they know not what they do," mean to you?

Prayer: Dear Lord, there are some things we cannot understand in this life. Help us to accept the truth that you give us and trust you in the questions we still have. This we ask in Jesus' name. Amen.

Reflection:

Exodus 34:29-32

Moses came down from Mount Sinai. As he came down from the mountain with the two tablets of the covenant in his hand, Moses did not know that the skin of his face shone because he had been talking with God. When Aaron and all the Israelites saw Moses, the skin of his face was shining, and they were afraid to come near him. But Moses called to them; and Aaron and all the leaders of the congregation returned to him, and Moses spoke with them. Afterwards all the Israelites came near, and he gave them in commandment all that the Lord had spoken with him on Mount Sinai.

Pondering and Meditating: Walking with Christ means living out our faith in everyday ways in everyday places. Disciples of Jesus don't usually wear halos or walk on water. That said, sometimes the joy of being close to God is unmistakably written on our face in our attitude. When in your life have you felt particularly close to God? Has the joy of the Lord ever made everything about life feel different? If so why do you believe God does not always keep us on that "high"?

Prayer: Dear Lord, I do not ask you for a feeling or a thrill. Only let me so walk with you that I will be changed on the inside and others might see the difference you have made. This I ask in Jesus' name. Amen.

Reflection:

Tuesday, February 5, 2013

Exodus 34:33-35

When Moses had finished speaking with them, he put a veil on his face; but whenever Moses went in before the Lord to speak with him, he would take the veil off, until he came out; and when he came out, and told the Israelites what he had been commanded, the Israelites would see the face of Moses, that the skin of his face was shining; and Moses would put the veil on his face again, until he went in to speak with him.

Pondering and Meditating: There is a stage in our faith when we might desperately want God to be real but be filled with doubts. Later there may come a time when we believe God hears our every word but for some reason we are not motivated to pray. Consider the example of Moses. Do you regularly enter into the Lord's presence to speak with him? If not, what prevents you from making time to spend with God? If you did make a decision to regularly spend more time with God, what difference do you believe it would make in your life?

Prayer: O God, sometimes we are like little children playing tricks. We knock on your door and run away before you can answer. Teach us, Lord, to be still in your presence. Help us to learn to speak and listen when we are alone with you. This we ask in Jesus' name. Amen.

Reflection:

Wednesday, February 6, 2013

Psalm 99

The Lord is king; let the peoples tremble! He sits enthroned upon the cherubim; let the earth quake! The Lord is great in Zion; he is exalted over all the peoples. Let them praise your great and awesome name. Holy is he! Mighty King, lover of justice, you have established equity; you have executed justice and righteousness in Jacob. Extol the Lord our God; worship at his footstool. Holy is he! Moses and Aaron were among his priests; Samuel also was among those who called on his name. They cried to the Lord, and he answered them. He spoke to them in the pillar of cloud; they kept his decrees, and the statutes that he gave them. O Lord our God, you answered them; you were a forgiving God to them, but an avenger of their wrongdoings. Extol the Lord our God, and worship at his holy mountain; for the Lord our God is holy.

Pondering and Meditating: God is more than words but words are the best tools we have for describing God. Psalm 99 uses masculine language ("God," "Lord" and "he") to speak of God. Today we are quick to point out that God is not a man, but even so these words make us think. What ideas about God are conveyed by the word "King" that we might have forgotten about today? How does the idea of God's absolute authority and power fit into your faith?

Prayer: O God, we use words to speak of you, but whatever words we use are not enough. Help us to worship you with our words, but even more so with our hearts. This we ask in Jesus' name. Amen.

Reflection:

Thursday, February 7, 2013

I Corinthians 3:12-15

Now if anyone builds on the foundation with gold, silver, precious stones, wood, hay, straw— the work of each builder will become visible, for the Day will disclose it, because it will be revealed with fire, and the fire will test what sort of work each has done. If what has been built on the foundation survives, the builder will receive a reward. If the work is burned, the builder will suffer loss; the builder will be saved, but only as through fire.

Pondering and Meditating: There is a strain of Christian thought that teaches that we are saved by God's grace and that nothing we do on earth is of eternal significance. The Bible however teaches something more profound. We are saved by grace and not by works (Ephesians 2:8-9); but we are also saved in order that we might do good works (Ephesians 2:10 completes the thought.) In that light the warning and the promise of today's passage is stern. Some Christians will enter heaven knowing they have wasted their time on earth; while others will do things that last forever. What are you doing right now that you believe really matters? Where are you wasting time? What do you want to do with the time you have left?

Prayer: O Lord, when your Son appears grant that my knee shall bow without shame. This I ask in Jesus' name. Amen.

Reflection:

Friday, February 8, 2013

I Corinthians 3:16-4:2

Do you not know that you are God's temple and that God's Spirit dwells in you? If anyone destroys God's temple, God will destroy that person. For God's temple is holy, and you are that temple. Do not deceive yourselves. If you think that you are wise in this age, you should become fools so that you may become wise. For the wisdom of this world is foolishness with God. For it is written, 'He catches the wise in their craftiness', and again, 'The Lord knows the thoughts of the wise, that they are futile.' So let no one boast about human leaders. For all things are yours, whether Paul or Apollos or Cephas or the world or life or death or the present or the future—all belong to you, and you belong to Christ, and Christ belongs to God. Think of us in this way, as servants of Christ and stewards of God's mysteries. Moreover, it is required of stewards that they should be found trustworthy.

Pondering and Meditating: The words of today's reading are relentless. Our lives do matter and ultimately we will stand before God and everything will fade away save the question of our faithfulness. What are you living for right now? What has God called you to be faithful to? What changes do you need to make in your priorities?

Prayer: O God, this is not the only life; but please give me grace and strength to run the race you have appointed to me on earth. This I ask in Jesus' name. Amen.

Reflection:

Saturday, February 9, 2013

Luke 9:28-36

Now about eight days after these sayings Jesus took with him Peter and John and James, and went up on the mountain to pray. And while he was praying, the appearance of his face changed, and his clothes became dazzling white. Suddenly they saw two men, Moses and Elijah, talking to him. They appeared in glory and were speaking of his departure, which he was about to accomplish at Jerusalem. Now Peter and his companions were weighed down with sleep; but since they had stayed awake, they saw his glory and the two men who stood with him. Just as they were leaving him, Peter said to Jesus, 'Master, it is good for us to be here; let us make three dwellings, one for you, one for Moses, and one for Elijah'-not knowing what he said. While he was saying this, a cloud came and overshadowed them; and they were terrified as they entered the cloud. Then from the cloud came a voice that said, 'This is my Son, my Chosen; listen to him!' When the voice had spoken, Jesus was found alone. And they kept silent and in those days told no one any of the things they had seen.

Pondering and Meditating: Peter saw Jesus standing beside two great historical leaders of the faith and he thought that was good. Then came the revelation from God and he saw Jesus alone. Why do you believe that Jesus is unique? Is this something you have been taught or something you own for yourself? Why? Do you still have questions?

Prayer: O God, I ask no vision, but grant that I might know Jesus for who he is, as much as I can on earth. Amen.

Reflection:

Luke 9:37-42

On the next day, when they had come down from the mountain, a great crowd met him. Just then a man from the crowd shouted, 'Teacher, I beg you to look at my son; he is my only child. Suddenly a spirit seizes him, and all at once he shrieks. It throws him into convulsions until he foams at the mouth; it mauls him and will scarcely leave him. I begged your disciples to cast it out, but they could not.' Jesus answered, 'Your faithless and perverse generation, how much longer must I be with you and bear with you? Bring your son here.' While he was coming, the demon dashed him to the ground in convulsions. But Jesus rebuked the unclean spirit, healed the boy, and gave him back to his father.

Pondering and Meditating: When Jesus came down from the Mount of Transfiguration he found the majority of his disciples caught up in an argument over how to help a young man. Sometimes it is better to argue than not to care. Who are the people that you have been frustrated by in your efforts to reach with the word of Christ? Are you able to care for people with the love of Christ, even when you don't know what to say?

Prayer: Dear God, help me to find time to spend alone with you and then out of that time fill me with love for everyone around me. This I ask in Jesus' name. Amen.

Reflection:

Deuteronomy 26:1-4, 11

When you have come into the land that the Lord your God is giving you as an inheritance to possess, and you possess it, and settle in it, you shall take some of the first of all the fruit of the ground, which you harvest from the land that the Lord your God is giving you, and you shall put it in a basket and go to the place that the Lord your God will choose as a dwelling for his name. You shall go to the priest who is in office at that time, and say to him, 'Today I declare to the Lord your God that I have come into the land that the Lord swore to our ancestors to give us.' When the priest takes the basket from your hand and sets it down before the altar of the Lord your God, Then you, together with the Levites and the aliens who reside among you, shall celebrate with all the bounty that the Lord your God has given to you and to your house.

Pondering and Meditating: People sometimes complain when the church talks about money and certainly that can be done in the wrong way. That said, from the very beginnings of the Bible the Lord linked his blessings to the responsibility to give. When and what are the Jewish people commanded to give to God? What do you think it means to us that the offerings mentioned here are to be given to the Levites and the aliens? Do you give with a willing or grudging heart?

Prayer: O God, forgive my greed and selfishness and teach me to become a person who gives willingly and joyfully. This I ask in Jesus' Name. Amen.

Reflection:

Tuesday, February 12, 2013

Deuteronomy 26:5-10

You shall make this response before the Lord your God: 'A wandering Aramean was my ancestor; he went down into Egypt and lived there as an alien, few in number, and there he became a great nation, mighty and populous. When the Egyptians treated us harshly and afflicted us, by imposing hard labour on us, we cried to the Lord, the God of our ancestors; the Lord heard our voice and saw our affliction, our toil, and our oppression. The Lord brought us out of Egypt with a mighty hand and an outstretched arm, with a terrifying display of power, and with signs and wonders; and he brought us into this place and gave us this land, a land flowing with milk and honey. So now I bring the first of the fruit of the ground that you, O Lord, have given me.' You shall set it down before the Lord your God and bow down before the Lord your God.

Pondering and Meditating: We live in a day and age where people, even many Christians, have cut themselves off from their past and their heritage. The Bible teaches us another way; part of knowing who we are is remembering where we came from. What people and places are parts of your spiritual heritage? How have they shaped who you are today? What parts of our United Methodist tradition resonate most with you?

Prayer: O God, we thank you for the men and women you have used in shaping who we are. Please help us not to forget them and please mold and shape us that one day people might give thanks for the role we played in their lives. This we ask in Jesus' Name. Amen.

Reflection:

Wednesday, February 13, 2013

Psalm 91:1-2

You who live in the shelter of the Most High, who abide in the shadow of the Almighty, will say to the Lord, 'My refuge and my fortress; my God, in whom I trust.'

Pondering and Meditating: One of the hardest things in the world to battle is worry. A word from our doctor, a downturn in the stock market, our child driving off alone; all of these things can keep us awake at night. How prone are you to worry? Do you trust that God is your refuge and fortress? If not, how can you learn to worry less?

Prayer: O God, we have so many burdens and fears and all too often we think we must handle everything on our own. Teach us, Lord. Teach us to surrender our silly worries over small things. Teach us also to trust you with the big problems that are more than we can handle. Teach us, please teach us, to believe the things we say we believe about you. This we ask in Jesus' Name. Amen.

Reflection:

Thursday, February 14, 2013

Psalm 91:9-16

Because you have made the Lord your refuge, the Most High your dwelling-place, no evil shall befall you, no scourge come near your tent. For he will command his angels concerning you to guard you in all your ways. On their hands they will bear you up, so that you will not dash your foot against a stone. You will tread on the lion and the adder, the young lion and the serpent you will trample under foot. Those who love me, I will deliver; I will protect those who know my name. When they call to me, I will answer them; I will be with them in trouble, I will rescue them and honour them. With long life I will satisfy them, and show them my salvation.

Pondering and Meditating: Sometimes it is hard to know how to take the words of the Bible. In Psalm 91 we are told that if we trust in God then God will rescue us from danger. Often that seems to be the case but at other times we run into the truth that bad things can happen to good people. Have you ever questioned God because God allowed you to go through a trial? When has God delivered you from some difficulty? How do you make sense of the struggles and sorrows we go though in this life?

Prayer: O God, we thank you for your blessings and we trust that your promises are true. Please help us to continue to trust you when times are hard. This we ask in Jesus' Name. Amen.

Reflection:

Romans 10:8-13

But what does it say? 'The word is near you, on your lips and in your heart' (that is, the word of faith that we proclaim); because if you confess with your lips that Jesus is Lord and believe in your heart that God raised him from the dead, you will be saved. For one believes with the heart and so is justified, and one confesses with the mouth and so is saved. The scripture says, 'No one who believes in him will be put to shame.' For there is no distinction between Jew and Greek; the same Lord is Lord of all and is generous to all who call on him. For, 'Everyone who calls on the name of the Lord shall be saved.'

Pondering and Meditating: Some people today read Romans 10:8 and believe it teaches us that God gives us authority and power to speak words of faith, which will produce miracles, faith and healing. The Scripture itself, however, says something different. We cannot claim wealth or healing with our words, but we actually can accept God's salvation offered to us in Jesus Christ. What does it say of believers today that they confuse earthly wealth with eternal salvation? Do you trust that you are "put right" with God through what Jesus Christ has done for us? If not, will you call on the Lord today and ask for his salvation?

Prayer: O God, help us not to trade your spiritual blessings for wealth that does not last. Help us to find you, and life, through Jesus Christ in whose name we pray. Amen.

Reflection:

Luke 4:1-8

Jesus, full of the Holy Spirit, returned from the Jordan and was led by the Spirit in the wilderness, where for forty days he was tempted by the devil. He ate nothing at all during those days, and when they were over, he was famished. The devil said to him, 'If you are the Son of God, command this stone to become a loaf of bread.' Jesus answered him, 'It is written, and "One does not live by bread alone." ' Then the devil led him up and showed him in an instant all the kingdoms of the world. And the devil said to him, 'To you I will give their glory and all this authority; for it has been given over to me, and I give it to anyone I please. If you, then, will worship me, it will all be yours.' Jesus answered him, 'It is written, "Worship the Lord your God, and serve only him."

Pondering and Meditating: Even Jesus could be tempted. This is because true purity and holiness only exist as the product of a conscious choice. Babies are innocent because they cannot fathom evil. Mature people have no business being innocent. We must purchase holiness and purity with our conscious decisions. When have you been tempted and given in? When have you been tempted and not given in? In what areas of your life do you need to begin to fight the battle to become a better man or woman?

Prayer: O God, help us to trust that your grace covers over all our sin and that your Holy Spirit can work within us so that we actually begin to live more as Jesus did. This we ask in Jesus' name. Amen.

Reflection:

Luke 4:9-13

Then the devil took him to Jerusalem, and placed him on the pinnacle of the temple, saying to him, 'If you are the Son of God, throw yourself down from here, for it is written, "He will command his angels concerning you, to protect you", and "On their hands they will bear you up, so that you will not dash your foot against a stone." ' Jesus answered him, 'It is said, "Do not put the Lord your God to the test." ' When the devil had finished every test, he departed from him until an opportune time.

Pondering and Meditating: Have you ever prayed for a sign? Have you ever wondered why God did not provide signs for everyone so that they would feel compelled to believe? Satan's third temptation of Jesus was to give that very thing to the crowds of Jerusalem. On what basis did Jesus say "no" to Satan? What does this teach us about our desires for God to prove himself to us? Even though God does not give us signs, God shows us what we need to see in order to believe. When has God been especially near to you so that you knew God was real?

Prayer: O God, each of us needs you in our lives and the way you speak to us is seldom the same from one person to another. I do not ask you for a dream or vision. I simply pray that you would help me to know and love you as I should. This we pray in Jesus' Name. Amen.

Reflection:

Tuesday, February 18, 2013

Genesis 15:1-7

After these things the word of the Lord came to Abram in a vision, 'Do not be afraid, Abram, I am your shield; your reward shall be very great.' But Abram said, 'O Lord God, what will you give me, for I continue childless, and the heir of my house is Eliezer of Damascus?' And Abram said, 'You have given me no offspring, and so a slave born in my house is to be my heir.' But the word of the Lord came to him, 'This man shall not be your heir; no one but your very own issue shall be your heir.' He brought him outside and said, 'Look towards heaven and count the stars, if you are able to count them.' Then he said to him, 'So shall your descendants be.' And he believed the Lord; and the Lord reckoned it to him as righteousness. Then he said to him, 'I am the Lord who brought you from Ur of the Chaldeans, to give you this land to possess.'

Pondering and Meditating: Abraham believed God, even when believing God tested his common sense. He and Sarah were childless but Abraham was willing to trust that God has the last word. When have you had to trust God when it was very hard to do so? What was the result? What do you think you might have done differently?

Prayer: O God, like Thomas, I want to see and then believe, but you call me to believe and then see. Please help me to walk with you when I can only see the next step and trust that you see all the landscape that is ahead. This I ask in Jesus' Name. Amen.

Reflection:

Genesis 15:8-12, 17-18

But he said, 'O Lord God, how am I to know that I shall possess it?' He said to him, 'Bring me a heifer three years old, a female goat three years old, a ram three years old, a turtle-dove, and a young pigeon.' He brought him all these and cut them in two, laying each half over against the other; but he did not cut the birds in two. And when birds of prey came down on the carcasses, Abram drove them away. As the sun was going down, a deep sleep fell upon Abram, and a deep and terrifying darkness descended upon him. When the sun had gone down and it was dark, a smoking fire-pot and a flaming torch passed between these pieces. On that day the Lord made a covenant with Abram, saying, 'To your descendants I give this land, from the river of Egypt to the great river, the river Euphrates.

Pondering and Meditating: Sometimes the parts of the Bible that seem strange to us made perfect sense to the people who were alive at the time. In this passage, God makes a covenant with Abraham using a ritual of Abraham's day. What does it reveal about God that God was willing to meet Abraham "on his level"? How is the coming of Jesus a continuation of this same divine quality? How might God be speaking to people in new ways today?

Prayer: O God, give me a mind that can understand your ancient words and a heart that is receptive to your word today. This I ask in the name of him that is the Word made flesh. Amen.

Reflection:

Wednesday, February 20, 2013

Psalm 27:1-6

The Lord is my light and my salvation; whom shall I fear? The Lord is the stronghold of my life; of whom shall I be afraid? When evildoers assail me to devour my flesh — my adversaries and foes — they shall stumble and fall. Though an army encamp against me, my heart shall not fear; though war rise up against me, yet I will be confident. One thing I asked of the Lord, that will I seek after: to live in the house of the Lord all the days of my life, to behold the beauty of the Lord, and to inquire in his temple. For he will hide me in his shelter in the day of trouble; he will conceal me under the cover of his tent; he will set me high on a rock. Now my head is lifted up above my enemies all around me, and I will offer in his tent sacrifices with shouts of joy; I will sing and make melody to the Lord.

Pondering and Meditating: The Lord is my light and my salvation. When we are close to God it is so easy to see our problems and challenges from the perspective of faith and it is almost impossible to fear. When has God been near to you in such a way that you were uplifted" by God's presence? Why are you not always in this elevated spiritual state? Is there anything you think you should change in your walk with Christ?

Prayer: O God, please be my strength and my shield, even when I forget who you are; but please help me not to forget as often. This I ask in Jesus' Name. Amen.

Reflection:

Thursday, February 21, 2013

Psalm 27:7-14

Hear, O Lord, when I cry aloud, be gracious to me and answer me! 'Come,' my heart says, 'seek his face!' Your face, Lord, do I seek. Do not hide your face from me. Do not turn your servant away in anger, you who have been my help. Do not cast me off, do not forsake me, O God of my salvation! If my father and mother forsake me, the Lord will take me up. Teach me your way, O Lord, and lead me on a level path because of my enemies. Do not give me up to the will of my adversaries, for false witnesses have risen against me, and they are breathing out violence. I believe that I shall see the goodness of the Lord in the land of the living. Wait for the Lord; be strong, and let your heart take courage; wait for the Lord!

Pondering and Meditating: The psalms are so incredibly honest. Psalm 27 begins with a statement of unshakable faith but finishes with an earnest plea that God would give the strength that is needed. How can our faith grow when it is tested? When your faith waivers do you turn to God or walk away? Can you think of a time when you have come through a trial victoriously in your faith?

Prayer: O God, you are the God of my heights and the God of my depths; the God of my joys and the God who is with me in my fears. Whatever this world may bring, help me to trust in you. This I ask in the name of him who promised to be with us to the end of the age. Amen.

Reflection:

Friday, February 22, 2013

Philippians 3:17-4:1

Brothers and sisters, join in imitating me, and observe those who live according to the example you have in us. For many live as enemies of the cross of Christ; I have often told you of them, and now I tell you even with tears. Their end is destruction; their god is the belly; and their glory is in their shame; their minds are set on earthly things. But our citizenship is in heaven, and it is from there that we are expecting a Savior, the Lord Jesus Christ. He will transform the body of our humiliation so that it may be conformed to the body of his glory, by the power that also enables him to make all things subject to himself. Therefore, my brothers and sisters, whom I love and long for, my joy and crown, stand firm in the Lord in this way, my beloved.

Pondering and Meditating: Today we find it easy to believe in heaven but hard to believe in hell, and yet Scripture paints a different picture. Christ is our Savior but those who "live as enemies of the cross" are destined for "destruction." Do you believe that the Bible is telling us the truth here? What do you believe about the idea of evil? If God wants everyone to be saved, why would some people be lost?

Prayer: O God, often we are blind because we see things only through the lenses of the world. Teach us to see and understand everything from the perspective of your Kingdom. This we ask in Jesus' name. Amen.

Reflection:

Luke 13:31-32

At that very hour some Pharisees came and said to him, 'Get away from here, for Herod wants to kill you.' He said to them, 'Go and tell that fox for me, "Listen, I am casting out demons and performing cures today and tomorrow, and on the third day I finish my work.

Pondering and Meditating: Some speak of the death of Jesus as a tragedy and in some ways it was; but it was also a victory and the accomplishment of a purpose. Jesus understood people, he knew what awaited him in Jerusalem; and yet he would not be diverted from his destiny. What does it mean to you that Jesus chose to die for the redemption of the world? What does it mean to you that he died for you personally? Do you have confidence that through Christ your sins are forgiven and you are a child of God? If not would you like to pray for that now?

Prayer: O God, it staggers the human mind that you once were born into our world to become one of us. Even more it is hard to accept that Christ once died for us. None of us can understand all that Christ did, but I pray that you would forgive me and grant me the life and salvation you came to make available to us all. This I ask in the name of Christ, who died, is risen, and will come again. Amen.

Reflection:

Luke 13:33-35

Yet today, tomorrow, and the next day I must be on my way, because it is impossible for a prophet to be killed away from Jerusalem." Jerusalem, Jerusalem, the city that kills the prophets and stones those who are sent to it! How often have I desired to gather your children together as a hen gathers her brood under her wings, and you were not willing! See, your house is left to you. And I tell you, you will not see me until the time comes when you say, "Blessed is the one who comes in the name of the Lord." '

Pondering and Meditating: It is always startling thatsome Christians can be prejudiced against the Jewish people. After all, Jesus was a Jew and even if his own people rejected him there is a clear scriptural promise that Jesus' love for his own people will one day be returned. (See Romans, chapters 9-11, especially 11:25-32 and Zechariah, chapters 12-14, especially 12:10-13:1.) Do you believe that God's plan still includes the fulfillment of God's promises to Abraham? How do you believe that will work? What does this mean for all the other nations of the world?

Prayer: O God of all the nations, we await with hope the return of Christ as King of kings and Lord of lords. Until that day comes, help us to look at all peoples through the lens of the cross and never to be ashamed of sharing the reason for the hope that is within us. This we pray in Jesus' Name. Amen.

Reflection:

MARCH

BISHOP THOMAS J. BICKERTON

I end each piece of correspondence with the same words: The Journey Continues, . . . Those words accurately summarize the theme of this month's readings. God's sustaining grace and ever present love has enabled the journey to continue from the time of creation until today. God's offer of forgiveness and reconciliation for those who have wandered is available for all those who believe. And God's resurrecting power brought new life to Jesus and a new vision of God's will and purpose for the world.

What is required is a sense of the holy in our midst, an anticipation that God will be at work among us, a joy in being a part of God's eternal plan, and a love that will give to others the same love we have received. As Peter says in Acts 10:34: "I truly understand that God shows no partiality, but in every nation anyone who fears him and does what is right is acceptable to him." With that kind of grace and love at work, there is no doubt that our God has made it possible for the journey to continue. Thanks be to God.

Monday, February 25, 2013

Isaiah 55:1-2

"Ho, everyone who thirsts, come to the waters; and you that have no money, come, buy and eat! Come, buy wine and milk without money and without price. Why do you spend your money for that which is not bread, and your labor for that which does not satisfy? Listen carefully to me, and eat what is good, and delight yourselves in rich food."

Pondering and Meditating: "Your money is no good here." But your trust and faith is. God has a free pass into a life rich in things that delight the soul. Have you listened carefully for the invitation God freely issues? Are you finding nourishment in the goodness of God? Is your soul today delighting in the abundance of God?

Prayer: Thank you, God, for your gracious invitation and for the abundance of your provisions. Grant to me the courage today to find joy and delight in you. Amen.

Reflection:

Tuesday, February 26, 2013

Isaiah 55:3-5

"Incline your ear, and come to me; listen, so that you may live. I will make with you an everlasting covenant, my steadfast, sure love for David. See, I made him a witness to the peoples, a leader and commander for the peoples. See, you shall call nations that you do not know, and nations that do not know you shall run to you, because of the Lord your God, the Holy One of Israel, for he has glorified you."

Pondering and Meditating: In order to delight in the Lord we have to "incline our ear" in God's direction. And when we do, we find joy for our soul and an everlasting covenant with our God. As a part of that covenant, God blesses us with good and wise leadership to keep us focused and open to God's guidance. Have you set aside some time each day for quiet reflection and listening? Do you find a sense of joy in the midst of your everyday? Make sure today to give thanks for and express thanks to the leaders who point you in the direction of the Lord.

Prayer: Gracious and loving God, we stand amazed at your care and love for us. You are my joy, my life, my blessing. Open my eyes today that I may see you. Open my ears today that I may hear you. Open my heart today that I may let you lead me. Amen.

Reflection:

Isaiah 55: 6-9

Seek the Lord while he may be found, call upon him while he is near; let the wicked forsake their way, and the unrighteous their thoughts; let them return to the Lord, that he may have mercy on them, and to our God, for he will abundantly pardon. For my thoughts are not your thoughts, nor are your ways my ways, says the Lord. For as the heavens are higher than the earth, so are my ways higher than your ways and my thoughts than your thoughts.

Pondering and Meditating: Now is the time to seek the Lord. There is a sense of urgency in the prophet for the people to turn from their way to God's way. Our inclinations are far different, at times, from God's. Now is the time to make a change. Is there a sense of urgency within you to seek out the way of the Lord? What is it that you need to confess today? What are the habits, feelings and attitudes that separate you from the way of the Lord?

Prayer: Holy One, you continue to love me in spite of my actions. I confess to you that my way is often far different than your way. Guide me today back onto the path which leads to you. Amen.

Reflection:

Psalm 63:1-8

O God, you are my God, I seek you, my soul thirsts for you; my flesh faints for you, as in a dry and weary land where there is not water. So I have looked upon you in the sanctuary, beholding your power and glory. Because your steadfast love is better than life, my lips will praise you. So I will bless you as long as I live; I will lift up my hands and call on your name. My soul is satisfied as with a rich feast, and my mouth praises you with joyful lips when I think of you on my bed, and meditate on you in the watches of the night; for you have been my help, and in the shadow of your wings I sing for joy. My soul clings to you; your right hand upholds me.

Pondering and Meditating: We cannot cling to God with our hands but we can with our souls. We have the opportunity to meditate on God's ways during the day and even into the nights when we cannot find sleep. The psalmist believes that this longing for God blesses God or makes God happy. Find a time in the morning when you wake and in the evening before you sleep to think about the place that God has in your heart.

Prayer: O God, fill my day with thoughts of you. Bless my life with your presence as I strive to bless you with a deeper devotion and love. Uphold me today, I pray. Amen.

Reflection:

Friday, March 1, 2013

I Corinthians 10: 1-5

I do not want you to be unaware, brothers and sisters, that our ancestors were all under the cloud, and all passed through the sea, and all were baptized into Moses in the cloud and in the sea, and all ate the same spiritual food, and all drank the same spiritual drink. For they drank from the spiritual rock that followed them, and the rock was Christ. Nevertheless, God was not pleased with most of them, and they were struck down in the wilderness.

Pondering and Meditating: Some things never change. People will be people. The Israelites received great blessings from God yet they followed their own way. The Corinthians were eager for awhile but grew complacent and undisciplined. What about us? What about you? To follow the ways of the Lord requires daily discipline and endurance. What are the spiritual habits you could establish to avoid repeating the behaviors of past generations?

Prayer: I desire you today, my God, but tomorrow I may be tempted with other agendas and concerns. Help me to seek you today, tomorrow and always. Keep me focused on what you have done for me and what I can do in response. Bless me with strength for the journey that lies ahead. Amen.

Reflection:

Saturday, March 2, 2013

I Corinthians 10:6-13

Now these things occurred as examples for us, so that we might not desire evil as they did. Do not become idolaters as some of them did; as it is written, "The people sat down to eat and drink, and they rose up to play." We must not indulge in sexual immorality as some of them did, and twenty-three thousand fell in a single day. We must not put Christ to the test, as some of them did, and were destroyed by the serpents. And do not complain as some of them did, and were destroyed by the destroyer. These things happened to serve as an example, and they were written down to instruct us, on whom the ends of the ages have come. So if you think you are standing, watch out that you do not fall. No testing has overtaken you that is not common to everyone. God is faithful, and he will not let you be tested beyond your strength, but with the testing he will also provide the way out so that you may be able to endure it."

Pondering and Meditating: Soon after being freed from slavery the Israelites grew weary, bored and afraid. Their lack of discipline led to grumbling, immorality and rash decisions. Like the Corinthians after them, we too run the risk of losing focus and perspective. Yet, there is a way through. God will "provide the way out so that you may be able to endure it." What are the things that cloud your vision and prohibit you from seeing God's faithful presence in your life?

Prayer: Lead me into the future, O God, with a sense of confidence that you will never leave me and that you alone will provide the way for me to follow. Amen.

Reflection:

Sunday, March 3, 2013

Luke 13: 1-9

At that very time there were some present who told him about the Galileans whose blood Pilate had mingled with their sacrifices. He asked them, "Do you think that because these Galileans suffered in this way they were worse sinners than all other Galileans? No, I tell you; but unless you repent, you will all perish as they did. Or those eighteen who were killed when the tower of Siloam fell on them – do you think they were worse offenders than all the others living in Jerusalem? No, I tell you; but unless you repent, you will all perish as they did." Then he told this parable: "A man had a fig tree planted in his vineyard; and he came looking for fruit on it and found none. So he said to the gardener, 'See here! For three years I have come looking for fruit on this fig tree, and still I find none. Cut it down! Why should it be wasting the soil?' He replied, 'Sir, let it alone for one more year, until I dig around it and put manure on it. If it bears fruit next year, well and good; but if not, you can cut it down.'"

Pondering and Meditating: Jesus linked a political calamity and a natural disaster to serve as signs of why we need to be prepared spiritually for the age to come. God gives us signs to show us the way and grace to turn to the way of the Lord. The opportunity is to respond in a timely manner. Where do you see the signs of God's guidance and grace?

Prayer: Gracious God, increase my awareness of your presence in my life. May I never take for granted the precious gift of your grace. Amen.

Reflection:

Joshua 5:9-12

The Lord said to Joshua, "Today I have rolled away from you the disgrace of Egypt. And so that place is called Gilgal to this day. While the Israelites were camped in Gilgal they kept the Passover in the evening on the fourteenth day of the month in the plains of Jericho. On the day after the Passover, on that very day, they ate the produce of the land, unleavened cakes and parched grain. The manna ceased on the day they ate the produce of the land, and the Israelites no longer had manna; they ate the crops of the land of Canaan that year.

Pondering and Meditating: The disgrace of slavery has been replaced with the abundance of a promised land. The chosen people will no longer be a people of the wilderness but a people of the land given to them by God's grace. While circumstances change, God's provisions do not. The manna ceases, but the produce of the land becomes their sustenance. God is still with them. Have you noticed the consistency of God's provisions in the midst of changing circumstances? No matter what conditions exist, God is faithful. Be on the watch today for the ways in which God provides in the midst of changing times.

Prayer: Holy One, I pause to thank you today for the simple reminder that you are a consistent presence for me in the midst of changing and uncertain times. Amen.

Reflection:

Tuesday, March 5, 2013

Psalm 32: 1-2

Happy are those whose transgression is forgiven, whose sin is covered. Happy are those to whom the Lord imputes no iniquity, and in whose spirit there is no deceit.

Pondering and Meditating: When we fully confess our sin to God the result is nothing less than complete forgiveness. This is the source of happiness or blessedness. Happiness does not come because there is no sin. Happiness is found when one realizes that their sin is covered and forgiven. But the key is the realization that sin should not be denied, excused or downplayed. Are you honest with yourself about your sinful life? What are the confessions you need to acknowledge? With humility, make those confessions today.

Prayer: Loving God, we stand amazed that you freely forgive our sins. Create within us today a spirit of honesty that will cause us to openly confess our transgressions to you. The psalmist reveals that happiness comes when sin is forgiven. Count us in that number as we fully confess our human sinfulness to you. Amen.

Reflection:

Psalm 32: 3-7

While I kept silence, my body wasted away through my groaning all day long. For day and night your hand was heavy upon me; my strength was dried up as by the heart of summer. Then I acknowledged my sin to you, and I did not hide my iniquity; I said, "I will confess my transgressions to the Lord," and you forgave the guilt of my sin. Therefore let all who are faithful offer prayer to you; at a time of distress, the rush of mighty waters shall not reach them. You are a hiding place for me; you preserve me from trouble; you surround me with glad cries of deliverance.

Pondering and Meditating: The process of finding happiness begins with making a full and honest confession before our God. When the soul keeps quiet and attempts to hide from God the realities of life, the end result is a heaviness of heart and a life of guilt. What a wonderful revelation to discover, however, that when we are honest with God, the Lord fully forgives. The key word in this passage is "therefore." Here is the result of confession: preservation and gladness! What is keeping you from experiencing that gladness today? What is holding you back from an open and honest relationship with God?

Prayer: For some reason, God, I still try to fool myself and hide my true self from you. I know that you know me better than I know myself. My faith assures me that you are a forgiving God yet my practices do not demonstrate that belief. Release me from me and help me to experience the complete joy of salvation through you. Amen.

Reflection:

Psalm 32:8-11

I will instruct you and teach you the way you should go; I will counsel you with my eye upon you. Do not be like a horse or a mule, without understanding, whose temper must be curbed with bit and bridle, else it will not stay near you. Many are the torments of the wicked, but steadfast love surrounds those who trust in the Lord. Be glad in the Lord and rejoice, O righteous, and shout for joy, all you upright in heart.

Pondering and Meditating: The psalmist ends with a revelation of the complete package God provides. We not only receive forgiveness when we confess, we also receive guidance along the way. God guides us in the way and keeps God's eye on us on the journey. As humans, we have the intelligence to know God's promises and seek them in our daily walk. This simple understanding is enough to cause us to rejoice and shout for joy. As you meditate on these words today, pray that you may have the strength to let you inhibitions go in order to experience the full benefits of God's love.

Prayer: God, why is it that you love us so? You not only promise to forgive, you show how interested you are in us by providing guidance and instruction along the way. Deepen our trust in you so that we might experience the fullness of your forgiving love. Amen.

Reflection:

Friday, March 8, 2013

II Corinthians 5:16-17

From now on, therefore, we regard no one from a human point of view, even though we once knew Christ from a human point of view, we know him no longer in that way. So if anyone is in Christ, there is a new creation: everything old has become new!

Pondering and Meditating: God effected creation in six days when the world was created. Later, God changed the lives of the Israelite people when they were delivered from exile in Egypt. They became a new creation with their entrance into the Promised Land. Now, Paul individualizes this concept when he says that when anyone is in Christ, they are a new creation. The old habits and tendencies have been replaced with new disciplines and norms. What makes such a change? It is the realization that life is from God and grace is sustaining. Our knowledge is far beyond earthly things and there is a new perspective on daily living. We are a new creation. As you journey through your day of busy routines and earthly rhythms, spend some time thinking today about godly things. Thank God for the life you have been given as a part of God's creation. Journal about the old habits and tendencies that need to be replaced in your life. Answer the question: What would it look like if I were to become a new creation in response to God's love for me?

Prayer: When I gaze upon the heavens and the work of your creation, O God, I wonder why you are so mindful of someone like me. Yet, I am a part of your creation too and for that I am thankful. Help me to respond to your love with a life that demonstrates that I am a new creation too. Amen.

Reflection:

Saturday, March 9, 2013

II Corinthians 5:18-21

All this is from God, who reconciled us to himself through Christ, and has given us the ministry of reconciliation; that is, in Christ God was reconciling the world to himself, not counting their trespasses against them, and entrusting the message of reconciliation to us. So we are ambassadors for Christ, since God is making his appeal through us; we entreat you on behalf of Christ, be reconciled to God. For our sake he made him to be sin who knew no sin so that in him we might become the righteousness of God.

Pondering and Meditating: In response to God's gift to us through Jesus Christ, Paul says that we now have a ministry of reconciliation. We are ambassadors for Christ and are called to represent God's message of reconciliation to the world and among all people. We do not live the Gospel for ourselves alone. As a new creation, we have been equipped to face the world for which Jesus died. We have good news to share based on a new realization within us. How will you be an ambassador for Christ today? What are the specific ways you can share your faith with another? How can you become a reconciler today among people who are divided?

Prayer: Use me, O Lord, as an instrument of your peace and as an ambassador of your reconciling love. Work through me today to be a witness of what it looks like to be a new creation. Amen.

Reflection:

Luke 15:1-3, 11b-32

Now all the tax collectors and sinners were coming near to listen to him. And the Pharisees and the scribes were grumbling and saying, "This fellow welcomes sinners and eats with them." So he told them this parable. (Read the story of the Prodigal Son found in Luke 15:11b-32)

Pondering and Meditating: "This fellow welcomes sinners and eats with them." This has been the pattern that God has established from the beginning of time. From Adam and Eve in the Old Testament to the Apostle Paul, the biblical story demonstrates that God's desire is to see the creation aligned with its intended purpose. We were created for joy yet our human tendency is to be like the prodigal son. We want to go and do it our own way. Yet, God returns the chosen people from exile, Jesus welcomes sinners and eats with them, and godly fathers welcome their wayward sons back into the family. This is the way of the Lord. Is it your way? How tempted are you to respond like the older brother who resents the grace offered to his younger sibling? To receive grace is an amazing gift. To transmit grace in the midst of sinners and those who disappoint us is another matter. Meditate today on how you can be more welcoming and gracious to all of God's children.

Prayer: O God, you welcomed me home when I strayed from you. As your ambassador and as a part of your new creation, give me the courage to transmit your grace to those around me, especially among those who are disappoint and let me down. Amen.

Reflection:

Monday, March 11, 2013

Isaiah 43:16-21

Thus says the Lord, who makes a way in the sea, a path in the mighty waters, who brings out chariot and horse, army and warrior; they lie down, they cannot rise, they are extinguished, quenched like a wick: Do not remember the former things, or consider the things of old. I am about to do a new thing; now it springs forth, do you not perceive it? I will make a way in the wilderness and rivers in the desert. The wild animals will honor me, the jackals and the ostriches; for I give water in the wilderness, rivers in the desert, to give drink to my chosen people, the people whom I formed for myself so that they might declare my praise.

Pondering and Meditating: The Israelites find themselves in exile again, this time at the hands of the Babylonians. But God is about to act once again. What God has done previously, God will do again. In the exile from Egypt, the water was turned into dry land. This time the desert will be turned into rivers in order to meet their needs. God is not limited to acting in the same old ways to accomplish new acts of salvation. God is not just a God of history. God uses current circumstances to accomplish God's will. God is relevant in any age at any time. Our God is a very present help in times of need. Ask yourself this question: "Where do I see God at work in the world around me today?"

Prayer: I thank you, God, for the historical record of the Bible. Help me today to realize, however, that you are a God of yesterday, today and tomorrow. Open my eyes to see you in the midst of every moment and day. Amen.

Reflection:

Tuesday, March 12, 2013

Psalm 126: 1-3

When the Lord restored the fortunes of Zion, we were like those who dream. Then our mouth was filled with laughter, and our tongue with shouts of joy; then it was said among the nations, "The Lord has done great things for them." The Lord has done great things for us, and we rejoiced.

Pondering and Meditating: The key word in this passage is the word "restored." Webster's Dictionary defines "restore" as to "give back" or "return." Living in exile the Israelites could only dream of returning to their former land. Yet God reversed their reality and fulfilled their most extravagant dreams. The result is a consistent response among God's people: laughter and joy. Recall today times in your life when you knew that God was at work in your life. What did you feel? Look around you today. Sense the awesome presence of God at work in the midst of creation. Reflect on how God has sustained you as a part of that creation. Smile! Laugh! Rejoice!

Prayer: Creator God, we are but a grain of sand in the grand scheme of your creation. Yet, you know us, love us, and claim us as your own. When we become consumed with the realities of life, you come to us again and again with encouragement and restoration. Free us today that we might laugh, rejoice, and sing your praises. Amen.

Reflection:

Psalm 126:4-6

Restore our fortunes, O Lord, like the watercourses in the Negeb. May those who sow in tears reap with shouts of joy. Those who go out weeping, bearing the seed for sowing, shall come home with shouts of joy, carrying their sheaves.

Pondering and Meditating: The work of God is accomplished through a radical reversal. Those who weep will reverse their emotions and shout for joy. The dry bed in the Negeb remained a wasteland where the survival of any living thing was unlikely. But in a moment, the rains begin and the wasteland is turned into a source of life. This is the ability for radical reversal that exists with our God. We are called to plant seeds in anticipation of a great harvest because our God can do miraculous things. Where is it that you find yourself doubting and cynical? What consumes your thoughts that take away from a spirit of anticipation and hope? God can even reverse a bad attitude or a destructive habit. Identify one or two things today that you can "give over" to God in anticipation of a radical reversal.

Prayer: Forgiving God, I confess to you today that at times I doubt your ability. Sometimes I plant seeds of cynicism that reflect my lack of faith in you. Forgive my human limitations today and give me a vision of new life so that I may bear witness to the glorious harvest brought forth by your hand. Amen.

Reflection:

Philippians 3:4b-9

If anyone else has reason to be confident in the flesh, I have more: circumcised on the eighth day, a member of the people of Israel, of the tribe of Benjamin, a Hebrew born of Hebrews; as to the laws, a Pharisee; as to zeal, a persecutor of the church; as to righteousness under the law, blameless. Yet whatever gains I had, these I have to regard as loss because of Christ. More than that, I regard everything as loss because of the surpassing value of knowing Christ Jesus my Lord. For his sake I have suffered the loss of all things, and I regard them as rubbish, in order that I may gain Christ and be found in him, not having a righteousness of my own that comes from the law, but one that comes through faith in Christ, the righteousness from God based on faith.

Pondering and Meditating: It is interesting to think about the things that we value and the things that discount. For the man named Saul, laws and the opportunity to persecute the church were things of value. But following his conversion, the man named Saul had a whole new set of priorities. The profits he once gained were now considered to be far less important. In fact, Paul considered them as rubbish – useless for his future life. What are you counting on to provide meaning and purpose for your life? What are the things that you value? Where does your relationship with Christ fit into those values?

Prayer: Thank you, gracious God, for the gift of salvation so freely offered to me today. Help me to put more priority in the gift of your Son than I do in the things of this world. Amen.

Reflection:

Philippians 3:10-14

I want to know Christ and the power of his resurrection and the sharing of his sufferings by becoming like him in his death, if somehow I may attain the resurrection from the dead. Not that I have already obtained this or have already reached the goal; but I press on to make it my own, because Christ Jesus has made me his own. Beloved, I do not consider that I have made it my own; but this one thing I do: forgetting what lies behind and straining forward to what lies ahead, I press on toward the goal for the prize of the heavenly call of God in Christ Jesus.

Pondering and Meditating: There are two very clear attributes of the Apostle Paul that stand out in this passage: humility and desire. Paul clearly realizes that he has not reached the goal and cannot obtain it without the claim of Christ Jesus upon his life. This spirit of humility puts him in the right place in order to press on toward his ultimate goal: to know Christ and experience the fullness of God. This was his desire. What is yours? What are the goals that you press for in your life? Paul reminds us that human goals have a limited profit while divine goals have eternal gain. What place do heavenly goals have in your daily life? Reflect today on the role that Jesus plays in your life.

Prayer: O God, the Scriptures show clearly the path toward happiness and joy. Guide us as we eagerly pursue those things that will honor you and bless our journey. Help us to cultivate a holy desire for more of you each day. Amen.

Reflection:

Saturday, March 16, 2013

John 12:1-3

Six days before the Passover Jesus came to Bethany, the home of Lazarus, whom he had raised from the dead. There they gave a dinner for him. Martha served, and Lazarus was one of those at the table with him. Mary took a pound of costly perfume made of pure nard, anointed Jesus' feet, and wiped them with her hair. The house was filled with the fragrance of the perfume.

Pondering and Meditating: This passage describes two wonderful gestures: a dinner in gratitude for the raising of Lazarus and the new life he had been given and the anointing of Jesus' feet by Mary. This is a gesture of ultimate love, a recognition of who Jesus was, what he had done, and what he was doing. This is only one of several Gospel stories where someone has been blessed by an encounter with Jesus. Although the gift does not compare with what Jesus did, no one can doubt the purity of Mary's intentions. God, through the Holy Spirit, has been at work in our lives today. Ponder today on those things that God has done for you. What are the specific actions you can do in response to God's gracious love?

Prayer: Lord, we pour out our hearts to you today in grateful appreciation for your acts of mercy and love. You have saved us and sustained us by your grace. Although it does not compare with what you have done, in this moment we pause to say a simple phrase: "thank you." Amen.

Reflection:

John 12:4-8

But Judas Iscariot, one of his disciples (the one who was about to betray him), said, "Why was this perfume not sold for three hundred denarii and the money given to the poor?" (He said this not because he cared about the poor, but because he was a thief; he kept the common purse and used to steal what was put in it.) Jesus said, "Leave her alone. She bought it so that she might keep it for the day of my burial. You always have the poor with you, but you do not always have me."

Pondering and Meditating: While Mary fully acknowledges the presence and the gracious acts of Jesus, Judas did not. He was more concerned with the price of the gift than the act of the giver. This highly negative characterization of Judas goes far in creating the contrast between one who recognizes the Savior and another who never understood who Jesus was and what he was doing. Often, in reality, there is a fine line between recognition and negligence. Judas was a disciple. He witnessed all of the gracious acts and miracles of Jesus. But he could not make the connection. This is a cautionary word for the modern Christian. We know the stories of Jesus. Yet we too run the risk of not sensing the presence of Christ in our midst. Pray today that God might grant you a renewed spirit of awareness and sensitivity.

Prayer: Lord, our lives are very busy and we are so easily distracted. We confess that there are times when we undeniably forget to acknowledge all that you have done for us. There are even times when we doubt your presence and deny your role in our lives. Forgive us we pray. Amen.

Reflection:

Monday, March 18, 2013

Psalm 118: 1-2

O give thanks to the Lord, for he is good; his steadfast love endures forever. Let Israel say, "His steadfast love endures forever."

Pondering and Meditating: Often in worship someone in leadership will shout, "God is good, all the time!" The congregation will respond, "And all the time, God is good!" If present, the writer of Psalm 118 would not hesitate to agree. The word "good" is one of the most common Hebrew words. It means ethical, honest, honorable, moral, right, just, righteous and trustworthy. But the writer does not stop there. He also uses the word "steadfast." Webster's Dictionary defines the word "steadfast" as: "firmly fixed in place, not subject to change." The psalmist surely picked the right word to describe the love of God. It is a love that is firmly fixed in place and is not subject to change. Throughout this month of devotions conversation has been centered on the unbreakable connection God has made with God's people. God is worthy to be praised because, quite simply, God will never give up on us. Meditate on those two words today: good and steadfast. What are your testimonies about the good and steadfast nature of our God?

Prayer: I give thanks to you, O Lord, for you are good; your steadfast love endures forever. May my voice be joined with many others in shouting to the heavens, "You, O God, are good all the time! And all the time, you are good!" Amen.

Reflection:

Tuesday, March 19, 2013

Psalm 118: 19-21

Open to me the gates of righteousness that I may enter through them and give thanks to the Lord. This is the gate of the Lord; the righteous shall enter through it. I thank you that you have answered me and have become my salvation.

Pondering and Meditating: The temple of God was meant for the righteous to enter and offer the sacrifices of righteousness. Righteous deeds were done within its walls, and righteous teachings sounded forth from its courts. There are many who long to enter so that they may give God proper worship and praise. These are the ones who recognize the life God has given, the salvation God has provided. These are the ones who are full of gratitude and praise. There are many others, however, who do not care whether or not the gates of God's house are opened or not. These are the ones who do not recognize God's role in their lives. These are the ones who see life from a self-centered viewpoint. These are the ones who seek praise for themselves and their fragile egos. How often do you pause to recognize the gates of righteousness that God has opened for you? Every day deserves to be the day when you take the time necessary to acknowledge God's gracious acts of salvation.

Prayer: So often I wander aimlessly through our days, O God, and do not recognize the gates of righteousness that have been opened for me. Your grace has sustained me and seen me through. Thank you for opening yourself to me this day and every day. Amen.

Reflection:

Wednesday, March 20, 2013

Psalm 118: 22-29

The stone that the builders rejected has become the chief cornerstone. This is the Lord's doing; it is marvelous in our eyes. This is the day that the Lord has made; let us rejoice and be glad in it. Save us, we beseech you, O Lord! O Lord, we beseech you, give us success! Blessed is the one who comes in the name of the Lord. We bless you from the house of the Lord. The Lord is God, and he has given us light. Bind the festal procession with branches, up to the horns of the altar. You are my God, and I will give thanks to you; you are my God, I will extol you. O give thanks to the Lord, for he is good, for his steadfast love endures forever.

Pondering and Meditating: Today a cornerstone mostly plays a ceremonial role. Inside a modern cornerstone you may find a historical record and items that tell the story of the date when the building was constructed. In ancient times a building would have a large cornerstone to support the weight of the structure. They were essential. The psalmist uses this metaphor to describe Israel: rejected by others but chosen determined to be essential by God. God's claim on their lives causes great joy and celebration to take place. Those words are so beautifully stated that they have been used by individuals and congregations for centuries. Spend some time with this passage today, replacing all the plural references to personal ones. Use it as a source of prayer and praise in your meditating.

Prayer: This is the day you have made, O God, and for that I am very thankful. You have saved me, sustained me and loved me from the time I was born. You have been and remain my light and my salvation. Amen.

Reflection:

Luke 19:28

After he had said this, he went on ahead, going up to Jerusalem.

Pondering and Meditating: Throughout the Gospel of Luke it is clear that this is a journey of Jesus to Jerusalem. He is going there to face rejection, suffering and death. Yet, even though the reader knows that this is Jesus' intent, for some reason the disciples do not understand this. They thought that it was a time for liberation from the Roman Empire or time for the final consummation of the Kingdom of God. It was not until they were filled with the Holy Spirit on the Day of Pentecost that they truly understood why this journey to Jerusalem was so necessary. Do you ever question God's involvement in your life? Do you ever wonder where God is or what God's intentions might be? While we tend to be critical of why the disciples just don't seem to "get it," there are distinct times when we don't "get it" either. Faith in God requires a great deal of trust, especially during times when we do not understand all of the specifics.

Prayer: Lord, I want to be the kind of disciple that follows you without question. Bless me with a greater trust and a deeper faith as I continue to find ways to follow you more closely. Amen.

Reflection:

Luke 19:29-34

When he had come near Bethphage and Bethany, at the place called the Mount of Olives, he sent two of the disciples, saying, "Go into the village ahead of you, and as you enter it you will find tied there a colt that has never been ridden. Untie it and bring it here. If anyone asks you, 'Why are you untying it?' just say this, 'The Lord needs it.'" So those who were sent departed and found it as he had told them. As they were untying the colt, its owners asked them, "Why are you untying the colt?" They said, "The Lord needs it."

Pondering and Meditating: Why did the Lord need a colt? Jesus' entry into Jerusalem on a colt was a fulfillment of the prophecy of Zechariah: "Rejoice greatly, O daughter of Zion. Shout aloud, O daughter of Jerusalem. Lo, your king comes to you; triumphant and victorious is he, and riding on an ass and upon a colt, the foal of an ass." Some thought that he should ride into Jerusalem on a white horse and lead a military revolution. Yet this was not the reason why he came. What? No weapons? No war? Turn the other cheek? Love one another? This was the message of the Messiah and the colt was a sign of peace that represented God's will and intention. What are the signs of peace that show our world today the true will and intention of God? How might you be one of those modern day signs of peace?

Prayer: Lord, your Son brought a new understanding to a misguided world. He used basic symbols to show the way of peace. Use me today, as an instrument of peace, in the midst of a world that still does not understand. Amen.

Reflection:

Luke 19:35- 38

Then they brought it to Jesus; and after throwing their cloaks on the colt, they set Jesus on it. As he rode along, people kept spreading their cloaks on the road. As he was now approaching the path down from the Mount of Olives, the whole multitude of the disciples began to praise God joyfully with a loud voice for all the deeds of power that they had seen, saying, "Blessed is the king who comes in the name of the Lord! Peace in the highest heaven!"

Pondering and Meditating: Jesus enters Jerusalem in meekness and humility as the Messiah who brings peace to his people. He came to bring us the Kingdom of God. He is the one who offers peace, joy and eternal life. Does this Messiah find a welcome entry into your heart and home? Do you consistently welcome him and adore him even when opposition arises?

Prayer: O God, I know that this adoring Palm Sunday crowd was made up of the very ones who just a few days later cried, "Crucify Him!" I pray that you would help me to consistently recognize the great deeds of your hand and to always shout my praises to you. Amen.

Reflection:

Sunday, March 24, 2013

Luke 19:39-40

Some of the Pharisees in the crowd said to him, "Teacher, order your disciples to stop." He answered, "I tell you, if these were silent, the stones would shout out."

Pondering and Meditating: Here, on the outskirts of the city, Jesus gives an unmistakable sign that he is the Messiah, the one to come. At this moment, Jesus wants his followers to affirm that he is the One they have waited for. If these followers do not declare to the world who they believe Jesus is, the stones will cry out. His death and resurrection in a few days will dispel years of misunderstanding. Old conceptions will die when he does. New understandings will rise when he is resurrected. This is no time to be silent. This is the time to proclaim, "This is the day the Lord has made. Let us rejoice and be glad in it!" The same is true for our day too. The 21st century is marked as a time when there is great skepticism about religion. It is a time when many people are trying to down-play any public displays of faith. This is no time to be silent. This is the time to proclaim Jesus as Lord and Messiah. As a modern day disciple, how will you give voice to your faith? Meditate on your life today and pray that God might bless you with an effective word of witness.

Prayer: Lord, I am tempted to be silent in the midst of opposition and resistance. I confess that there are distinct times when I would rather blend into the crowd than to stand up and proclaim my faith. Bless me with courage and strength to proclaim my faith as a modern day disciple of Jesus, my Lord. Amen.

Reflection:

Monday, March 25, 2013

Psalm 36:5-11

Your steadfast love, O Lord, extends to the heavens, your faithfulness to the clouds. Your righteousness is like the mighty mountains, your judgments are like the great deep; you save humans and animals alike, O Lord. How precious is your steadfast love, O God! All people may take refuge in the shadow of your wings. They feast on the abundance of your house, and you give them drink from the river of your delights. For with you is the fountain of life; in your light we see light. O continue your steadfast love to those who know you, and your salvation to the upright of heart! Do not let the foot of the arrogant tread on me, or the hand of the wicked drive me away. There the evildoers lie prostrate; they are thrust down, unable to rise.

Pondering and Meditating: This is an all-encompassing Psalm. God's mercy extends beyond humans to animals. God's love is precious like an expensive stone. God is like a bird that provides refuge under its wings. God is like a gracious host who extravagantly provides for her guests. God is like a fountain that provides life and a light that breaks the darkness. This is the magnitude of our God's love. As we enter this Holy Week, may we remember the wideness of God's love as best described in John 3:16, "For God so loved the world that he gave his only Son, so that everyone who believes in him may not perish but may have eternal life." Meditate today on the vastness of God's love for the world and for you.

Prayer: During this holiest of weeks, create within me a clean heart, O God, and enable me to see the height and depth of your great love. Amen.

Reflection:

I Corinthians 1:18-25

For the message about the cross is foolishness to those who are perishing, but to us who are being saved it is the power of God. For it is written, "I will destroy the wisdom of the wise, and the discernment of the discerning I will thwart." Where is the one who is wise? Where is the scribe? Where is the debater of this age? Has not God made foolish the wisdom of the world? For since, in the wisdom of God, the world did not know God through wisdom, God decided, through the foolishness of our proclamation, to save those who believe. For Jews demand signs and Greeks desire wisdom, but we proclaim Christ crucified, a stumbling block to Jews and foolishness to Gentiles, but to those who are called, both Jews and Greeks, Christ (is) the power of God and the wisdom of God. For God's foolishness is wiser than human wisdom, and God's weakness is stronger than human strength.

Pondering and Meditating: The source of all Christian teaching is a concept that many would call foolish: Jesus Christ crucified, dead and buried who three days later rose into new life. What is a commonly understood message for us is not so easily understood in other places. Once again, this reality challenges us to deepen our faith and resolve. May this be your prayer today: that God might bless you with the stamina and courage you need to be a fool for Christ.

Prayer: Strengthen my determination today, O God, and bless me as I represent you to a world that struggles to understand. Amen.

Reflection:

Hebrews 12:1-3

Therefore, since we are surrounded by so great a cloud of witnesses, let us also lay aside every weight and the sin that clings so closely, and let us run with perseverance the race that is set before us, looking to Jesus the pioneer and perfecter of our faith, who for the sake of the joy that was set before him endured the cross, disregarding its shame, and has taken his seat at the right hand of the throne of God. Consider him who endured such hostility against himself from sinners, so that you may not grow weary or lose heart.

Pondering and Meditating: Whether it is running a race or playing a game, the key to success is focus. The race of life is a painful one. It is an endurance test of will. There will be mental, emotional and spiritual challenges throughout the race. There will be weights that hinder us and sins that hold us back. In the midst of it all, the key is to remain focused. The writer of Hebrews provides for us the best focal point for the journey: Jesus, the pioneer and perfecter of our faith. He is the one who endured hostility and opposition. He is the one who will see us through on our journey as well. He is the one who is our focal point so that we might not grow weary and lose heart. How might fixing our gaze on Jesus help us in our Christian journey? How can his example give us hope and encouragement?

Prayer: Lord God, in the day to day grind of life it is so easy to lose focus and perspective. Give us the strength we need to turn our eyes upon Jesus each day and be guided by his inspiration and grace. Amen.

Reflection:

John 13:31-35

When he had gone out, Jesus said, "Now the Son of Man has been glorified, and God has been glorified in him. If God has been glorified in him, God will also glorify him in himself and will glorify him at once. Little children, I am with you only a little longer. You will look for me; and as I said to the Jews so now I say to you, 'Where I am going, you cannot come.' I give you a new commandment, that you love one another. Just as I have loved you, you also should love one another. By this everyone will know that you are my disciples, if you have love for one another."

Pondering and Meditating: There is a chain reaction in our understanding of the Gospel message. God loved the world so much he sent his only begotten son. In response, God's son loved us so much that he gave his life in order that we may live with abundance and joy. And, in response, we are called to love one another so that others may know that we are followers of God. This is not a love that is driven by a duty. It is a love that flows out of communion with Christ. We are loved. In response we love. On this day when Jesus washed his disciple's feet and brought new meaning to a loaf of bread and a cup of wine, let us consider how we might give ourselves to others in service and love.

Prayer: Thank you, Lord Jesus, for the ways in which you continue to inspire and bless us on our journey. Thank you for your sacrificial love and for the inspiration you provide that leads us to love our neighbor as you love us. Amen.

Reflection:

Friday, March 29, 2013

Good Friday
John 19:16b-18, 25b-30

So they took Jesus; and carrying the cross by himself, he went out to what is called The Place of the Skull, which in Hebrew is called Golgotha. There they crucified him, and with him two others, one on either side, with Jesus between them. ... Meanwhile, standing near the cross of Jesus were his mother, and his mother's sister, Mary the wife of Clopas, and Mary Magdalene. When Jesus saw his mother and the disciple whom he loved standing beside her, he said to his mother, "Woman, here is your son." Then he said to the disciple, "Here is your mother." And from that hour the disciple took her into his own home. After this, when Jesus knew that all was now finished, he said (in order to fulfill the Scripture), "I am thirsty." A jar full of sour wine was standing there. So they put a sponge full of wine on a branch of hyssop and held it to his mouth. When Jesus had received the wine, he said, "It is finished." Then he bowed his head and gave up his spirit.

Pondering and Meditating: The death of Christ on the cross is a sign of God's mercy and amazing love. On this cross our sin has been redeemed and the way to peace, joy and righteousness has been found. The way of Jesus is a way of love and sacrifice. Are you ready to take up your cross each day and follow the Lord Jesus in the way of sacrificial love?

Prayer: Lord Jesus, the stories of this Holy Week reveal that you loved us to the very end. Give me the courage today to take up my cross each day with humility and in gratitude for your amazing love. Amen.

Reflection:

Saturday, March 30, 2013

Holy Saturday
Matthew 27:57-61

When it was evening, there came a rich man from Arimathea, named Joseph, who was also a disciple of Jesus. He went to Pilate and asked for the body of Jesus; then Pilate ordered it to be given to him. So Joseph took the body and wrapped it in a clean cloth and laid it in his own new tomb, which he had hewn in the rock. He then rolled a great stone to the door of the tomb and went away. Mary Magdalene and the other Mary were there, sitting opposite the tomb.

Pondering and Meditating: Joseph of Arimathea was a good and righteous man who was a follower of Jesus. We know that he sought to honor Jesus in his death by giving him a proper burial. We can assume that this was a man who was very disappointed by the turn of events that led to Jesus' death. Yet, even in the midst of his sorrow and loss, this man honored Jesus to the end and did not abandon him. As you meditate on the devotion of this unknown disciple, pray that even in the midst of hurt and disappointment you will be able to stand next to Jesus to the very end.

Prayer: Thank you, Lord, for inspiration from a simple man named Joseph. Give us the courage to honor Jesus with the same devotion he showed. Amen.

Reflection:

Easter Sunday
Acts 10:34-43

Then Peter began to speak to them: "I truly understand that God shows no partiality, but in every nation anyone who fears him and does what is right is acceptable to him. You know the message he sent to the people of Israel, preaching peace by Jesus Christ – he is Lord of all. That message spread throughout Judea, beginning in Galilee after the baptism that John announced: how God anointed Jesus of Nazareth with the Holy Spirit and with power; how he went about doing good and healing all who were oppressed by the devil, for God was with him. We are witnesses to all that he did both in Judea and in Jerusalem. They put him to death by hanging him on a tree; but God raised him on the third day and allowed him to appear, not to all the people but to us who were chosen by God as witnesses, and who ate and drank with him after he rose from the dead. He commanded us to preach to the people and to testify that he is the one ordained by God as judge of the living and the dead. All the prophets testify about him that everyone who believes in him receives forgiveness of sins through his name."

Pondering and Meditating: We serve a God who shows no partiality. We serve a God who anointed Jesus with the Holy Spirit. We serve a God who raised Jesus from the dead. We serve a God who commanded us to testify that Jesus is the Son of God. We serve a God who forgives in Jesus' name. Meditate today, with a thankful heart, on all that God has done.

Prayer: Thank you, God, for the life of Jesus and for your amazing resurrection power. Amen.

Reflection:

APRIL

Rev. Eugene W. Matthews

My Christian, nurturing development as a young lad took place on a three point charge in Northern Anne Arundel County. Out of necessity, as the congregation awaited the arrival of the pastor, the Exhorters (an ancient name for Lay Speakers), would lead the gathered congregants in what was called an "Experience Meeting." Today's terminology is "Praise and Worship."

During that time, many of the saints of that day would either sing a hymn or testify as to how they had "experienced" God in their daily activity in the past week and their life. Some of those testimonies still live in my memory today. In a confessional moment, I must admit that I have incorporated some of them in my sermons over the years and have passed them on to several younger family members.

The readings, reflective and meditative and pondering moments for this month, are reflective times to dwell upon the "experiences" of those people who gave witness to the risen Christ in their lives. Some of them touched him, and some heard him, some felt his breath upon them and one in particular had visions about him even while exiled.

This opportunity to write for this month provided me with another chance to "experience" the Risen Christ.

May it be the same for you.

John 20: 19 – 23

When it was evening on that day, the first day of the week, and the doors of the house where the disciples had met were locked for fear of the Jews, Jesus came and stood among them and said, "Peace be with you." After he said this, he showed them his hands and his side. Then the disciples rejoiced when they saw the Lord. Jesus said to them again, "Peace be with you. As the Father has sent me, so I send you." When he had said this, he breathed on them and said to them, "Receive the Holy Spirit. If you forgive the sins of any, they are forgiven them; if you retain the sins of any, they are retained."

Pondering and Meditating: There is an old Country and Western love ballad titled, "Make the World Go Away." In this passage the disciples were afraid of the unknown following the crucifixion of Jesus. Do you remember a time in your life when you have felt confused, frustrated, baffled to the extent that you wanted to lock the door behind you? What or to whom did you turn in that moment? What of your spiritual disciplines provided you with the greatest relief?

Prayer: Dear God, in the most trying and distressful moments of our lives we realize that it is you who enters into our lives to unlock our troubled minds and situations. It is with that knowledge that we continue to give you thanks and praise for the peace that you often speak to our hearts.

Reflection:

Tuesday April 2, 2013

John 20: 24-31

But Thomas (who was called the Twin), one of the twelve, was not with them when Jesus came. So the other disciples told him, "We have seen the Lord." But he said to them, "Unless I see the mark of the nails in his hands, and put my finger in the mark of the nails and my hand in his side, I will not believe." A week later his disciples were again in the house and Thomas was with them. Although the doors were shut, Jesus came and stood among them and said, "Peace be with you." Then he said to Thomas, "Put your finger here and see my hands. Reach out your hand and put it in my side. Do not doubt but believe." Thomas answered him, "My Lord and my God!" Jesus said to him, "Have you believed because you have seen me? Blessed are those who have not seen and yet have come to believe."

Pondering and Meditating: There are times when a tragedy takes place and the phrase is uttered he/she was at the wrong place at the wrong time. The tragedy regarding Thomas was not his doubting, it is human nature to doubt; but Thomas missed the blessing of being with the Lord. Do you think you've missed a blessing lately by being absent from worship, or Bible study or even a committee meeting? Do you sense that you have been a blessing to someone this past week?

Prayer: Gracious and loving God you are merciful good and kind and have blessed me in countless ways. Now use me as your vessel to bless others along the way. Amen.

Reflection:

Wednesday, April 3, 2013

Acts 5: 27- 32

When they had brought them, they had them stand before the council. The high priest questioned them, saying, "We gave you strict orders not to teach in this name, yet here you have filled Jerusalem with your teaching and you are determined to bring this man's blood on us." But Peter and the apostles answered, "We must obey God rather than any human authority. The God of our ancestors raised up Jesus, whom you had killed by hanging him on a tree. God exalted him at his right hand as Leader and Saviour, so that he might give repentance to Israel and forgiveness of sins. And we are witnesses to these things, and so is the Holy Spirit whom God has given to those who obey him."

Pondering and Meditating: There are many challenges, choices and options that we face in our lives daily. They include how we dress, colors of the car we purchase, food we eat, and sometimes how we choose to exercise our faith. As Christians, the latter options must always be based upon our relationship with Christ. How comfortable are you in witnessing to your faith? Can you speak truth to power? Have you ever found yourself in a setting when you heard someone impugn another person's character? How did you handle it?

Prayer: O Lord, I pray that your Holy Spirit will strengthen me that in times of choices and options, I will respond in faith and in a manner that will bring honor and glory to your name. Amen.

Reflection:

Thursday, April 4, 2013

Psalm 118:14 – 16

The Lord is my strength and my might; he has become my salvation. There are glad songs of victory in the tents of the righteous: "The right hand of the Lord does valiantly; the right hand of the Lord is exalted; the right hand of the Lord does valiantly."

Pondering and Meditating: Through the ages, the Psalters as well as the hymns and gospel songs of the church have brought joy and solace to the hearts of Christian believers. There are too many to cite but a few of them are "How Great Thou Art," "When The Storms of Life Are Raging," "Joy To The World" and of course the popular "Blessed Assurance." Some comforting Psalms are: The Lord is My Shepherd (23), The Lord is My Light and Salvation (27) and certainly Make a Joyful Noise Unto The Lord (100). What are the hymns of the church and passages of Scripture that are most meaningful to you in your life? When and where have you most needed them?

Prayer: O God: "My faith looks up to thee, O Lamb of Calvary, Savior divine. Now hear me while I pray, take all my guilt away, O let me from this day be holy thine." Amen.

Reflection:

Friday April 5, 2013

Psalm 118: 24

This is the day that the Lord has made; let us rejoice and be glad in it.

Pondering and Meditating: There is a popular gospel song that begins with the line: "One day at a time sweet Jesus, that's all I'm asking of you" There are several days that we do not feel exhilarated and on top of the world. Frankly speaking, those are the times when it may not be cloud covered or rain in the forecast but the elements of our souls are drear and gloomy and downcast. The psalmist, however, reminds us that regardless of the circumstances God has created this day and we need to be glad and live it to the fullest. How do you handle days when you get off to a rough start? In the tradition of John Wesley, how is your soul today? What actions will you take today to ensure that you will use this day as another opportunity to rejoice in the Lord?

Prayer: Dear God, thank you for this day and the chance to live it out fully and to your glory. In the final refrain of that same gospel tune, this is my prayer: "Tomorrow may never be mine, so help me today, show me the way, one day at a time." Amen.

Reflection:

Revelation 1: 4-7

John to the seven churches that are in Asia: Grace to you and peace from him who is and who was and who is to come, and from the seven spirits who are before his throne, and from Jesus Christ, the faithful witness, the firstborn of the dead, and the ruler of the kings of the earth. To him who loves us and freed us from our sins by his blood, and made us to be a kingdom, priests serving his God and Father, to him be glory and dominion forever and ever. Amen. Look! He is coming with the clouds; every eye will see him, even those who pierced him; and on his account all the tribes of the earth will wail. So it is to be. Amen.

Pondering and Meditating: The Apostle John found himself exiled and near death but even in his terminal, lonely condition he realized that he was not alone and apart from God. Marooned on the Island of Patmos, he received a vision from God and he wrote to seven churches admonishing and encouraging their faith in the risen Christ. The issues he centered upon are not foreign to those we face today as individuals and congregations. They focus upon the faith, fire and fruit of our lives. How committed are you and your congregation to your ministry? Think about ways that you can be helpful in establishing goals to become more fruitful in your ministry.

Prayer: O Lord, help me to deepen my faith, set me on fire, give me more zeal to be a disciple for the transformation of the world. Hallelujah! Hallelujah! Amen!

Reflection:

Sunday, April 7, 2013

Revelation 1: 8

"I am the Alpha and the Omega," says the Lord God, who is and who was and who is to come, the Almighty.

Pondering and Meditating: There are some who have called the first Sunday after Easter low Sunday, which mainly refers to the slippage of church attendance after the Easter Sunday crowd has left. As believers in Christ, the afterglow of the resurrected Lord should still be fresh in our souls. "Christ the Lord is Risen Today" surely is our theme song today. The revelator has reassured the One who was revealed to us in flesh was, and will be forever more. This is a day to give adoration, thanksgiving and the highest praise and sing prayerfully the Doxology.

Prayer: Praise God from whom all blessings flow, praise God all creatures here below, praise God above ye heavenly host, Praise Father, Son and Holy Ghost. Amen!

Reflection:

Acts 9: 1-6

Meanwhile Saul, still breathing threats and murder against the disciples of the Lord, went to the high priest and asked him for letters to the synagogues at Damascus, so that if he found any who belonged to the Way, men or women, he might bring them bound to Jerusalem. Now as he was going along and approaching Damascus, suddenly a light from heaven flashed around him. He fell to the ground and heard a voice saying to him, "Saul, Saul, why do you persecute me?' He asked, "Who are you, Lord?' The reply came, "I am Jesus, whom you are persecuting. But get up and enter the city, and you will be told what you are to do. "

Pondering and Meditating: Some changes in life can be difficult to accept especially if they come at us suddenly. They may take the form of a sudden passing of a loved one, loss of a job or loss of friendship. Other changes may come gradually such as aging, a birth of a child or preparing to move to another location. As one experiences change, either dramatically or gradually, much of how we handle them depends upon our maturity, spirituality and depth of faith. Spend a few moments reflecting upon some of the changes that have occurred in your life. Have some of them happened recently? How did you sense that God was in the midst of any of the changes that you have experienced?

Prayer: Lord, I thank you that you remain with us constantly throughout every movement in our life. For all the times that you have carried us through the winding roads of life, I offer to you our thanks and praise. Amen.

Reflection:

Monday, April 9, 2013

Acts 9: 8- 11, 13-15

Saul got up from the ground, and though his eyes were open, he could see nothing; so they led him by the hand and brought him into Damascus. For three days he was without sight, and neither ate nor drank. Now there was a disciple in Damascus named Ananias. The Lord said to him in a vision, "Ananias." He answered, "Here I am, Lord." The Lord said to him, "Get up and go to the street called Straight, and at the house of Judas look for a man of Tarsus named Saul. But Ananias answered, "Lord, I have heard from many about this man, how much evil he has done to your saints in Jerusalem; and here he has authority from the chief priests to bind all who invoke your name." But the Lord said to him, "Go, for he is an instrument whom I have chosen to bring my name before Gentiles and kings and before the people of Israel."

Pondering and Meditating: There is the hymn that in some cases has become a meaningful phrase that affirms that "God moves in a mysterious way." Not only that but God often communicates in an unusual way so that sometimes it may come through nature, a child's laughter or in the form of another's voice. Sometimes the call of God to a particular ministry may come to us. Where and how have you sensed God communicating with you?

Prayer: O God, make me to know your ways. Help me to listen with an open ear and heart for your voice. Use me, even me, O Lord, as a vessel of thine. In Christ name I pray. Amen.

Reflection:

Monday, April 10, 2013

Psalm 30: 1-3

I will extol you, O Lord, for you have drawn me up, and did not let my foes rejoice over me. O Lord my God, I cried to you for help, and you have healed me. O Lord, you brought up my soul from Sheol, restored me to life from among those gone down to the Pit.

Pondering and Meditating: This is a Psalm of thanksgiving recognizing the occasion of the dedication of the temple to God. The Psalmist said: "I will extol you, O Lord," meaning I am praising you, O Lord, and then he recited the reasons for the praise of thanksgiving. He extolled God for healing, deliverance and even for being brought back from the dead. Since we are a few days from the experience of Easter, we can see this from the lens of the resurrection. You know that every day is a day of thanksgiving, so for what are you extolling God for today? How well do you relate to the aspect of healing and restoration? Have you witnessed to it to anyone concerning any of those experiences?

Prayer: Gracious Lord, may I never fail to give thanks every day for your unmerited grace and favor that you have bestowed on me in the past and that which I know awaits me in the future, Amen.

Reflection:

Psalm 30: 4- 5

Sing praises to the Lord, O you his faithful ones, and give thanks to his holy name. For his anger is but for a moment; his favour is for a lifetime. Weeping may linger for the night, but joy comes with the morning.

Pondering and Meditating: Many people have felt, or known of people who have gone through what is known as the "Dark Night of The Soul." Some may have called it deep depression or being in the dumps. Whatever may have caused this dilemma, it leads to a long night of weeping. The answer and relief comes in the morning of their lives when through the power of the Holy Spirit, Jesus steps in. Take time to seek someone around you who you think may be in a midnight situation. Think of the various ways either through prayer, a card, an e-mail or a telephone call that you might be able to bring the sun rising joy of a new day. Do you know of someone? Will you agree to become their messenger of hope?

Prayer: O God, into all of our lives the clouds gather and the rains fall. But in all of this we know behind each cloud filled day, the sun is shining. Amen.

Reflection:

John 21: 1-5

After these things Jesus showed himself again to the disciples by the Sea of Tiberias; and he showed himself in this way. Gathered there together were Simon Peter, Thomas called the Twin, Nathanael of Cana in Galilee, the sons of Zebedee, and two others of his disciples. Simon Peter said to them, "I am going fishing." They said to him, "We will go with you." They went out and got into the boat, but that night they caught nothing. Just after daybreak, Jesus stood on the beach; but the disciples did not know that it was Jesus. Jesus said to them, "Children, you have no fish, have you?' They answered him, "No."

Pondering and Meditating: There is probably no one who has not left their home or office and pro-ceeded to the car and discovered that they have left the keys behind. If it has happened to you, you know you were not equipped to drive your car. The disciples were trying to fish that day, but they did not become equipped until Jesus arrived. Can you think of a moment in time when you were trying to figure out a situation and Jesus showed up? How did he get your attention? How did the conversation start?

Prayer: O God, thank you for coming into my life, just when I was at the end of my rope. Lord, thank you for tying a knot at the end of the rope and in enabling me to hang on a little longer. In Jesus' name I pray. Amen.

Reflection:

John 21:15-19

When they had finished breakfast, Jesus said to Simon Peter, "Simon son of John, do you love me more than these?' He said to him, "Yes, Lord; you know that I love you." Jesus said to him, "Feed my lambs." A second time…the third time, "Simon son of John, do you love me?' Peter felt hurt because he said to him the third time, "Do you love me?' And he said to him, "Lord, you know everything; you know that I love you." Jesus said to him, "Feed my sheep. Very truly, I tell you, when you were younger, you used to fasten your own belt and to go wherever you wished. But when you grow old, you will stretch out your hands, and someone else will fasten a belt around you and take you where you do not wish to go." After this he said to him, "Follow me."

Pondering and Meditating: The challenge came in the form of a question to Simon Peter: "Do you love me more than these?" Jesus was making an inquiry about Peter's commitment to discipleship. What Jesus was specifically asking is, are you willing to tend to the lives of others? Peter, will you feed the hungry and visit the sick or is fishing more important in your life? To those of us reflecting today, are there any "more than these" in your life? What about your discipleship? Are you holding back feeling that you are unable to commit your total self to feeding the lambs and sheep?

Prayer: Lord, I thank you for your tender care for me that is exhibited through your abiding presence in my life. I commit myself this day and each day to be a living witness in response to your faithfulness to me. Amen.

Reflection:

Sunday April 14, 2013

Revelation 5: 11- 14

Then I looked, and I heard the voice of many angels surrounding the throne and the living creatures and the elders; they numbered myriads of myriads and thousands of thousands, singing with full voice, "Worthy is the Lamb that was slaughtered to receive power and wealth and wisdom and might and honor and glory and blessing!" Then I heard every creature in heaven and on earth and under the earth and in the sea, and all that is in them, singing, "To the one seated on the throne and to the Lamb be blessing and honor and glory and might forever and ever!" And the four living creatures said, "Amen." And the elders fell down and worshipped.

Pondering and Meditating: Here we read about the concluding features of John's vision that gives witness to the splendor of the divine throne of God. He saw that there was only one who was worthy to open the scroll that was in the hand of the One who occupied the throne. That one was Jesus the Lamb, who was slain for all humankind. In this same vision, there are a host of angelic voices that were heard, reminiscent of the voices that sang at Jesus' birth. Christ's presence comes through a daily walk with him. Has he opened up your heart to a new walk with him? Have you heard angelic voices lately? What were they singing?

Prayer: Holy Lord, you are worthy to be praised, for you often spring up within me with new melodies of your divine presence. For the continued vision of your splendor, I offer thanks and praise to you this day. Amen.

Reflection:

John 10:22-24

At that time the festival of the dedication took place in Jerusalem. It was winter, and Jesus was walking in the temple, in the portico of Solomon. So the Jews gathered around him and said to him, "How long will you keep us in suspense? If you are the Messiah, tell us plainly."

Pondering and Meditating: Sometimes the questions that we are asked are more intriguing than the answers. More importantly is what relates to who is asking and why. Is there a hidden agenda? Often it is said that in the legal profession one should not ask a question to which one does not already know the answer. Those who questioned Jesus most likely had a hint, but they were trying to entrap him. Have you ever felt as though someone was testing you when they asked you about your faith? Did you feel intimidated? How certain are you about your commitment to Christ? Are you bold to speak a word about God?

Prayer: O God, help me to never be timid, weak or ashamed to respond to inquiries about my faith in you. I truly love you, Lord, and I want the whole world to hear my testimony about my commitment to you. Amen.

Reflection:

Tuesday, April 16, 2013

John 10:25- 30

Jesus answered, "I have told you, and you do not believe. The works that I do in my Father's name testify to me; but you do not believe, because you do not belong to my sheep. My sheep hear my voice. I know them, and they follow me. I give them eternal life, and they will never perish. No one will snatch them out of my hand. What my Father has given me is greater than all else, and no one can snatch it out of the Father's hand. The Father and I are one."

Pondering and Meditating: Today is the continuing saga from yesterday's reading as Jesus responds to the questioning about his authority and identity. Amazingly, he had performed many miracles but apparently this was not proof enough for his interrogators. When did you first experience the existence of Christ in your life? Have there been moments you can point to? How many persons have you led to Christ?

Prayer: O God, help me to be a bearer of Good News to those whom I meet. In Jesus name, I pray. Amen

Reflection:

Psalm 23:1

The Lord is my shepherd, I shall not want.

Pondering and Meditating: There is an age-old story of an oratorical contest in which people were invited to recite their favorite poem, Scripture or quotation. In this scene a young, educated erudite young man stood an enunciated Psalm 23 very eloquently. Following him an elderly woman stood, who had not matriculated to the level of the young man, but proceeded to recite the same psalm. Following the presentations, the judges awarded the prize to the seasoned saint. When asked to explain their decision, the answer was that the young man knew the psalm, but the woman was acquainted with the shepherd. How well are we acquainted with the shepherd? Do you know him well enough to introduce others to him? What was the nature of your last conversation? The shepherd knows the sheep, how well does he know you?

Prayer: I am thankful, O Lord, that because of your death and resurrection, I have been at liberty to converse with you daily. I have felt comfortable and have been strengthened through our many conversations. Amen.

Reflection:

Psalm 23:2- 23

He makes me lie down in green pastures; he leads me beside still waters; he restores my soul. He leads me in right paths for his name's sake. Even though I walk through the darkest valley, I fear no evil; for you are with me; your rod and your staff — they comfort me. You prepare a table before me in the presence of my enemies; you anoint my head with oil; my cup overflows. Surely goodness and mercy shall follow me all the days of my life, and I shall dwell in the house of the Lord my whole life long.

Pondering and Meditating: Sometimes a passage of Scripture can be read purely for its aesthetics and not necessarily for study purposes .One such example is Psalm 23. This is perhaps the most memorized passage of Scripture. It is often read at funerals and recited before people undergo surgery and quoted often beside those who are sick. This pastoral setting conjures up all types of images which bring healing, strength and renewal. When has this psalm been most meaningful to you? What are some of the images that come to mind? Has it helped you overcome shadows? When have you felt renewed?

Prayer: Surely goodness and mercy shall follow me all the days of my life and I shall dwell in the house of the Lord my whole life long. Amen.

Reflection:

Acts 9:36-43

Now in Joppa there was a disciple whose name was Tabitha, which in Greek is Dorcas. She was devoted to good works and acts of charity. At that time she became ill and died. When they had washed her, they laid her in a room upstairs. Since Lydda was near Joppa, the disciples, who heard that Peter was there, sent two men to him with the request, "Please come to us without delay." So Peter got up and went with them; and when he arrived, they took him to the room upstairs. All the widows stood beside him, weeping and showing tunics and other clothing that Dorcas had made while she was with them. Peter put all of them outside, and then he knelt down and prayed. He turned to the body and said, "Tabitha, get up." Then she opened her eyes, and seeing Peter, she sat up. He gave her his hand and helped her up. Then calling the saints and widows, he showed her to be alive. This became known throughout Joppa, and many believed in the Lord.

Pondering and Meditating: This is an interesting scene in which we witness Peter, who has been transformed from one who once denied his Lord to one who has now opened himself to the power of the risen Christ. Peter has been summoned to pray for Dorcas, a woman of exemplary faith who, through his prayer, was restored to life. Even today there are evidences of lives and relationships that have been resurrected. What testimonies of restored lives have you seen? Do you believe?

Prayer: O God, I know that prayer can change things. First, I ask that you change my heart, O God, to be more like you. Amen.

Reflection:

Revelation 7: 9

After this I looked, and there was a great multitude that no one could count, from every nation, from all tribes and peoples and languages, standing before the throne and before the Lamb, robed in white, with palm branches in their hands.

Pondering and Meditating: John visualizes a magnificent, multicultural scene that almost defies our most vivid imagination. There are so many people representing all nations, tribes, ethnicities and languages that it is impossible to count them. Can this be similar to what heaven may be like? What would it look like to have a little of this type of experience here on earth and not wait for it to occur in the hereafter? Is this a possibility? How can we begin? How can you help?

Prayer: O God, enable us o have a "Taste of Glory Divine" right here on earth and let it begin with me, Amen

Reflection:

Revelation 7: 10-15

They cried out in a loud voice, saying, "Salvation belongs to our God who is seated on the throne, and to the Lamb!" And all the angels stood around the throne and around the elders and the four living creatures, and they fell on their faces before the throne and worshipped God, singing, "Amen! Blessing and glory and wisdom and thanksgiving and honor and power and might be to our God forever and ever! Amen." Then one of the elders addressed me, saying, "Who are these, robed in white, and where have they come from?' I said to him, "Sir, you are the one that knows." Then he said to me, "These are they who have come out of the great ordeal; they have washed their robes and made them white in the blood of the Lamb. For this reason they are before the throne of God, and worship him day and night within his temple, and the one who is seated on the throne will shelter them.

Pondering and Meditating: There is no substitute for sensing the awareness of the nearness of the Lord on a continuing, daily basis. Those who are acquainted with the Wesleyan heritage, as contained in the General Rules, have been encouraged to practice the Means of Grace in order to maintain a closer walk with God. They are: worshipping, family and public prayer, Holy Communion, reading the Scriptures, fasting and abstinence. Which one of these practices has been most meaningful to you?

Prayer: Lord, help me to realize that I can't make this journey through life without your holding my hand. I promise from this day forward to keep a closer walk with thee. Amen

Reflection:

Acts 11:1-9

Now the apostles and the believers who were in Judea heard that the Gentiles had also accepted the word of God. So when Peter went up to Jerusalem, the circumcised believers criticized him, saying, "Why did you go to uncircumcised men and eat with them?' Then Peter began to explain it to them, step by step, saying, "I was in the city of Joppa praying, and in a trance I saw a vision. There was something like a large sheet coming down from heaven, being lowered by its four corners; and it came close to me. As I looked at it closely I saw four-footed animals, beasts of prey, reptiles, and birds of the air. I also heard a voice saying to me, "Get up, Peter; kill and eat." But I replied, "By no means, Lord; for nothing profane or unclean has ever entered my mouth." But a second time the voice answered from heaven, "What God has made clean, you must not call profane."

Pondering and Meditating: Some Jewish members of the early church believed that because the Law was given to Moses, one had to be a Jew to receive salvation. There were others who believed that if the Gentiles followed the traditions they, in turn, would receive salvation. The voice of God proclaimed that God excludes no one from the gift of salvation through the work of Christ .Whom do you most admire for speaking out about social justice? When given the opportunity, have you spoken truth to power?

Prayer: Open my eyes, O God, to see that none around me feel that they are treated unfairly or excluded in any setting. Open my mouth that I may speak in moments where the Gospel of acceptance needs to be a reality. Open my heart, so that I may truly love all of my neighbors as I love myself. Amen.

Reflection:

Acts 11:16

And I remembered the word of the Lord, how he had said, "John baptized with water, but you will be baptized with the Holy Spirit."

Pondering and Meditating: The Baptism of our Lord Sunday, traditionally observed in January, has always been a special worship moment for me. I especially am moved at the time of the renewal of the baptismal vow that says, "Remember your baptism and be thankful." I am privileged to say that I vividly recall that at the age of three, I stood with my family in my great grandfather's modest living room as he baptized me. He was a local pastor and I admired and stood in awe of him as a man of God. I bear his middle name and, even until this day, believe that I was truly baptized that evening by the Holy Spirit. How have you been marked by your baptism? Has it made a difference in your witness?

Prayer: O Lord, through faith I know that not only have I been washed, but I have been empowered through the Holy Spirit to live out my covenant of baptism Amen

Reflection:

Psalm 148: 1-7

Praise the Lord! Praise the Lord from the heavens; praise him in the heights! Praise him, all his angels; praise him, all his host! Praise him, sun and moon; praise him, all you shining stars! Praise him, you highest heavens, and you waters above the heavens! Let them praise the name of the Lord, for he commanded and they were created. He established them forever and ever; he fixed their bounds, which cannot be passed. Praise the Lord from the earth, you sea monsters and all deeps.

Pondering and Meditating: The Psalms consist mainly of a collection of songs, prayers and poetry to express thanksgiving and praise to God. Some of them are laments, some poems, and many relate to a range of human experiences. In the 148th Psalm, the Psalmist is inviting the whole creation to praise God. There are many facets, customs and ways to praise God. Have you ever been in a setting when someone says, "let's give God some praise?" How does that make you feel? Do you feel comfortable in audibly praising God? Are other ways more appropriate for you?

Prayer: O Lord, I want to praise you with my hands, my feet, my tongue but most of all I want to praise you with my life. Hallelujah! Amen.

Reflection:

Thursday April 25, 2013

Revelation 21: 1- 4

Then I saw a new heaven and a new earth; for the first heaven and the first earth had passed away, and the sea was no more. And I saw the holy city, the new Jerusalem, coming down out of heaven from God, prepared as a bride adorned for her husband. And I heard a loud voice from the throne saying, "See, the home of God is among mortals. He will dwell with them; they will be his peoples, and God himself will be with them; he will wipe every tear from their eyes. Death will be no more; mourning and crying and pain will be no more for the first things have passed away."

Pondering and Meditating: I am certain that images flood into your mind when you think of heaven. John gives an apocalyptic view of what it is like where there is no more death disease or pain. Jesus stated that the Kingdom of God can be realized within each of us. Moreover; he instructed his disciples to pray that the Kingdom would come on earth as it is in heaven. What comes to mind when you think about heaven? How has the definition Jesus gave been realized in your life? Where have you seen signs of the Kingdom? What can you do to enhance the realization of bringing heaven to earth?

Prayer: Thy Kingdom come on earth ,as it is in heaven, for thine is the Kingdom, the Power and the Glory forever. Amen.

Reflection:

Revelation 21:5-6

And the one who was seated on the throne said, "See, I am making all things new." Also he said, "Write this, for these words are trustworthy and true." Then he said to me, "It is done! I am the Alpha and the Omega, the beginning and the end. To the thirsty I will give water as a gift from the spring of the water of life."

Pondering and Meditating: The reading for today connects with yesterday's vision from John, who described some new situations of a heavenly place and visualized an atmosphere of serenity, one that is void of tears and death. Newness is a key word in this latest theme. Where have you experienced a sense of newness in your life? Is there in your opinion, an opportunity for freshness in the life of the church? Where are the places around you that need to be renewed?

Prayer: O God, send the fresh winds of change and renewal in my soul and into the dry places of the hearts of all humankind. I pray this to the one that makes all things new. Amen.

Reflection:

John 13 31:33

When he had gone out, Jesus said, "Now the Son of Man has been glorified, and God has been glorified in him. If God has been glorified in him, God will also glorify him in himself and will glorify him at once. Little children, I am with you only a little longer. You will look for me; and as I said to the Jews so now I say to you, "Where I am going, you cannot come."

Pondering and Meditating: This is an interesting passage to read because the context of the scene is prior to Jesus' crucifixion and yet it is placed in the lectionary near the end of the Easter season. No doubt this entire passage is foreshadowing his earthly end, but these two verses are pointing to his resurrection and his coexistence with God. What do you think of when you hear about the glorification of God in Christ? In what way is the glorification of Christ manifested in your life? What can you do to glorify his name today?

Prayer: O God, to you I offer the highest praise and give you the glory and honor that is due your Holy Name. Amen.

Reflection:

John 13:34

I give you a new commandment, that you love one another. Just as I have loved you, you also should love one another.

Pondering and Meditating: There are volumes of poems, sonnets, hymns and songs written about love. Most of love from the human perspective reflects something on the emotional level. Jesus is speaking of a new paradigm that relates to the depth of love that he had for his disciples and the world, which he was willing to give his life for. Therefore, he was leaving instructions for his followers to enter into a love relationship that would be capable of keeping their community together. To use a phrase from one of the classic tunes: How deep is your love? What practices to you engage in to keep the covenants of love in your life?

Prayer: O Lord, because you loved me, I know that my sins are forgiven and I am set free from eternal death. I pledge to not only love you with my whole heart, but to love my neighbor as myself. In Jesus' name, I pray. Amen.

Reflection:

MAY 2012

REV. BYRON E. BROUGHT

These passages this month are leading up to the Pentecost. God is on the move. The stories are powerful and energetic. God is not on the sidelines; God is the main player.

The assignment to write these devotional pieces was challenging in several ways. First, I tend to think in concrete terms, but many of these passages pushed me to think in more spiritualized terms. Secondly, the daily lectionary forced me to break up passages in ways that I don't normally do. This created the opportunity for different interpretations, and placed the emphasis on different parts of Scripture than it would have had the passage been taken as a whole. Finally, it's a humbling prospect to imagine that my stream of thoughts might be used to lead your prayer life and meditations.

As I read through these sacred and beautiful passages, I rejoiced in knowing that the full range and depth of our human emotion and experience is contained within them.

During this season, allow God to lead you like the rush of a mighty wind.

Monday, April 29, 2013

Acts 16: 9-10

During the night Paul had a vision: there stood a man of Macedonia pleading with him and saying, "Come over to Macedonia and help us." When he had seen the vision, we immediately tried to cross over to Macedonia, being convinced that God had called us to proclaim the good news to them.

Pondering and Meditating: God's presence in Acts is absolute. When was the last time you were convinced that God was calling you? When was the last time you were able to make yourself completely available to God?

Prayer: Be thou my vision, O Lord of my heart, naught be all else to me, save that thou art; Thou my best thought by day or by night, waking or sleeping, thy presence my light. Amen. (Ancient Irish hymn, Eleanor Hull, Translation)

Reflection:

Tuesday, April 30, 2013

Acts 16: 11-15

We set sail from Troas and took a straight course to Samothrace, the following day to Neapolis, and from there to Philippi, which is a leading city of the district of Macedonia and a Roman colony. We remained in this city for some days. On the sabbath day we went outside the gate by the river, where we supposed there was a place of prayer; and we sat down and spoke to the women who had gathered there. A certain woman named Lydia, a worshiper of God, was listening to us; she was from the city of Thyatira and a dealer in purple cloth. The Lord opened her heart to listen eagerly to what was said by Paul. When she and her household were baptized, she urged us, saying, "If you have judged me to be faithful to the Lord, come and stay at my home." And she prevailed upon us.

Pondering and Meditating: What walls had to come down for Paul to speak freely with the women of Philippi? What walls had to come down for Lydia to invite these strangers into her home? How do boundaries protect us? How do walls keep us apart?

Prayer: "Open the eyes of my heart, Lord. I want to see you." Amen. (Michael W. Smith)

Reflection:

Psalm 67

May God be gracious to us and bless us and make his face to shine upon us, that your way may be known upon earth, your saving power among all nations. Let the peoples praise you, O God; let all the peoples praise you. Let the nations be glad and sing for joy, for you judge the peoples with equity and guide the nations upon earth. Let the peoples praise you, O God; let all the peoples praise you. The earth has yielded its increase; God, our God, has blessed us. May God continue to bless us; let all the ends of the earth revere him.

Pondering and Meditating: Psalm 67 gives thanks to God for a good harvest, and asks God that the blessings will continue. May is a good time for planting. Have you thought about starting a garden? Consider making it a spiritual exercise – from seed, to harvest, to table … thanks be to God.

Prayer: "For the fruit of all creation, thanks be to God. Gifts bestowed on every nation, thanks be to God. For the plowing, sowing, reaping, silent growth while we are sleeping, Future needs in earth's safekeeping, thanks be to God." Amen. (Fred Pratt Green)

Reflection:

Thursday, May 2, 2013

Revelation 21:10, 22-27

And in the spirit he carried me away to a great, high mountain and showed me the holy city Jerusalem coming down out of heaven from God. I saw no temple in the city, for its temple is the Lord God the Almighty and the Lamb. And the city has no need of sun or moon to shine on it, for the glory of God is its light, and its lamp is the Lamb. The nations will walk by its light, and the kings of the earth will bring their glory into it. Its gates will never be shut by day — and there will be no night there. People will bring into it the glory and the honor of the nations. But nothing unclean will enter it, nor anyone who practices abomination or falsehood, but only those who are written in the Lamb's book of life.

Pondering and Meditating: What a wonderful image: the city needs no sun or moon. God's light is enough. From the creation stories, we learn that the sun is not the source of light. Yes, you'll have to put your physics on the back burner for a moment. God's love is the source of light. I find great comfort in that; do you? How does that thought illuminate you?

Prayer: God, thank you for your new creation with each new day. Thank you for the way that you recreate us, and restore us. Thank you for the way that you allow us to see you differently, now that we know we have been redeemed. Amen.

Reflection:

Friday, May 3, 2013

Revelation 22:1-5

Then the angel showed me the river of the water of life, bright as crystal, flowing from the throne of God and of the Lamb through the middle of the street of the city. On either side of the river is the tree of life with its twelve kinds of fruit, producing its fruit each month; and the leaves of the tree are for the healing of the nations. Nothing accursed will be found there any more. But the throne of God and of the Lamb will be in it, and his servants will worship him; they will see his face, and his name will be on their foreheads. And there will be no more night; they need no light of lamp or sun, for the Lord God will be their light, and they will reign forever and ever.

Pondering and Meditating: "Mercy me," sings a song called, I Can Only Imagine, in which they envision the moment when they see God face-to-face. What will they do? Will they sing? Will they dance? Will they be too overcome with awe to do anything? How do you think you will respond? What will be the crowning moment?

Prayer: Holy God, thank you for revealing your face to us in Jesus. Thank you for revealing your face to us in our sisters and brothers. Thank you for revealing your face to us in the beauty of the world around us. Allow us to reflect a small part of your glory. Amen.

Reflection:

Saturday, May 4, 2013

John 14: 23-24

Jesus answered him, "Those who love me will keep my word, and my Father will love them, and we will come to them and make our home with them. Whoever does not love me does not keep my words; and the word that you hear is not mine, but is from the Father who sent me.

Pondering and Meditating: Our home is in God. God's home is in us. It's a wonderful relationship. In this life, we wander like pilgrims searching for a place that we can truly belong – a place, which we might call home. Are you at home with God? Are you at peace? Or are you still searching, and wandering, knowing that you won't be home until you reach your final destination?

Prayer: "Our hearts are restless until they find rest in thee." Amen. (Augustine)

Reflection:

Sunday, May 5, 2013

John 14: 25-29

I have said these things to you while I am still with you. But the Advocate, the Holy Spirit, whom the Father will send in my name, will teach you everything, and remind you of all that I have said to you. Peace I leave with you; my peace I give to you. I do not give to you as the world gives. Do not let your hearts be troubled, and do not let them be afraid. You heard me say to you, "I am going away, and I am coming to you." If you loved me, you would rejoice that I am going to the Father, because the Father is greater than I. And now I have told you this before it occurs, so that when it does occur, you may believe.

Pondering and Meditating: I read this passage at almost every memorial service. It brings comfort to those who hear it; it brings comfort to me as I am speaking. It feels good to be comforted, especially as I am trying to comfort others. What is it about God's promise that gives you peace? What is it about God's presence that gives you peace?

Prayer: Fear-destroying God, thank you for being our hope, our strength and our refuge. Thank you for the confidence to face the future unafraid. Thank you for your presence, which never abandons us and never leaves us alone. Amen.

Reflection:

Monday, May 6, 2013

Acts16: 16-18

One day, as we were going to the place of prayer, we met a slave girl who had a spirit of divination and brought her owners a great deal of money by fortune telling. While she followed Paul and us, she would cry out, "These men are slaves of the Most High God, who proclaim to you a way of salvation." She kept doing this for many days. But Paul, very much annoyed, turned and said to the spirit, "I order you in the name of Jesus Christ to come out of her." And it came out that very hour.

Pondering and Meditating: As we pass through this world, we meet some really annoying people. I always find humor in Paul's response, because I can imagine the people in my life who take pleasure in chipping away at my sanity. If only I could cast out spirits in the name of Jesus Christ. Early on in my ministry, a colleague gave me some advice, "Don't let others rob you of your joy in life." Those words have stuck with me over the years. I hope you'll find inspiration in those words as well. What annoys you? How do you overcome it?

Prayer: God, perhaps our words and actions are annoying to you. Thank you for your grace in always listening to what we have to say. Refine our prayer that it may become to your ears like children's laughter. Amen.

Reflection:

Acts 16: 19-24

But when her owners saw that their hope of making money was gone, they seized Paul and Silas and dragged them into the marketplace before the authorities. When they had brought them before the magistrates, they said, "These men are disturbing our city; they are Jews and are advocating customs that are not lawful for us as Romans to adopt or observe." The crowd joined in attacking them and the magistrates had them stripped of their clothing and ordered them to be beaten with rods. After they had given them a severe flogging, they threw them into prison and ordered the jailer to keep them securely. Following these instructions, he put them in the innermost cell and fastened their feet in the stocks.

Pondering and Meditating: City life: busy, on the move, commerce, trade, action, progress – how does the Gospel threaten our hope of making money? How does the Gospel invite us to reorganize our priorities? Do we love God or money more?

Prayer: God, you know that we're a people with multiple loves. Show us the way to find our true love in you. Amen.

Reflection:

Acts 16: 25-33

About midnight Paul and Silas were praying and singing hymns to God, and the prisoners were listening to them. Suddenly there was an earthquake, so violent that the foundations of the prison were shaken; and immediately all the doors were opened and everyone's chains were unfastened. When the jailer woke up and saw the prison doors wide open, he drew his sword and was about to kill himself, since he supposed that the prisoners had escaped. But Paul shouted in a loud voice, "Do not harm yourself, for we are all here." The jailer called for lights, and rushing in, he fell down trembling before Paul and Silas. Then he brought them outside and said, "Sirs, what must I do to be saved?" They answered, "Believe on the Lord Jesus, and you will be saved, you and your household." They spoke the word of the Lord to him and to all who were in his house. At the same hour of the night he took them and washed their wounds; then he and his entire family were baptized without delay.

Pondering and Meditating: What "chains" are preventing you from living in the fullness of the life to which you've been called? What would that life of fullness look like for you?

Prayer: "Long my imprisoned spirit lay, fast bound in sin and nature's night; Thine eye diffused a quickening ray – I woke, the dungeon flamed with light; My chains fell off, my heart was free, I rose, went forth, and followed Thee." Amen. (Charles Wesley, 1738)

Reflection:

Psalm 97

The Lord is king! Let the earth rejoice; let the many coastlands be glad! Clouds and thick darkness are all around him; righteousness and justice are the foundation of his throne. Fire goes before him, and consumes his adversaries on every side. His lightnings light up the world; the earth sees and trembles. The mountains melt like wax before the Lord, before the Lord of all the earth. The heavens proclaim his righteousness; and all the peoples behold his glory. All worshippers of images are put to shame, those who make their boast in worthless idols; all gods bow down before him. Zion hears and is glad, and the towns of Judah rejoice, because of your judgments, O God. For you, O Lord, are most high over all the earth; you are exalted far above all gods. The Lord loves those who hate evil; he guards the lives of his faithful; he rescues them from the hand of the wicked. Light dawns for the righteous, and joy for the upright in heart. Rejoice in the Lord, O you righteous, and give thanks to his holy name!

Pondering and Meditating: It's hard to imagine mountains melting like wax. If we were to watch a video of the history of the earth, condensed into a minute long segment, then we would see mountains rise and fall at a far faster pace than wax melting. This psalm disrupts my sense of security, and confirms my sense of security at the same time. How do you feel knowing that the things of this world are not eternal? How do you feel knowing that you are?

Prayer: Transcendent God, how can we possibly thank you enough for sharing eternity with us? Amen.

Reflection:

Friday, May 10, 2013

Revelation 22: 12-17, 20-21

"See, I am coming soon; my reward is with me, to repay according to everyone's work. I am the Alpha and the Omega, the first and the last, the beginning and the end." Blessed are those who wash their robes, so that they will have the right to the tree of life and may enter the city by the gates. "It is I, Jesus, who sent my angel to you with this testimony for the churches. I am the root and the descendant of David, the bright morning star." The Spirit and the bride say, "Come." And let everyone who hears say, "Come." And let everyone who is thirsty come. Let anyone who wishes take the water of life as a gift. … The one who testifies to these things says, "Surely I am coming soon." Amen. Come, Lord Jesus! The grace of the Lord Jesus be with all the saints. Amen.

Pondering and Meditating: One of the many challenges of the Christian life is to balance this paradox: on the one hand we are to remain faithful to our calling in this world and faithfully execute the duties that have been given to us. On the other hand, we are to be mindful of our other world hope, as we anxiously await the "coming soon" return of Jesus Christ. How do we balance these hopes? How is this a challenge for you?

Prayer: Jesus, we want you to come soon. But we also want to live life to the fullest with the time that we have and with the knowledge we have. Help us live faithfully in this tension, knowing that life and life eternal are both given to us as gifts. Amen.

Reflection:

Saturday, May 11, 2013

John 17: 20-24

I ask not only on behalf of these, but also on behalf of those who will believe in me through their word, that they may all be one. As you, Father, are in me and I am in you, may they also be in us, so that the world may believe that you have sent me. The glory that you have given me I have given them, so that they may be one, as we are one, I in them and you in me, that they may become completely one, so that the world may know that you have sent me and have loved them even as you have loved me. Father, I desire that those also, whom you have given me, may be with me where I am, to see my glory, which you have given me because you loved me before the foundation of the world.

Pondering and Meditating: At the heart of this beautiful prayer is love. "We" and "me" come together in this passage. How does your life reflect the idea that you are one with God? How does your life reflect the idea that you are one with your sisters and brothers in faith?

Prayer: Thank you, Jesus, for praying for us. Thank you for obscuring the line, which separates us. Let us be worthy of the life that you have dreamed. Amen.

Reflection:

Sunday, May 12, 2013

John 17: 25-26

"Righteous Father, the world does not know you, but I know you; and these know that you have sent me. I made your name known to them, and I will make it known, so that the love with which you have loved me may be in them, and I in them."

Pondering and Meditating: "What a friend we have in Jesus." How could we know God apart from Jesus? Yes, we would have a witness, but our witness would come up short. In Jesus, we finally know a God, who reverses our preconceptions, who transforms our expectations and who redeems our prejudices. Only God can do that. Who is God to you? How do you share God with others?

Prayer: Revealing God, open our hearts, open our minds, open our lives to a life of sacred relationship with you and our neighbors. Amen.

Reflection:

Monday, May 13, 2013

Acts 2: 1-4

When the day of Pentecost had come, they were all together in one place. And suddenly from heaven there came a sound like the rush of a violent wind, and it filled the entire house where they were sitting. Divided tongues, as of fire, appeared among them, and a tongue rested on each of them. All of them were filled with the Holy Spirit and began to speak in other languages, as the Spirit gave them ability.

Pondering and Meditating: I don't like violent wind. It scares me. That reaction may, on some subconscious level, awaken a childhood memory when our family was caught by surprise by a quickly approaching storm. Lightning struck the outside of our home, very near where we were standing outside on the porch. It feels like the weather is out of control when the wind blows that hard. I brace myself for whatever damage is coming to the house and the yard. But the Pentecost wind isn't destructive; it's creative. Have you ever experienced God, "like the rush of a violent wind?" What was created?

Prayer: Holy Spirit, blow around us. Holy Spirit, blow right through us. Holy Spirit, blow against us. Amen.

Reflection:

Acts 2: 5-13

Now there were devout Jews from every nation under heaven living in Jerusalem. And at this sound the crowd gathered and was bewildered, because each one heard them speaking in the native language of each. Amazed and astonished, they asked, "Are not all these who are speaking Galileans? And how is it that we hear, each of us, in our own native language? Parthians, Medes, Elamites, and residents of Mesopotamia, Judea and Cappadocia, Pontus and Asia, Phrygia and Pamphylia, Egypt and the parts of Libya belonging to Cyrene, and visitors from Rome, both Jews and proselytes, Cretans and Arabs — in our own languages we hear them speaking about God's deeds of power." All were amazed and perplexed, saying to one another, "What does this mean?" But others sneered and said, "They are filled with new wine."

Pondering and Meditating: Rev. Kenda Creasy Dean of Princeton Theological Seminary, once spoke of the youth today not as the "lawless" generation, but of the "aweless" generation. Young people today just aren't impressed by anything. The Pentecost experience was amazing and astonishing, but perhaps we've heard it all before and we're no longer moved. What does it take to amaze and astonish us? What does God have to do to get our attention?

Prayer: Holy Spirit, move in us once again. Save us from bland and lukewarm faith. We pray not that we might be entertained, but that we might be awed by your power. Unite us together as your one great family. Amen.

Reflection:

Acts 2: 14-21

But Peter, standing with the eleven, raised his voice and addressed them, "Men of Judea and all who live in Jerusalem, let this be known to you, and listen to what I say. Indeed, these are not drunk, as you suppose, for it is only nine o'clock in the morning. No, this is what was spoken through the prophet Joel: "In the last days it will be, God declares that I will pour out my Spirit upon all flesh, and your sons and your daughters shall prophesy, and your young men shall see visions, and your old men shall dream dreams. Even upon my slaves, both men and women, in those days I will pour out my Spirit; and they shall prophesy. And I will show portents in the heaven above and signs on the earth below, blood, and fire, and smoky mist. The sun shall be turned to darkness and the moon to blood, before the coming of the Lord's great and glorious day. Then everyone who calls on the name of the Lord shall be saved.'

Pondering and Meditating: It's not your average fisherman's chatter. When I was a water taxi captain in Annapolis, we would occasionally listen in on the fishermen chatter over the marine radio. Where is the Spanish mackerel biting? Where are the rockfish jumping? What would transform this rough-hewn fisherman, with bloodied and blistered hands, into a Joel-quoting prophet? How has God transformed your life?

Prayer: Holy Spirit, fill us with the confidence that we need to be your voice to the world. Amen.

Reflection:

Psalm 104: 24-34

O Lord, how manifold are your works! In wisdom you have made them all; the earth is full of your creatures. Yonder is the sea, great and wide, creeping things innumerable are there, living things both small and great. There go the ships, and Leviathan that you formed to sport in it. These all look to you to give them their food in due season; when you give to them, they gather it up; when you open your hand, they are filled with good things. When you hide your face, they are dismayed; when you take away their breath, they die and return to their dust. When you send forth your spirit, they are created; and you renew the face of the ground. May the glory of the Lord endure forever; may the Lord rejoice in his works – who looks on the earth and it trembles, who touches the mountains and they smoke. I will sing to the Lord as long as I live; I will sing praise to my God while I have being. May my meditation be pleasing to him, for I rejoice in the Lord.

Pondering and Meditating: A whale singing … a wolf howling … a donkey braying … a bird chirping – all these things are praising God. The creation witnesses to the goodness of God. Where do you see God in creation? How does the natural order affirm your faith?

Prayer: Good and wonderful God, we thank you for "all things bright and beautiful, all creatures great and small." We trust that you care for even the smallest of your creation, and we trust that you call on us to care for your world. Thanks be to God. Amen.

Reflection:

Romans 8: 14-17

For all who are led by the Spirit of God are children of God. For you did not receive a spirit of slavery to fall back into fear, but you have received a spirit of adoption. When we cry, "Abba! Father!" it is that very Spirit bearing witness with our spirit that we are children of God, and if children, then heirs, heirs of God and joint heirs with Christ – if, in fact, we suffer with him so that we may also be glorified with him.

Pondering and Meditating: The term "children of God" gets batted around from time-to-time within various Christian circles. It's a nice idea to think of every person as a child of God, but Paul had a far more specific designation. For Paul, a child of God was one who was "led by the Spirit of God." Is it more comforting for you to think of every human being as children of God? Is it more comforting for you to think only of those who are "led by the Spirit" as children of God?

Prayer: Mommy and Daddy God, thank you for adopting us. Without you, we are orphaned in the world. With you, we are part of a wonderful family. It's your desire to claim the whole world as your faithful children, and we pray for the redemption of the whole creation. Amen.

Reflection:

John 14: 8-16

Philip said to him, "Lord, show us the Father, and we will be satisfied." Jesus said to him, "Have I been with you all this time, Philip, and you still do not know me? Whoever has seen me has seen the Father. How can you say, 'Show us the Father'? Do you not believe that I am in the Father and the Father is in me? The words that I say to you I do not speak on my own; but the Father who dwells in me does his works. Believe me that I am in the Father and the Father is in me; but if you do not, then believe me because of the works themselves. Very truly, I tell you, the one who believes in me will also do the works that I do and, in fact, will do greater works than these, because I am going to the Father. I will do whatever you ask in my name, so that the Father may be glorified in the Son. If in my name you ask me for anything, I will do it. If you love me, you will keep my commandments. And I will ask the Father, and he will give you another Advocate, to be with you forever. This is the Spirit of truth, whom the world cannot receive, because it neither sees him nor knows him."

Pondering and Meditating: Jesus sounds frustrated. I'd hate to think that I was on the receiving end of Jesus' frustration, and yet I'm sure that my words and actions have failed him a thousand times. Jesus said, "If you love me, you will keep my commandments." But what if we don't? Does it mean we don't love him if we forget or mess up? How do we demonstrate our love as fallen people?

Prayer: Bind us, Lord, so closely to you that we cannot help but fall in love with you. Amen.

Reflection:

Sunday, May 19, 2013

John 14: 25-27

"I have said these things to you while I am still with you. But the Advocate, the Holy Spirit, whom the Father will send in my name, will teach you everything, and remind you of all that I have said to you. Peace I leave with you; my peace I give to you. I do not give to you as the world gives. Do not let your hearts be troubled, and do not let them be afraid."

Pondering and Meditating: Jesus doesn't give to us as the world gives. What does the world give you? Security? Wealth? Fame? Power? What's good about that? What's bad about that? What does Jesus give?

Prayer: The things of this world are pretty cool, God. They give me the happiness that I'm seeking. But I know that they won't last forever. Show me the joy that knows no end, from the source that is everlasting – the joy of your kingdom. Amen.

Reflection:

Proverbs 8: 1-4

Does not wisdom call, and does not understanding raise her voice? On the heights, beside the way, at the crossroads she takes her stand; beside the gates in front of the town, at the entrance of the portals she cries out: "To you, O people, I call, and my cry is to all that live."

Pondering and Meditating: Is "understanding" mad at me? Why is she raising her voice? The only time people raise their voice at me is when they're mad. But here, "understanding" doesn't seem angry. It sounds like she has something important to say. What does she want to tell us? How would greater understanding and greater wisdom be beneficial to our lives?

Prayer: O God, your friend wisdom has a lot of good things to teach us. May we respect her, and may we learn a thing or two of the understanding that she imparts. Amen.

Reflection:

Proverbs 8: 5-21

"O simple ones, learn prudence; acquire intelligence, you who lack it. Hear, for I will speak noble things, and from my lips will come what is right; for my mouth will utter truth; wickedness is an abomination to my lips. All the words of my mouth are righteous; there is nothing twisted or crooked in them. They are all straight to one who understands and right to those who find knowledge. Take my instruction instead of silver, and knowledge rather than choice gold; for wisdom is better than jewels, and all that you may desire cannot compare with her. I, wisdom, live with prudence, and I attain knowledge and discretion. The fear of the Lord is hatred of evil. Pride and arrogance and the way of evil and perverted speech I hate. I have good advice and sound wisdom; I have insight, I have strength. By me kings reign, and rulers decree what is just; by me rulers rule, and nobles, all who govern rightly. I love those who love me, and those who seek me diligently find me. Riches and honor are with me, enduring wealth and prosperity. My fruit is better than gold, even fine gold, and my yield than choice silver. I walk in the way of righteousness, along the paths of justice, endowing with wealth those who love me, and filling their treasuries."

Pondering and Meditating: Does wickedness ever leave our lips? How about pride and arrogance? You can't pass through this world without hearing some kind of profanity. Maybe it's even come out of our mouths. How does "wisdom" call us to a higher standard of living?

Prayer: O God, let my words be pleasing to your ears. Amen.

Reflection:

Wednesday, May 22, 2013

Proverbs 8: 22-31

The Lord created me at the beginning of his work, the first of his acts of long ago. Ages ago I was set up, at the first, before the beginning of the earth. When there were no depths I was brought forth, when there were no springs abounding with water. Before the mountains had been shaped, before the hills, I was brought forth – when he had not yet made earth and fields, or the world's first bits of soil. When he established the heavens, I was there, when he drew a circle on the face of the deep, when he made firm the skies above, when he established the fountains of the deep, when he assigned to the sea its limit, so that the waters might not transgress his command, when he marked out the foundations of the earth, then I was beside him, like a master worker; and I was daily his delight, rejoicing before him always, rejoicing in his inhabited world and delighting in the human race.

Pondering and Meditating: In the words of the late Dr. Bruce M. Metzger, "Wisdom is all delight, rejoicing before God and delighting in his human creatures." Where do you see "wisdom" at the heart of all creation? When do you rejoice before God? What gives you delight?

Prayer: Thank you, Lord, for the things of this world, which dance to your greater glory. Thank you for the witness of wisdom. Thank you for the witness of creation, which sings of the story of your amazing grace.

Reflection:

Romans 5: 1-5

Therefore, since we are justified by faith, we have peace with God through our Lord Jesus Christ, through whom we have obtained access to this grace in which we stand; and we boast in our hope of sharing the glory of God. And not only that, but we also boast in our sufferings, knowing that suffering produces endurance, and endurance produces character, and character produces hope, and hope does not disappoint us, because God's love has been poured into our hearts through the Holy Spirit that has been given to us.

Pondering and Meditating: I don't know of too many people who can be convinced of the benefits of suffering. In my attempts to explain it, I inevitably water down the concept of suffering by spiritualizing it. I met a Russian woman once who told me that Americans don't spend time grieving. We shun sadness and hurt, and quickly find the salve to heal our wounds. Russians, on the other hand, spend much of their lives grieving. I don't know enough to agree or disagree with her, but I thought it was an interesting commentary. Is there real benefit in suffering? Is it spiritual or material, or both? When have you suffered and found that it leads to hope?

Prayer: Forgive us, Lord, for passing over our guilt too quickly. Forgive us, Lord, for dwelling on our hurts for too long. Let there be a season of grief. Let there be an even longer season of healing and hope. Amen.

Reflection:

John 16: 1-4

"I have said these things to you to keep you from stumbling. They will put you out of the synagogues. Indeed, an hour is coming when those who kill you will think that by doing so they are offering worship to God. And they will do this because they have not known the Father or me. But I have said these things to you so that when their hour comes you may remember that I told you about them. I did not say these things to you from the beginning, because I was with you."

Pondering and Meditating: This is a timely example of the need for the greater wisdom and understanding to which we were just called in Proverbs. The pathetic reality of this part of John's Gospel is that evil exists. Jesus' followers are faced with persecution, and with the realization that people kill for God. Ignorance is everywhere. Where have you seen evil twist God's word? Who suffers when religion gets so distorted?

Prayer: Dear Lord, forgive us our sins, as we forgive those who sin against us. Amen.

Reflection:

John 16: 4b-11

"I did not say these things to you from the beginning, because I was with you. But now I am going to him who sent me; yet none of you asks me, 'Where are you going?' But because I have said these things to you, sorrow has filled your hearts. Nevertheless I tell you the truth: it is to your advantage that I go away, for if I do not go away, the Advocate will not come to you; but if I go, I will send him to you. And when he comes, he will prove the world wrong about sin and righteousness and judgment: about sin, because they do not believe in me; about righteousness, because I am going to the Father and you will see me no longer; about judgment, because the ruler of this world has been condemned."

Pondering and Meditating: It's nice to know that somebody's got our back. Jesus promised us that the Holy Spirit will do just that. How in the world could we make it without this divine presence? When do you feel the presence of the Spirit? How does the Holy Spirit help encourage you and strengthen you?

Prayer: "Spirit of the living God, fall afresh on me. Spirit of the living God, fall afresh on me. Melt me, mold me, fill me, use me. Spirit of the living God, fall afresh on me." Amen. (Daniel Iverson)

Reflection:

Sunday, May 26, 2013

John 16: 12-15

"I still have many things to say to you, but you cannot bear them now. When the Spirit of truth comes, he will guide you into all the truth; for he will not speak on his own, but will speak whatever he hears, and he will declare to you the things that are to come. He will glorify me, because he will take what is mine and declare it to you. All that the Father has is mine. For this reason I said that he will take what is mine and declare it to you."

Pondering and Meditating: Why was Jesus on such a time crunch? Couldn't he have stayed a little longer? Would another year or two have changed everything? There was so much to do, so much to say, so much good still waiting to be accomplished. Couldn't we linger with him just a little while more?

Prayer: God, we feel blessed that you spent some time in this world in flesh and blood. And we thank you for your constant presence with us in your Holy Spirit. Draw near and dear to us, that we may be secure. Amen.

Reflection:

Monday, May 27, 2013

I Kings 18: 20-21

So Ahab sent to all the Israelites, and assembled the prophets at Mount Carmel. Elijah then came near to all the people, and said, "How long will you go limping with two different opinions? If the Lord is God, follow him; but if Baal, then follow him." The people did not answer him a word.

Pondering and Meditating: What idols command our thoughts and attention? What idols command our devotion? What would we have to give up if we were to shift our devotion to God?

Prayer: Thank you, God, for your patience with us. It seems a small thing to ask for our unconditional love in response to yours. But we are a trinket people, who form attachments to each new thing that comes down the pike. Center our thoughts that you might remain at the center of our lives

Reflection:

Kings 18: 22-28

Then Elijah said to the people, "I, even I only, am left a prophet of the Lord; but Baal's prophets number four hundred fifty. Let two bulls be given to us; let them choose one bull for themselves, cut it in pieces, and lay it on the wood, but put no fire to it; I will prepare the other bull and lay it on the wood, but put no fire to it. Then you call on the name of your god and I will call on the name of the Lord; the god who answers by fire is indeed God." All the people answered, "Well spoken!" Then Elijah said to the prophets of Baal, "Choose for yourselves one bull and prepare it first, for you are many; then call on the name of your god, but put no fire to it." So they took the bull that was given them, prepared it, and called on the name of Baal from morning until noon, crying, "O Baal, answer us!" But there was no voice, and no answer. They limped about the altar that they had made. At noon Elijah mocked them, saying, "Cry aloud! Surely he is a god; either he is meditating, or he has wandered away, or he is on a journey, or perhaps he is asleep and must be awakened." Then they cried aloud and, as was their custom, they cut themselves with swords and lances until the blood gushed out over them.

Pondering and Meditating: It's a showdown in the "Everything's Going to be OK Corral." I laugh when Elijah mocks his enemies, but I feel guilty about it too. That's not what I teach and preach. Is it ever appropriate to mock our enemies?

Prayer: God, allow me to demonstrate that you are to be praised, without having to demonstrate that my enemies are fools. Amen.

Reflection:

I Kings 18: 31-39

First he repaired the altar of the Lord that had been thrown down; Elijah took twelve stones, according to the number of the tribes of the sons of Jacob, to whom the word of the Lord came, saying, "Israel shall be your name"; with the stones he built an altar in the name of the Lord. Then he made a trench around the altar, large enough to contain two measures of seed. Next he put the wood in order, cut the bull in pieces, and laid it on the wood. He said, "Fill four jars with water and pour it on the burnt offering and on the wood." Then he said, "Do it a second time"; and they did it a second time. Again he said, "Do it a third time"; and they did it a third time, so that the water ran all around the altar, and filled the trench also with water. At the time of the offering of the oblation, the prophet Elijah came near and said, "O Lord, God of Abraham, Isaac, and Israel, let it be known this day that you are God in Israel, that I am your servant, and that I have done all these things at your bidding. Answer me, O Lord, answer me, so that this people may know that you, O Lord, are God, and that yo.. have turned their hearts back." Then the fire of the Lord fell and consumed the burnt offering, the wood, the stones, and the dust, and even licked up the water that was in the trench. When all the people saw it, they fell on their faces and said, "The Lord indeed is God; the Lord indeed is God."

Pondering and Meditating: What sign have you received to know your faith is real? What sign are you waiting for?

Prayer: Wonderful God, burn brightly in our hearts and consume our doubts. Amen.

Reflection:

Thursday, May 30, 2013

I Kings 8: 22-23

Then Solomon stood before the altar of the Lord in the presence of all the assembly of Israel, and spread out his hands to heaven. He said, "O Lord, God of Israel, there is no God like you in heaven above or on earth beneath, keeping covenant and steadfast love for your servants who walk before you with all their heart,

Pondering and Meditating: The long-awaited temple has been built and dedicated. Where is your sacred space? Where do you feel close to God? What have you dedicated to the Lord?

Prayer: Thank you, God, for the times when we're able to give our best to you. May our lives be filled with sacred moments that we set apart for you. Amen.

Reflection:

I Kings 8: 41-43

"Likewise when a foreigner, who is not of your people Israel, comes from a distant land because of your name – for they shall hear of your great name, your mighty hand, and your outstretched arm – when a foreigner comes and prays toward this house, then hear in heaven your dwelling place, and do according to all that the foreigner calls to you, so that all the peoples of the earth may know your name and fear you, as do your people Israel, and so that they may know that your name has been invoked on this house that I have built.

Pondering and Meditating: How is your church a witness to the community? How does your building welcome first-time guests? How does your building invite others to participate? How easy is your church to find?

Prayer: God, we pray that the message that we proclaim with our architecture and our designs will be just as welcoming as our hearts and minds. Amen.

Reflection:

Galatians 1: 1-12

Paul an apostle – sent neither by human commission nor from human authorities, but through Jesus Christ and God the Father, who raised him from the dead – and all the members of God's family who are with me, To the churches of Galatia: Grace to you and peace from God our Father and the Lord Jesus Christ, who gave himself for our sins to set us free from the present evil age, according to the will of our God and Father, to whom be the glory forever and ever. Amen. I am astonished that you are so quickly deserting the one who called you in the grace of Christ and are turning to a different gospel – not that there is another gospel, but there are some who are confusing you and want to pervert the gospel of Christ. But even if we or an angel from heaven should proclaim to you a gospel contrary to what we proclaimed to you, let that one be accursed! As we have said before, so now I repeat, if anyone proclaims to you a gospel contrary to what you received, let that one be accursed! Am I now seeking human approval or God's approval? Or am I trying to please people? If I were still pleasing people, I would not be a servant of Christ. For I want you to know that the gospel that was proclaimed by me is not of human origin; for I did not receive it from a human source, nor was I taught it, but I received it through a revelation of Jesus Christ.

Pondering and Meditating: Does saving face with our friends matter more than telling the truth? Does our acceptance in popular circles matter more than doing the right thing?

Prayer: Forgive us, loving God, for moments when we desert you for the thrill of short-lived praise. Amen.

Reflection:

Luke 7:1-9

After Jesus had finished all his sayings in the hearing of the people, he entered Capernaum. A centurion there had a slave whom he valued highly, and who was ill and close to death. When he heard about Jesus, he sent some Jewish elders to him, asking him to come and heal his slave. When they came to Jesus, they appealed to him earnestly, saying, "He is worthy of having you do this for him, for he loves our people, and it is he who built our synagogue for us." And Jesus went with them, but when he was not far from the house, the centurion sent friends to say to him, "Lord, do not trouble yourself, for I am not worthy to have you come under my roof; therefore I did not presume to come to you. But only speak the word, and let my servant be healed. For I also am a man set under authority, with soldiers under me; and I say to one, 'Go,' and he goes, and to another, 'Come,' and he comes, and to my slave, 'Do this,' and the slave does it." When Jesus heard this he was amazed at him, and turning to the crowd that followed him, he said, "I tell you, not even in Israel have I found such faith."

Pondering and Meditating: The relationship between centurion and slave in this passage doesn't meet my expectations. They sound more like friends. What accounts for the centurion's humility and faith? Is it that the threat of death changes our values and our priorities? What do we learn in that shift? How does it change us?

Prayer: Holy God, may we be so humble as to confess that we are not worthy to have you in our homes. But so hopeful that you might come anyway. Amen.

Reflection:

JUNE

REV. ANDERS R. LUNT

God has a way of breaking into our lives. Sometimes we welcome such intrusions, especially when we are seeking forgiveness, healing or direction. But, when we're honest, there are times when we just wish God wouldn't "meddle" so much in our lives. When God breaks into our daily lives change always results. The way we relate to others' changes is often as a result of change in the way we see ourselves and understand our purpose in life. Values change and even the direction of our lives can change under the influence of God's intruding presence.

This month, we'll have daily opportunities to contemplate in Scripture some of the ways God has entered and changed lives. Perhaps, as a result, we'll experience our own lives changing in ways that make us more the people God created and calls us to be as followers of Jesus.

Monday, June 3, 2013

1 Kings 17:8-10

Then the word of the Lord came to him, saying, "Go now to Zarephath, which belongs to Sidon, and live there; for I have commanded a widow there to feed you." So he set out and went to Zarephath.

Pondering and Meditating: I've often wondered what plans Elijah might have had before receiving this word from the Lord. If you're at all like me, you likely have plans for yourself, plans for the weekend, plans for next week or even next month. Imagine throwing them all out the window, or at the very least putting them on hold, to go to a place where you've never been with no idea what may lie ahead. Elijah went, we assume, because he trusted God to provide. Where might God be calling you to go? What personal plans might you be called to put on hold in order to follow God's plan for you? How can you trust God more?

Prayer: God of the ages, give me a mind and heart open to discerning your plan for my life. Give me a vision of where you want me to go, what you want me to do. And then give me courage to follow, trusting that you will provide all that is needed for the journey. Amen.

Reflection:

1 Kings 17:13-16

Elijah said to her, "Do not be afraid; go and do as you have said; but first make me a little cake of it and bring it to me, and afterwards make something for yourself and your son. For thus says the Lord the God of Israel: The jar of meal will not be emptied and the jug of oil will not fail until the day that the Lord sends rain on the earth." She went and did as Elijah said, so that she as well as he and her household ate for many days. The jar of meal was not emptied, neither did the jug of oil fail, according to the word of the Lord that he spoke by Elijah.

Pondering and Meditating: The widow in this story was afraid to share her meager food with a stranger in a time of drought and famine. She had trouble imagining how she could feed her son and herself, let alone a third mouth. How often does an attitude of scarcity lead us to be afraid? How much more often does it limit our willingness to share what we have with others? God promises that when we are seeking to serve God and others in God's name there will always be enough. Where is an attitude of scarcity causing you to be afraid or holding you back from sharing? How might you move to an attitude of abundance and trust?

Prayer: Gracious and loving God, help me to trust that you will provide for my needs so that I might share what you provide with others in your name. Amen.

Reflection:

Wednesday, June 5, 2013

Psalm 146:1-6

Praise the Lord! Praise the Lord, O my soul! I will praise the Lord as long as I live; I will sing praises to my God all my life long. Do not put your trust in princes, in mortals, in whom there is no help. When their breath departs, they return to the earth; on that very day their plans perish. Happy are those whose help is the God of Jacob, whose hope is in the Lord their God, who made heaven and earth, the sea, and all that is in them; who keeps faith forever;

Pondering and Meditating: Who do you trust? Lately, it seems the number of institutions and individuals deemed worthy of our trust has shrunk dramatically. Yet, implicitly, we all trust someone or something. Some trust in wealth or education; others seek security in possessions or accomplishments and trust that these will bring fulfillment. The Psalmist helps us see that only God is worthy of lasting trust. "In God we trust," is more than a motto or inscription on money. It is a way of life ... the only way ... that leads to fulfillment, peace, contentment and — according to the Psalmist — happiness.

Prayer: Lord God, strip away from my life all false trust in anything other than you. Lead me to faith that places my life and my future totally in your hands. Amen.

Reflection:

Thursday, June 6, 2013

Galatians 1:11-12

For I want you to know, brothers and sisters, that the gospel that was proclaimed by me is not of human origin; for I did not receive it from a human source, nor was I taught it, but I received it through a revelation of Jesus Christ.

Pondering and Meditating: Learning to trust God to provide is a gradual process of growing in confidence. We discover that we can trust God to provide for our basic needs, to enable us to help others, to lead us "in right paths." But how about trusting God to enable us to share our faith with others? That's where many of us become tongue-tied, lose any confidence in ourselves or our ability to say the right thing. Paul reminds us, though, that proclaiming the Gospel does not depend on our ability or on anything of human origin. As God did with many of the prophets and with Paul, God will put words in our mouth when we risk telling the "old, old story of Jesus and his love." Who do you see, perhaps every day, in your neighborhood or workplace who has never heard the story that could transform their life if they only heard it from you?

Prayer: God, open my mouth that I might bear gladly the warm truth everywhere of Jesus and his love. Amen.

Reflection:

Luke 7:11-13

Soon afterwards he went to a town called Nain, and his disciples and a large crowd went with him. As he approached the gate of the town, a man who had died was being carried out. He was his mother's only son, and she was a widow; and with her was a large crowd from the town. When the Lord saw her, he had compassion for her and said to her, "Do not weep."

Pondering and Meditating: Even now, approaching the beginning of summer, I can hear the profound opening words of Handel's "Messiah," sung by a solo voice: "Comfort; comfort my people, says your God." The words are from Isaiah 40, but the meaning is expressed throughout Scripture: God comes to comfort us in our pain and suffering. Jesus' compassion for the widow in Nain is simply one more expression of God's nature. No matter how deep our sorrow, no matter how excruciating our pain, we are not alone. There is one who cares and always comes to bring comfort. Have you shared your deep pain with God? Where has God come, where is God coming right now to bring comfort to you?

Prayer: Gracious and loving God, help me to trust you enough to bare my soul and share my pain with you — even though I may not have told another soul. Hear my prayer and bring me comfort as is your nature, through Jesus Christ our Lord. Amen.

Reflection:

Saturday, June 8, 2013

Luke 7:14-17

Then he came forward and touched the bier, and the bearers stood still. And he said, "Young man, I say to you, rise!" The dead man sat up and began to speak, and Jesus gave him to his mother. Fear seized all of them; and they glorified God, saying, "A great prophet has risen among us!" and "God has looked favorably on his people!" This word about him spread throughout Judea and all the surrounding country.

Pondering and Meditating: In a Family Circus cartoon strip from more than 20 years ago, two children are portrayed looking out a window. "Wow," says Billy, "I see trees and grass and birds and clouds." His sister, though, says, "I see smears and fingerprints and flyspecks and dust." To which the little boy responds, "Windows are for looking through, Dolly, not at!" I wonder if maybe the same ought to be said of miracles in the Bible. Could these events, as C.S. Lewis suggests, be simply signs that help us see God's activity everywhere in the world. Is new life that results from joining of sperm and egg any less miraculous than a virgin birth? Or healing produced through medical intervention any less dramatic than so called "faith healing?" Perhaps Jesus' raising of a young man can help us see the ways God is always raising us from death to new life.

Prayer: God of power and love, help me to see those places in me and in my life where you are overcoming forces of evil and death and bringing new life through Jesus Christ. Amen.

Reflection:

Sunday, June 9, 2013

Psalm 30:10-12

Hear, O Lord, and be gracious to me! O Lord, be my helper!" You have turned my mourning into dancing; you have taken off my sackcloth and clothed me with joy, so that my soul may praise you and not be silent. O Lord my God, I will give thanks to you forever.

Pondering and Meditating: What a wonderful feeling when mourning is transformed into dancing, when sorrow doesn't go away, but recedes to the point where we can see a brighter day. How freeing to remove the old, dirty sackcloth of guilt or anxiety and be clothed with joy. How tempting it is to focus inward, to wallow in our new joy in much the same way we might have been consumed by sorrow or guilt. But then we encounter those two little words — in some ways, perhaps, the most important words in the Bible — "so that." God turns mourning into dancing, replaces sackcloth with joy so that we can praise God and give thanks to God forever. God provides abundance in our lives, gives confidence and trust in God, puts words in our mouths, comforts in pain, and brings new life so that we can love and serve God and our neighbor in all that we do. How are you using God's blessings in your life to bless others?

Prayer: God of amazing grace and love, awaken in me a new awareness of all you have done for me, and lead me to discover how I can be a blessing to others in your name. Amen.

Reflection:

1 Kings 21:1-4

Later the following events took place: Naboth the Jezreelite had a vineyard in Jezreel, beside the palace of King Ahab of Samaria. And Ahab said to Naboth, "Give me your vineyard, so that I may have it for a vegetable garden, because it is near my house; I will give you a better vineyard for it; or, if it seems good to you, I will give you its value in money." But Naboth said to Ahab, "The Lord forbid that I should give you my ancestral inheritance." Ahab went home resentful and sullen because of what Naboth the Jezreelite had said to him; for he had said, "I will not give you my ancestral inheritance." He lay down on his bed, turned away his face, and would not eat.

Pondering and Meditating: Poor Ahab! His offer to buy Naboth's vineyard is rejected outright. We can assume that, as king of Samaria, Ahab was used to getting what he wanted. In this case, when that didn't happen, he went home and pouted. Does this sound at all familiar? Though not a king, have you ever been resentful and sullen because of not getting something you wanted? When things don't turn out the way we want, when someone else wins the prize or gets the promotion we deserve, it can be all too tempting to react with bitterness and sulking. In some cases, the experience can even lead us to resent others or do something we might later regret.

Prayer: Gracious God, give me grace to deal with disappointment without becoming bitter and resentful. Help me to give thanks for what I do have rather than envious of what I don't. Amen.

Reflection:

1 Kings 21:16-20

As soon as Ahab heard that Naboth was dead, Ahab set out to go down to the vineyard of Naboth the Jezreelite, to take possession of it. Then the word of the Lord came to Elijah the Tishbite, saying: Go down to meet King Ahab of Israel, who rules in Samaria; he is now in the vineyard of Naboth, where he has gone to take possession. You shall say to him, "Thus says the Lord: Have you killed, and also taken possession?" You shall say to him, "Thus says the Lord: In the place where dogs licked up the blood of Naboth, dogs will also lick up your blood." Ahab said to Elijah, "Have you found me, O my enemy?" He answered, "I have found you. Because you have sold yourself to do what is evil in the sight of the Lord,

Pondering and Meditating: Ahab's wife, Jezebel, has arranged for Naboth to be killed so that Ahab can have the vineyard he coveted. Ignoring the injustice, Ahab goes to enjoy his new possession. But God intrudes, in the person of the prophet Elijah, who confronts Ahab with his sin and the accompanying consequences. Before jumping to condemn Ahab, we might want to consider how often we conveniently overlook our own injustice in pursuit of achieving our desires. Are there ways God is prodding you to confront your own sin? Are you living with consequences of your own sinful actions to which you were led because the end seemed to justify the means? Who might be playing the role of Elijah for you?

Prayer: Righteous God, strip away any false pretense or rationalization that has enabled me to hide from my own sin. Lead me to repent and seek forgiveness. Amen.

Reflection:

Wednesday, June 12, 2013

Psalm 32:1-5

Happy are those whose transgression is forgiven, whose sin is covered. Happy are those to whom the Lord imputes no iniquity, and in whose spirit there is no deceit. While I kept silence, my body wasted away through my groaning all day long. For day and night your hand was heavy upon me; my strength was dried up as by the heat of summer. Then I acknowledged my sin to you, and I did not hide my iniquity; I said, "I will confess my transgressions to the Lord," and you forgave the guilt of my sin.

Pondering and Meditating: Confess my transgressions and God will forgive me. It's easy to say, but much harder to actually do in many cases. We're not bad people, and can't imagine what led us to do such bad things. Not wanting to deal head-on with our sin, we try to ignore it, bury our guilt so deep inside it cannot be retrieved much less confronted. The problem, of course, is that such buried guilt and sin never go away. It begins to eat away at us, can even cause illness if not expressed. Many of us know what the Psalmist is talking about, with bodies wasting away and day-long groaning. God invites us to let it out, come clean, confess our sin no matter how awful, no matter how guilty and ashamed we feel. For the promise is that God will forgive, that nothing we have done or may do can separate us from God's love and grace in Jesus Christ. What are you waiting for?

Prayer: Gracious and loving God, forgive me for all the foolish, hurtful things I've done. Give me a clean heart, restore my soul, and help me to leave behind my guilt and shame and serve you with joy. Amen.

Reflection:

Galatians 2:15-16

We ourselves are Jews by birth and not Gentile sinners; yet we know that a person is justified not by the works of the law but through faith in Jesus Christ. And we have come to believe in Christ Jesus, so that we might be justified by faith in Christ, and not by doing the works of the law, because no one will be justified by the works of the law.

Pondering and Meditating: Most folks on the street — or even in church pews — might well describe the Ten Commandments as rules that, if obeyed, lead to reward from God. Even those who might not put it that way sometimes live as if living right is the way to earn God's favor. It's logical; it makes sense. Except according to Paul, it doesn't work that way. We are justified — brought into right relationship with God — not by what we do, but only through faith in Jesus Christ. Are you tirelessly striving to earn God's love, attempting to prove you're good enough to inherit eternal life? God's love is free, a gift to be received, not a reward to be earned. How can you accept the gift today?

Prayer: Loving God, help me get it through my thick skull that your love for me has nothing to do with my being good, but only with your goodness and love. Open my heart and my life to receive the gift of your love and grace in Jesus Christ. Amen.

Reflection:

Friday, June 14, 2013

Galatians 2:19-21

For through the law I died to the law, so that I might live to God. I have been crucified with Christ; and it is no longer I who live, but it is Christ who lives in me. And the life I now live in the flesh, I live by faith in the Son of God, who loved me and gave himself for me. I do not nullify the grace of God; for if justification comes through the law, then Christ died for nothing.

Pondering and Meditating: We do good works because God loves us not in order to earn God's love. When we understand that God loves us "just as we are," we want to do good in order to express our gratitude and love to God. In a very real sense, the person we once were exists no more. Acceptance of God's grace and love in Jesus puts us under new management. No longer do we live for ourselves, but for Christ. In fact, Paul says, Christ lives in us. How is God using you to be Christ in the world today? To whom can you be Christ?

Prayer: Transforming God, put a new and right spirit within me. Make me an instrument of your love. May your love overflow through me in ways that touch others with the love of Christ. Amen.

Reflection:

Luke 7:36-39

One of the Pharisees asked Jesus to eat with him, and he went into the Pharisee's house and took his place at the table. And a woman in the city, who was a sinner, having learned that he was eating in the Pharisee's house, brought an alabaster jar of ointment. She stood behind him at his feet, weeping, and began to bathe his feet with her tears and to dry them with her hair. Then she continued kissing his feet and anointing them with the ointment. Now when the Pharisee who had invited him saw it, he said to himself, "If this man was a prophet, he would have known who and what kind of woman this is who is touching him— that she is a sinner."

Pondering and Meditating: Jesus is certainly full of surprises. First, he accepts a dinner invitation from one of the Pharisees — the very people who are always trying to trip him up, get him in trouble. And then he lets a known sinner, a woman at that, touch him in very personal — even intimate — ways. You'd think Jesus would be more careful about the kinds of people he associates with. But, maybe that's the point. Jesus associates with anyone who wants to be close to him. While there may be times we resent Jesus' openness to people with whom we might not want to associate, isn't it encouraging to know that — even at our worst — here is room for us with Jesus. Who have you unintentionally prevented from coming close to Jesus? What is keeping you from getting closer to Jesus?

Prayer: Lord, lead me closer to Jesus this day. Amen.

Reflection:

Sunday, June 16, 2013

Luke 7: 40-48

Jesus spoke up and said to him, "Simon, I have something to say to you." "Teacher," he replied, "speak." "A certain creditor had two debtors; one owed five hundred denarii, and the other fifty. When they could not pay, he canceled the debts for both of them. Now which of them will love him more?" Simon answered, "I suppose the one for whom he canceled the greater debt." And Jesus said to him, "You have judged rightly." Then turning toward the woman, he said to Simon, "Do you see this woman? I entered your house; you gave me no water for my feet, but she has bathed my feet with her tears and dried them with her hair. You gave me no kiss, but from the time I came in she has not stopped kissing my feet. You did not anoint my head with oil, but she has anointed my feet with ointment. Therefore, I tell you, her sins, which were many, have been forgiven; hence she has shown great love. But the one to whom little is forgiven, loves little." Then he said to her, "Your sins are forgiven."

Pondering and Meditating: Jesus gives a new equation: Great forgiveness equals great love. Reflect on the forgiveness you have received from a loving God and consider how your great love can be expressed in grateful response.

Prayer: Forgiving God, make me aware of opportunities to demonstrate my love for you in grateful response to your great love for me. Amen.

Reflection:

Monday, June 17, 2013

1 Kings 19:1-5a

Ahab told Jezebel all that Elijah had done, and how he had killed all the prophets with the sword. Then Jezebel sent a messenger to Elijah, saying, "So may the gods do to me, and more also, if I do not make your life like the life of one of them by this time tomorrow." Then he was afraid; he got up and fled for his life, and came to Beer-sheba, which belongs to Judah; he left his servant there. But he himself went a day's journey into the wilderness, and came and sat down under a solitary broom tree. He asked that he might die: "It is enough; now, O Lord, take away my life, for I am no better than my ancestors." Then he lay down under the broom tree and fell asleep.

Pondering and Meditating: Elijah appears to be giving up. Realizing he is neither fast enough nor strong enough to get away from Jezebel's wrath, he lays down under a tree to die. Have you ever wanted to give up? Ever convinced yourself there was no point going on because the forces against you were too overwhelming? The story tells us that Elijah was visited by an angel, rose to eat, and traveled to Horeb where he met God. Is it possible God has sent an angel to you in your wilderness, someone to remind you that even though you may not be up to the challenges facing you, God is, and will sustain you?

Prayer: Powerful God, remind me that you are strongest when I acknowledge my weakness and dependence on you. Give me courage to trust and keep going despite obstacles and opposition. Amen.

Reflection:

Tuesday, June 18, 2013

1 Kings 19: 9-12

At that place he came to a cave, and spent the night there. Then the word of the Lord came to him, saying, "What are you doing here, Elijah?" He answered, "I have been very zealous for the Lord, the God of hosts; for the Israelites have forsaken your covenant, thrown down your altars, and killed your prophets with the sword. I alone am left, and they are seeking my life, to take it away." He said, "Go out and stand on the mountain before the Lord, for the Lord is about to pass by." Now there was a great wind, so strong that it was splitting mountains and breaking rocks in pieces before the Lord, but the Lord was not in the wind; and after the wind an earthquake, but the Lord was not in the earthquake; and after the earthquake a fire, but the Lord was not in the fire; and after the fire a sound of sheer silence.

Pondering and Meditating: Our world has become obsessed with spectacles. Events don't seem important unless accompanied by bigger, better, splashier celebrations. But Elijah didn't encounter God's presence in wind, earthquake or fire. Instead, God became present in a "sound of sheer silence." Is it possible our bigger, louder events have prevented us from encountering God in silence? Do we even allow ourselves times of silence at all? Even our prayers and worship can involve too much talking and too little listening for God.

Prayer: Loving God, help me to be still and know that you are God. Give me the gift of silence in which I can better discern your presence. Amen.

Reflection:

Wednesday, June 19, 2013

Psalm 42:1-2

As a deer longs for flowing streams, so my soul longs for you, O God. My soul thirsts for God, for the living God. When shall I come and behold the face of God?

Pondering and Meditating: Can you remember ever being really thirsty? Probably the closest thing to real thirst many of us have experienced is the time of nothing by mouth after midnight when preparing for surgery or medical testing. We do, though, know something about intense longing. We may long for relief from pain, for healing, for a break from endless work and pressure. Some even long for a time when the Orioles will have a winning team again! These longings tend to become all-consuming and can easily take control of our lives. Perhaps that's the point the Psalmist is making: is our longing for God's presence so strong that it controls every aspect of our existence? What would it be like to want to live in relationship with God more than anything else? More than financial security, success, fame or accomplishments? How might your life and relationships change if your soul longed for God that much?

Prayer: Loving God, fill me with desire for you, for your love and presence to become the center of my life and thoughts daily. Amen.

Reflection:

Psalm 42: 5-8

Why are you cast down, O my soul, and why are you disquieted within me? Hope in God; for I shall again praise him, my help and my God. My soul is cast down within me; therefore I remember you from the land of Jordan and of Hermon, from Mount Mizar. Deep calls to deep at the thunder of your cataracts; all your waves and your billows have gone over me. By day the Lord commands his steadfast love, and at night his song is with me, a prayer to the God of my life.

Pondering and Meditating: Memory can be both a curse and a blessing. Failures, disappointments and life's embarrassing moments can be hard to forget. Why is it that we so often seem prone to remember bad experiences better than good? Perhaps we need to practice recalling those times when we have been blessed by God's loving presence. Then, when our souls are downcast and disquieted, we will be able to draw strength from our memory of being wrapped in God's abiding love. By day or by night, at all times and in all places, our help is in the loving presence of our God.

Prayer: Ever present God, recall to my mind those times when I have keenly felt your presence and leaned on your everlasting arms. Help me to celebrate and to trust your never-failing love in Jesus Christ. Amen.

Reflection:

Luke 8:27-30

As he stepped out on land, a man of the city who had demons met him. For a long time he had worn no clothes, and he did not live in a house but in the tombs. When he saw Jesus, he fell down before him and shouted at the top of his voice, "What have you to do with me, Jesus, Son of the Most High God? I beg you, do not torment me" — for Jesus had commanded the unclean spirit to come out of the man. (For many times it had seized him; he was kept under guard and bound with chains and shackles, but he would break the bonds and be driven by the demon into the wilds.) Jesus then asked him, "What is your name?" He said, "Legion"; for many demons had entered him.

Pondering and Meditating: We modern folks tend not to put much stock in the idea of demon possession. But aren't there forces, unclean spirits, in each of us that can control us and cause us to do things we regret, things that can separate us from others? The first step toward physical healing is identifying the cause of illness. In much the same way, the first step toward emotional and spiritual healing might be naming the particular "demons" that live in and control us. Before we can be healed we must first acknowledge and name the unclean spirits that afflict us.

Prayer: Healing God, I confess that I am often under the influence of unclean forces. I name then now, so that you can free me from the chains and shackles that have so long bound me. I pray in Jesus' name, Amen.

Reflection:

Saturday, June 22, 2013

Luke 8: 35-36

Then people came out to see what had happened, and when they came to Jesus, they found the man from whom the demons had gone sitting at the feet of Jesus, clothed and in his right mind. And they were afraid. Those who had seen it told them how the one who had been possessed by demons had been healed

Pondering and Meditating: The man whose demons were legion has been healed and freed by Jesus. As we might expect, this dramatic healing attracted lots of attention and caused some to be afraid in the presence of one whose power was so great that even demons obeyed him. One of the problems with demons themselves is the way they tend to take control of our lives. And we are people who don't like to be out of control. Perhaps we fear being out of control more than the demons themselves. At least they are familiar (since we've lived with them so long!). If we give over control of our lives to Jesus we're never sure where it might lead. Are we clinging to the security of known demons and missing the freedom and uncertainty found in following Jesus?

Prayer: Gracious and loving God, give us courage to leave security of the familiar behind and follow Jesus. Though we may not know where he will lead us, we can know that he will never leave us. And that gives us confidence for the uncertain future. Amen.

Reflection:

Sunday, June 23, 2013

Galatians 3: 26-28

(F)or in Christ Jesus you are all children of God through faith. As many of you as were baptized into Christ have clothed yourselves with Christ. There is no longer Jew or Greek, there is no longer slave or free, there is no longer male and female; for all of you are one in Christ Jesus.

Pondering and Meditating: We Christians are a very diverse people. From all walks of life, liberal and conservative, Republican and Democrat, young and old, representing many different denominations, nationalities and ethnicities, we claim to be one body in Christ. Certainly it is not our unity of thought, practice or worship that enables us to make this claim. The tie that binds us, the only thing we really have in common is our relationship with Jesus Christ as Lord. Through Christ we are "all children of God through faith." We may disagree or even fight (as we often do) but we are bound together by ties that are stronger than those forces that push us apart. How would our life in community be different if we always focused on our oneness in Christ Jesus? Is there a brother or sister in Christ from whom you have been estranged? What would it take for you to be reconciled in the name of Christ who makes us one?

Prayer: Uniting God, help me to focus on the love of Christ that unites me with other Christians more than the differences that divide us from each other. Use me to create unity within the body of Christ. Amen.

Reflection:

2 Kings 2: 1-2

Now when the Lord was about to take Elijah up to heaven by a whirlwind, Elijah and Elisha were on their way from Gilgal. Elijah said to Elisha, "Stay here; for the Lord has sent me as far as Bethel." But Elisha said, "As the Lord lives, and as you yourself live, I will not leave you."

Pondering and Meditating: In today's world, commitment often seems to be a vanishing quality. At least 50 percent of marriages end in divorce. Fewer young adults express a desire to marry. Employees switch jobs more often and employers no longer seem to invest in long-term workers. Even professional athletes change teams frequently in pursuit of the highest compensation. Frequently, the only commitment evident is one individual's to "me, myself, and I." Before casting stones, though, perhaps we ought to examine our own record. Do we sacrifice self-interest in order to serve the needs of those to whom we have made commitments? Do we pursue personal agendas sometimes at the expense of other's needs? Elisha has committed to serve Elijah as a disciple. Despite uncertainty and perhaps danger, he affirms, "I will not leave you."

Prayer: Faithful God, keep me committed to following you, and help me to serve you and others, in the name of Jesus, who lived for you and gave himself for me and the world. Amen.

Reflection:

2 Kings 2:13-14

He picked up the mantle of Elijah that had fallen from him, and went back and stood on the bank of the Jordan. He took the mantle of Elijah that had fallen from him, and struck the water, saying, "Where is the Lord, the God of Elijah?" When he had struck the water, the water was parted to the one side and to the other, and Elisha went over.

Pondering and Meditating: Despite popular mythology, none of us can claim to be a self-made person. From parents who gave life and nurtured us, to teachers and mentors who helped us learn about ourselves and the world, and spiritual parents who guided us to faith, we have received a foundation on which we build. Elisha picked up the mantle of Elijah that had fallen to him and carried forward the prophetic ministry. What mantles have fallen to you? Whose example or teaching has blessed you? Have you built on that foundation? Are there some mantles still laying around that you need to pick up and carry forward?

Prayer: Challenging God, recall to my mind the blessings I have received from those who have gone before me in the faith. Give me deeper appreciation for what I have inherited, and renewed commitment to carry blessings forward so that I might bless others, in Jesus' name. Amen.

Reflection:

Psalm 16:5-11

The Lord is my chosen portion and my cup; you hold my lot. The boundary lines have fallen for me in pleasant places; I have a goodly heritage. I bless the Lord who gives me counsel; in the night also my heart instructs me. I keep the Lord always before me; because he is at my right hand, I shall not be moved. Therefore my heart is glad, and my soul rejoices; my body also rests secure. For you do not give me up to Sheol, or let your faithful one see the Pit. You show me the path of life. In your presence there is fullness of joy; in your right hand are pleasures forevermore.

Pondering and Meditating: In the midst of our own uncertainty and search for "the good life," God shows us the path of life that leads to fullness of joy and eternal pleasures. Why, then, do we so often chase momentary pleasures, or find ourselves being led down paths that lead to death and destruction? Our actions reflect what occupies the center of our lives and attention. The Psalmist provides life-giving advice: "Keep the Lord always before me."

Prayer: Faithful God, give me wisdom to make you the center of my life. Guide me to make decisions and commitments that lead me closer to you and the fullness of joy that is found in serving you above all else. Amen.

Reflection:

Thursday, June 27, 2013

Galatians 5:13-14

For you were called to freedom, brothers and sisters; only do not use your freedom as an opportunity for self-indulgence, but through love become slaves to one another. For the whole law is summed up in a single commandment, "You shall love your neighbor as yourself."

Pondering and Meditating: Freedom is a great blessing. Throughout the Bible, though, we find stories reminding us that God never gives blessings as a reward for past service. Instead, the blessings we receive are intended to equip us to serve God and others in God's name. Some have said the only freedom we really have is freedom to decide who or what we will serve. Paul encourages the Galatians to use their freedom to serve others rather than themselves. His example and ours was Jesus, who "emptied himself, taking the form of a slave." When rings are exchanged as part of the wedding vows, couples commit themselves with these words: "With all that I am, and all that I have, I honor you." Whom do we honor with our lives? How can we live so that our actions — not just our words — give honor to God and others in God's name?

Prayer: Loving God, help me to love and serve you and others in all that I do, in the name of Jesus Christ. Amen.

Reflection:

Friday, June 28, 2013

Galatians 5: 22-25

By contrast, the fruit of the Spirit is love, joy, peace, patience, kindness, generosity, faithfulness, gentleness, and self-control. There is no law against such things. And those who belong to Christ Jesus have crucified the flesh with its passions and desires. If we live by the Spirit, let us also be guided by the Spirit.

Pondering and Meditating: The goal for those who follow Christ is to become like Christ. The Bible reminds us that we cannot serve two masters. We can't serve God and wealth, or God and success, God and pleasure, God and personal fulfillment. The center of our lives determines the margins. Paul helps us to see that if the Spirit is our guide then our actions will embody Christ. How present are these fruits of the Spirit in our daily living? What do the margins of our lives say about the center? What can you do today to be more firmly rooted in Christ so that your life will produce more of the Spirit's fruits?

Prayer: Generous God, guide me to center my life around you and your love and grace toward me. Make me open to your Spirit, so that it fills me and overflows in fruits that touch and transform others in your name. Amen.

Reflection:

Luke 9:51-56

When the days drew near for him to be taken up, he set his face to go to Jerusalem. And he sent messengers ahead of him. On their way they entered a village of the Samaritans to make ready for him; but they did not receive him, because his face was set toward Jerusalem. When his disciples James and John saw it, they said, "Lord, do you want us to command fire to come down from heaven and consume them?" But he turned and rebuked them. Then they went on to another village.

Pondering and Meditating: No one enjoys rejection. Yet those who follow Jesus have to get used to being rejected because of the direction they have chosen to go. Following Jesus often brings us into conflict with the values and desires of others. What we learn from Jesus' example helps us see that our response to those who reject us is not to lash out in anger, but simply to move on. The mission compels us to keep moving forward in faith. Where have you allowed the opinions or approval of others to lead you away from God's direction for your life? How might God be calling you today to get back on track to carry out your role in God's mission?

Prayer: Guiding God, show me the way you want me to go, and give me courage to follow you, even at the expense of losing the acclaim or approval of others. In Jesus' name. Amen.

Reflection:

Sunday, June 30, 2013

Luke 9:57-62

As they were going along the road, someone said to him, "I will follow you wherever you go." And Jesus said to him, "Foxes have holes, and birds of the air have nests; but the Son of Man has nowhere to lay his head." To another he said, "Follow me." But he said, "Lord, first let me go and bury my father." But Jesus said to him, "Let the dead bury their own dead; but as for you, go and proclaim the kingdom of God." Another said, "I will follow you, Lord; but let me first say farewell to those at my home." Jesus said to him, "No one who puts a hand to the plow and looks back is fit for the kingdom of God."

Pondering and Meditating: The decision to follow Jesus has serious consequences. Jesus calls us to place him first in our priorities. Nothing and no one can be allowed to become more important than following Jesus. Other commitments become secondary, and the way we fulfill them reflects our decision to love and serve Jesus above all else. What have you allowed to occupy first place in your life? How would you have to change in order to make following Jesus your highest priority?

Prayer: Gracious and loving God, strengthen my will to respond in gratitude for your love and grace by putting you first in my life, through Jesus Christ our Lord. Amen.

Reflection:

JULY 2013

REV. STEPHANIE VADER

The Scriptures for the month of July speak about one of the overarching themes of the Bible, which is the power of possibility. God, the Bible tells us, is always doing a new thing, focused on what can be. While we human beings tend to get trapped in the facts. "Jjust give me the facts," we say. Notice in the Bible readings for this month how God brings the power of possibility to people who can only "see" the facts. The gifts of God and the power of possibility in the Bible always come as a surprise and not in the ways we imagine.

While we get trapped in our circumstances and become people who make decisions too often based in fear, we hear the promise in the Bible that with God all things are possible. Hafiz, the 14th century Iranian Sufi poet, says, "Fear is the cheapest room in the house. I'd like to see you in better living conditions." That is what God wants for us, to be people who are set free to see the power of possibility because we follow a living God who is always doing something new and surprising.

Søren Kierkegaard wrote, "If I were to wish for anything, I should not wish for wealth and power, but for the passionate sense of what can be, for the eye, which, ever young and ardent, sees the possible. Pleasure disappoints, possibility never. And what wine is so sparkling, what so fragrant, what so intoxicating as possibility?"

This month as you read the devotions for each day notice the powerful gifts from God that come as a surprise wrapped in a disguise.

2 Kings 5:1-7

Naaman, commander of the army of the king of Aram, was a great man and in high favour with his master, because by him the Lord had given victory to Aram. The man, though a mighty warrior, suffered from leprosy. Now the Arameans on one of their raids had taken a young girl captive from the land of Israel, and she served Naaman's wife. She said to her mistress, 'If only my lord were with the prophet who is in Samaria! He would cure him of his leprosy.' So Naaman went in and told his lord just what the girl from the land of Israel had said. And the king of Aram said, 'Go then, and I will send along a letter to the king of Israel.' He went, taking with him ten talents of silver, six thousand shekels of gold, and ten sets of garments. He brought the letter to the king of Israel, which read, 'When this letter reaches you, know that I have sent to you my servant Naaman, that you may cure him of his leprosy.' When the king of Israel read the letter, he tore his clothes and said, 'Am I God, to give death or life, that this man sends word to me to cure a man of his leprosy? Just look and see how he is trying to pick a quarrel with me.'

Pondering and Meditation: In the upside down world of the Bible, a young slave girl tells her powerful masters who to seek if they want to be healed of illness. When have you heard a message of healing from an unexpected source?

Prayer: Today may I be open to healing from unexpected sources. Amen.

Reflection:

2 Kings 5:8-14

But when Elisha the man of God heard that the king of Israel had torn his clothes, he sent a message to the king, 'Why have you torn your clothes? Let him come to me, that he may learn that there is a prophet in Israel.' So Naaman came with his horses and chariots, and halted at the entrance of Elisha's house. Elisha sent a messenger to him, saying, 'Go, wash in the Jordan seven times, and your flesh shall be restored and you shall be clean.' But Naaman became angry and went away, saying, "I thought that for me he would surely come out, and stand and call on the name of the Lord his God, and would wave his hand over the spot, and cure the leprosy! Are not Abana and Pharpar, the rivers of Damascus, better than all the waters of Israel Could I not wash in them, and be clean?" He turned and went away in a rage. But his servants approached and said to him, "Father, if the prophet had commanded you to do something difficult, would you not have done it? How much more, when all he said to you was, 'Wash, and be clean'"? So he went down and immersed himself seven times in the Jordan, according to the word of the man of God; his flesh was restored like the flesh of a young boy, and he was clean.

Pondering and Meditation: Have you ever been asked to do something very simple and refused because of your pride? Do you, like Naaman, expect healings to be exciting?

Prayer: May I be open to the simple healing blessings in my life: a kind word, a good meal, a beautiful flower. Amen.

Reflection:

Wednesday July 3, 2013

Psalm 30

I will extol you, O Lord, for you have drawn me up, and did not let my foes rejoice over me. O Lord my God, I cried to you for help, and you have healed me. O Lord, you brought up my soul from Sheol, restored me to life from among those gone down to the Pit. Sing praises to the Lord, O you his faithful ones, and give thanks to his holy name. For his anger is but for a moment; his favor is for a lifetime. Weeping may linger for the night, but joy comes with the morning. As for me, I said in my prosperity, "I shall never be moved." By your favor, O Lord, you had established me as a strong mountain; you hid your face; I was dismayed. To you, O Lord, I cried, and to the Lord I made supplication: "What profit is there in my death, if I go down to the Pit? Will the dust praise you? Will it tell of your faithfulness? Hear, O Lord, and be gracious to me! O Lord, be my helper!" You have turned my mourning into dancing; you have taken off my sackcloth and clothed me with joy, so that my soul may praise you and not be silent. O Lord my God, I will give thanks to you for ever.

Pondering and Meditation: Do you know anyone who is clothed with joy? What helps you to be clothed with joy? Do something today that clothes you with joy.

Prayer: God, I want to be clothed with joy today. Amen.

Reflection:

Thursday, July 4, 2013

Isaiah 66:10-14

Rejoice with Jerusalem, and be glad for her, all you who love her; rejoice with her in joy, all you who mourn over her – that you may nurse and be satisfied from her consoling breast; that you may drink deeply with delight from her glorious bosom. For thus says the Lord: I will extend prosperity to her like a river, and the wealth of the nations like an overflowing stream; and you shall nurse and be carried on her arm, and dandled on her knees. As a mother comforts her child, so I will comfort you; you shall be comforted in Jerusalem. You shall see, and your heart shall rejoice; your bodies shall flourish like the grass; and it shall be known that the hand of the Lord is with his servants, and his indignation is against his enemies.

Pondering and Meditation: The Psalmist speaks of God as being like a mother who gives comfort from her consoling breast. Have you ever thought of God as being like a breast-feeding mother offering you comfort? What are the things that bring you comfort? Make a list of some of things that bring you comfort and put that list up in a visible location so you can be reminded in times of distress of how to find comfort.

Prayer: May I both find and give comfort today. Amen.

Reflection:

Friday July 5, 2013

Psalm 66:1-9

Make a joyful noise to God, all the earth; sing the glory of his name; give to him glorious praise. Say to God, "How awesome are your deeds! Because of your great power, your enemies cringe before you. All the earth worships you; they sing praises to you, sing praises to your name." Come and see what God has done: he is awesome in his deeds among mortals. He turned the sea into dry land; they passed through the river on foot. There we rejoiced in him, who rules by his might forever, whose eyes keep watch on the nations – let the rebellious not exalt themselves. Bless our God, O peoples, let the sound of his praise be heard, who has kept us among the living, and has not let our feet slip.

Pondering and Meditation: The Psalmist praises God when remembering the mighty deeds of salvation that God has done in the past for the people of Israel. When we remember God's mighty deeds of salvation how can we not believe? What mighty deed of salvation has God done in your life? Often we only see the mighty deeds of God when we look back. Where do you see the activity of God in your life when you look back?

Prayer: When I remember, how can I not believe in your mighty deeds of salvation. Amen.

Reflection:

Saturday July 6, 2013

Galatians 6:1-10

My friends, if anyone is detected in a transgression, you who have received the Spirit should restore such a one in a spirit of gentleness. Take care that you yourselves are not tempted. Bear one another's burdens, and in this way you will fulfil the law of Christ. For if those who are nothing think they are something, they deceive themselves. All must test their own work; then that work, rather than their neighbour's work, will become a cause for pride. For all must carry their own loads. Those who are taught the word must share in all good things with their teacher. Do not be deceived; God is not mocked, for you reap whatever you sow. If you sow to your own flesh, you will reap corruption from the flesh; but if you sow to the Spirit, you will reap eternal life from the Spirit. So let us not grow weary in doing what is right, for we will reap at harvest time, if we do not give up. So then, whenever we have an opportunity, let us work for the good of all, and especially for those of the family of faith.

Pondering and Meditation: Do you know someone who does not grow weary in doing what is right? What disciplines do they practice to keep them from growing weary in doing what is right? What keeps you from growing weary?

Prayer: God I want to do what is right today, help me! Amen.

Reflection:

Sunday July 7, 2013

Luke 10:1-11

After this the Lord appointed seventy others and sent them on ahead of him in pairs to every town and place where he himself intended to go. He said to them, "The harvest is plentiful, but the labourers are few; therefore ask the Lord of the harvest to send out labourers into his harvest. Go on your way. See, I am sending you out like lambs into the midst of wolves. Carry no purse, no bag, no sandals; and greet no one on the road. Whatever house you enter, first say, 'Peace to this house!' And if anyone is there who shares in peace, your peace will rest on that person; but if not, it will return to you. Remain in the same house, eating and drinking whatever they provide, for the labourer deserves to be paid. Do not move about from house to house. Whenever you enter a town and its people welcome you, eat what is set before you; cure the sick who are there, and say to them, 'The kingdom of God has come near to you.' But whenever you enter a town and they do not welcome you, go out into its streets and say, 'Even the dust of your town that clings to our feet, we wipe off in protest against you. Yet know this: the kingdom of God has come near.'"

Pondering and Meditation: The Kingdom of God has come near to you. Do you believe you can catch glimpses of the Kingdom of God? Talk to someone today about a time when you caught a glimpse of the Kingdom of God.

Prayer: Lord, today I want to catch a glimpse of the Kingdom of God and share that news with someone. Amen.

Reflection:

Amos 7:7-9

This is what he showed me: the Lord was standing beside a wall built with a plumb-line, with a plumb-line in his hand. And the Lord said to me, "Amos, what do you see?" And I said, "A plumb-line." Then the Lord said, "See, I am setting a plumb-line in the midst of my people Israel; I will never again pass them by; the high places of Isaac shall be made desolate, and the sanctuaries of Israel shall be laid waste, and I will rise against the house of Jeroboam with the sword."

Pondering and Meditation: Most biblical scholars believe that the book of Amos is the earliest example of the prophetic books of the Bible. The prophetic books of the Bible are a group of writings that are unique in their character: they tell of prophecies of an approaching judgment upon God's people based on the people failing to live by the standards of God. Amos can be summarized in the following sentence: "The end has come upon my people Israel." (8:2) Amos prophecies that the people of Israel might lose the Promised Land, something that no one had ever suggested before. In the ancient theology of Israel, the loss of the Promised Land would mean an end to Israel. Are there things in your life that need to end, things that must die? The process of transformation involves death, not a physical death, but a dying to old fears, attitudes, habits, knee-jerk reactions. What fears, attitudes, habits and knee-jerk reactions need to die in your life to make room for God?

Prayer: Help me to see the things in my life that need to die to make room for you. Amen.

Reflection:

Amos 7:10-17

Then Amaziah, the priest of Bethel, sent to King Jeroboam of Israel, saying, "Amos has conspired against you in the very centre of the house of Israel; the land is not able to bear all his words. For thus Amos has said, 'Jeroboam shall die by the sword, and Israel must go into exile away from his land.'" And Amaziah said to Amos, "O seer, go, flee away to the land of Judah, earn your bread there, and prophesy there; but never again prophesy at Bethel, for it is the king's sanctuary, and it is a temple of the kingdom." Then Amos answered Amaziah, "I am no prophet, nor a prophet's son; but I am a herdsman, and a dresser of sycamore trees, and the Lord took me from following the flock, and the Lord said to me, 'Go, prophesy to my people Israel.' Now therefore hear the word of the Lord. You say, 'Do not prophesy against Israel, and do not preach against the house of Isaac.' Therefore, thus says the Lord: 'Your wife shall become a prostitute in the city, and your sons and your daughters shall fall by the sword, and your land shall be parceled out by line; you yourself shall die in an unclean land, and Israel shall surely go into exile away from its land.'"

Pondering and Meditation: Amaziah, priest of a royal sanctuary, felt that he got to decide what happens there. But God chooses to speak through Amos. God does what God wants and chooses whom to work with and through. Do you try to limit who God can work through?

Prayer: I want to listen to whomever you choose to speak through. Amen.

Reflection:

Psalm 82

God has taken his place in the divine council; in the midst of the gods he holds judgment: "How long will you judge unjustly and show partiality to the wicked? Give justice to the weak and the orphan; maintain the right of the lowly and the destitute. Rescue the weak and the needy; deliver them from the hand of the wicked." They have neither knowledge nor understanding, they walk around in darkness; all the foundations of the earth are shaken. I say, "You are gods, children of the Most High, all of you; nevertheless, you shall die like mortals, and fall like any prince." Rise up, O God, judge the earth; for all the nations belong to you!

Pondering and Meditation: The Psalmist says that God gives justice to the weak and the orphan and cares for the rights of the lowly and destitute. Do you treat those who are weak and lowly with justice and work for their rights? When was the last time you stood up for the rights of someone who had no power or voice in your community?

Prayer: May I notice those in my community who are powerless and find a way to speak up for them. Amen.

Reflection:

Thursday July 11, 2013

Deuteronomy 30:9-14

And the Lord your God will make you abundantly prosperous in all your undertakings, in the fruit of your body, in the fruit of your livestock, and in the fruit of your soil. For the Lord will again take delight in prospering you, just as he delighted in prospering your ancestors, when you obey the Lord your God by observing his commandments and decrees that are written in this book of the law, because you turn to the Lord your God with all your heart and with all your soul. Surely, this commandment that I am commanding you today is not too hard for you, nor is it too far away. It is not in heaven, that you should say, "Who will go up to heaven for us, and get it for us so that we may hear it and observe it?" Neither is it beyond the sea, that you should say, "Who will cross to the other side of the sea for us, and get it for us so that we may hear it and observe it?" No, the word is very near to you; it is in your mouth and in your heart for you to observe.

Pondering and Meditation: Do you love the Lord your God with all your heart and soul? Can you think of someone in your church or community that loves the Lord with all their heart and soul? How might your life be different if you loved the Lord with all your heart and soul?

Prayer: I want to love you, Lord, with all my heart and soul but I find it hard to do. Have mercy on me. Amen.

Reflection:

Friday July 12, 2013

Psalm 25: 1-10

To you, O Lord, I lift up my soul. O my God, in you I trust; do not let me be put to shame; do not let my enemies exult over me. Do not let those who wait for you be put to shame; let them be ashamed who are wantonly treacherous. Make me to know your ways, O Lord; teach me your paths. Lead me in your truth, and teach me, for you are the God of my salvation; for you I wait all day long. Be mindful of your mercy, O Lord, and of your steadfast love, for they have been from of old. Do not remember the sins of my youth or my transgressions; according to your steadfast love remember me, for your goodness' sake, O Lord! Good and upright is the Lord; therefore he instructs sinners in the way. He leads the humble in what is right, and teaches the humble his way. All the paths of the Lord are steadfast love and faithfulness, for those who keep his covenant and his decrees.

Pondering and Meditation: Do you trust in the steadfast love God has for you? Look back on your life and spend a few minutes thinking about a time when you were shown mercy even though you didn't deserve it? Pass that mercy on today to someone you meet.

Prayer: I will rejoice in your steadfast love and mercy, O God. Amen.

Reflection:

Colossians 1:3-10

In our prayers for you we always thank God, the Father of our Lord Jesus Christ, for we have heard of your faith in Christ Jesus and of the love that you have for all the saints, because of the hope laid up for you in heaven. You have heard of this hope before in the word of the truth, the gospel that has come to you. Just as it is bearing fruit and growing in the whole world, so it has been bearing fruit among yourselves from the day you heard it and truly comprehended the grace of God. This you learned from Epaphras, our beloved fellow-servant. He is a faithful minister of Christ on your behalf, and he has made known to us your love in the Spirit. For this reason, since the day we heard it, we have not ceased praying for you and asking that you may be filled with the knowledge of God's will in all spiritual wisdom and understanding, so that you may lead lives worthy of the Lord, fully pleasing to him, as you bear fruit in every good work and as you grow in the knowledge of God.

Pondering and Meditation: What does it look like to love the saints? Do you believe that you are surrounded by a great cloud of witnesses who watch you as you run the race of your life?

Prayer: Help me to remember the lives of the saints who continue to teach me through the witness of their lives.

Reflection:

Sunday July 14, 2013

Luke 10:29-37

But wanting to justify himself, he asked Jesus, "And who is my neighbor?" Jesus replied, "A man was going down from Jerusalem to Jericho, and fell into the hands of robbers, who stripped him, beat him, and went away, leaving him half dead. Now by chance a priest was going down that road; and when he saw him, he passed by on the other side. So likewise a Levite, when he came to the place and saw him, passed by on the other side. But a Samaritan while travelling came near him; and when he saw him, he was moved with pity. He went to him and bandaged his wounds, having poured oil and wine on them. Then he put him on his own animal, brought him to an inn, and took care of him. The next day he took out two denarii, gave them to the innkeeper, and said, "Take care of him; and when I come back, I will repay you whatever more you spend." Which of these three, do you think, was a neighbour to the man who fell into the hands of the robbers? He said, "The one who showed him mercy." Jesus said to him, "Go and do likewise."

Pondering and Meditation: Are you available to help those who call out to you or do you act like the priest and Levite and pass by on the other side?

Prayer: Sometimes I just want to pass by on the other side, and so I ask for the strength to show mercy and kindness to all the neighbors you send to me on this day. Amen.

Reflection:

Amos 8: 17- 12

The Lord has sworn by the pride of Jacob: Surely I will never forget any of their deeds. Shall not the land tremble on this account and everyone mourn who lives in it, and all of it rise like the Nile, and be tossed about and sink again, like the Nile of Egypt? On that day, says the Lord God, I will make the sun go down at noon, and darken the earth in broad daylight. I will turn your feasts into mourning, and all your songs into lamentation; I will bring sackcloth on all loins, and baldness on every head; will make it like the mourning for an only son, and the end of it like a bitter day. The time is surely coming, says the Lord God, when I will send a famine on the land; not a famine of bread, or a thirst for water, but of hearing the words of the Lord. They shall wander from sea to sea, and from north to east; they shall run to and fro, seeking the word of the Lord, but they shall not find it.

Pondering and Meditation: Have you ever felt like God was silent, like you were living in a time of famine and could not hear the words of the Lord? The saints speak about living through what they call "a dark night of the soul" when it seems that the Lord is silent.

Prayer: Help me to remember that you are with me even when I cannot hear your voice, O God. Amen.

Reflection:

Tuesday July 16, 2013

Psalm 52

Why do you boast, O mighty one, of mischief done against the godly? All day long you are plotting destruction. Your tongue is like a sharp razor, you worker of treachery. You love evil more than good, and lying more than speaking the truth. You love all words that devour, O deceitful tongue. But God will break you down forever; he will snatch and tear you from your tent; he will uproot you from the land of the living. The righteous will see, and fear, and will laugh at the evildoer, saying, "See the one who would not take refuge in God, but trusted in abundant riches, and sought refuge in wealth!" But I am like a green olive tree in the house of God. I trust in the steadfast love of God forever and ever. I will thank you for ever, because of what you have done. In the presence of the faithful I will proclaim your name, for it is good.

Pondering and Meditation: Do you think the tongue can be like a sharp razor? A sharp razor tongue can inflict great damage on a faith community. What practices help you discipline your tongue so that it builds up your community of faith rather than damaging it?

Prayer: I want to use my tongue to build up today and I know I will need your help to do it. Amen.

Reflection:

Genesis 18:1-8

The Lord appeared to Abraham by the oaks of Mamre, as he sat at the entrance of his tent in the heat of the day. He looked up and saw three men standing near him. When he saw them, he ran from the tent entrance to meet them, and bowed down to the ground. He said, "My lord, if I find favour with you, do not pass by your servant. Let a little water be brought, and wash your feet, and rest yourselves under the tree. Let me bring a little bread, that you may refresh yourselves, and after that you may pass on – since you have come to your servant." So they said, "Do as you have said." And Abraham hastened into the tent to Sarah, and said, "Make ready quickly three measures of choice flour, knead it, and make cakes." Abraham ran to the herd, and took a calf, tender and good, and gave it to the servant, who hastened to prepare it. Then he took curds and milk and the calf that he had prepared, and set it before them; and he stood by them under the tree while they ate.

Pondering and Meditation: Abraham and Sarah offer their guests the gift of hospitality with a warm greeting (Abraham runs to greet them), a foot washing, a cool tree to sit under and a fine meal. Abraham and Sarah get an A+ for hospitality. If you had to give yourself a hospitality grade for how you treat guests who come to your church, what grade would you give? Do you spend all your time at church talking with people you already know?

Prayer: Help me to not be cautious about offering the gifts of hospitality. Amen.

Reflection:

Thursday July 18, 2013

Psalm 15

O Lord, who may abide in your tent? Who may dwell on your holy hill? Those who walk blamelessly, and do what is right, and speak the truth from their heart; who do not slander with their tongue, and do no evil to their friends, nor take up a reproach against their neighbors; in whose eyes the wicked are despised, but who honor those who fear the Lord; who stand by their oath even to their hurt; who do not lend money at interest, and do not take a bribe against the innocent. Those who do these things shall never be moved.

Pondering and Meditation: Imagine yourself dwelling in a tent with God? What would you talk about with God? Would you and God stay awake all night talking or would you just be silent before the Almighty?

Prayer: Dear God: I want to be someone who walks blameless and does what is right so I can sleep tonight in the tent with you, but I am going to need lots of help. Amen.

Reflection:

Friday July 19, 2013

Colossians 1:15-20

He is the image of the invisible God, the firstborn of all creation; for in him all things in heaven and on earth were created, things visible and invisible, whether thrones or dominions or rulers or powers – all things have been created through him and for him. He himself is before all things, and in him all things hold together. He is the head of the body, the church; he is the beginning, the firstborn from the dead, so that he might come to have first place in everything. For in him all the fullness of God was pleased to dwell, and through him God was pleased to reconcile to himself all things, whether on earth or in heaven, by making peace through the blood of his cross.

Pondering and Meditating: When our Christian ancestors proclaimed in the first centuries that Jesus is Lord, they were making a statement not only of faith but also a political statement. After all, Caesar also claimed the title Lord, so to proclaim Jesus is Lord was understood by the Roman authorities to be a threat to the Lordship of Caesar. Paul proclaims in this passage that all things, including thrones, dominions, rulers and powers were created through Jesus and for Jesus. To Paul, Christians proclaiming Jesus is Lord means that we are citizens of the Kingdom of God first and foremost. Our allegiance as Christians is to Christ and modeling our life after his life rather than to any particular country, political party, ideology or philosophy. Have you ever had a time when your allegiance to Jesus was in conflict with your allegiance to another power? How did you resolve your conflict?

Prayer: Let my life reflect that Jesus is Lord. Amen.

Reflection:

Saturday, July 20, 2013

Colossians 1:24-28

I am now rejoicing in my sufferings for your sake, and in my flesh I am completing what is lacking in Christ's afflictions for the sake of his body, that is, the church. I became its servant according to God's commission that was given to me for you, to make the word of God fully known, the mystery that has been hidden throughout the ages and generations but has now been revealed to his saints. To them God chose to make known how great among the Gentiles are the riches of the glory of this mystery, which is Christ in you, the hope of glory. It is he whom we proclaim, warning everyone and teaching everyone in all wisdom, so that we may present everyone mature in Christ.

Pondering and Meditation: What does a person who is mature in Christ act like? How would you describe someone who you believe is mature in Christ? Interview someone you think is mature in Christ and find out what disciplines they practice to help them stay in love with God?

Prayer: Dear Jesus, I want to be counted as mature in you. Help me discern how to do that. Amen.

Reflection:

Luke 10:38-42

Now as they went on their way, he entered a certain village, where a woman named Martha welcomed him into her home. She had a sister named Mary, who sat at the Lord's feet and listened to what he was saying. But Martha was distracted by her many tasks; so she came to him and asked, "Lord, do you not care that my sister has left me to do all the work by myself? Tell her then to help me." But the Lord answered her, "Martha, Martha, you are worried and distracted by many things; there is need of only one thing. Mary has chosen the better part, which will not be taken away from her."

Pondering and Meditation: Whenever I host a party I have a difficult time stopping myself from cleaning up while my guests are still there, when the meal is over I want to clear the table, and do the dishes. When my guests are leaving I realize that although my kitchen and home is cleaned up I missed out on interacting with my guests, which is why I had a party in the first place. Surely, when guests are in our home, talking with them is more important than cleaning, but that can be hard to practice for those of us who, like Martha, just want to get stuff done. What great conversations or opportunities have you missed out on because you got too preoccupied with getting stuff done?

Prayer: Today I want to be more like Mary and not be distracted by the many things I feel I need to get done. Amen.

Reflection:

Monday July 22, 2013

Hosea 1:2-9

When the Lord first spoke through Hosea, the Lord said to Hosea, "Go, take for yourself a wife of whoredom and have children of whoredom, for the land commits great whoredom by forsaking the Lord." So he went and took Gomer, daughter of Diblaim, and she conceived and bore him a son. And the Lord said to him, "Name him Jezreel; for in a little while I will punish the house of Jehu for the blood of Jezreel, and I will put an end to the kingdom of the house of Israel. On that day I will break the bow of Israel in the valley of Jezreel." She conceived again and bore a daughter. Then the Lord said to him, "Name her Lo-ruhamah, for I will no longer have pity on the house of Israel or forgive them. But I will have pity on the house of Judah, and I will save them by the Lord their God; I will not save them by bow, or by sword, or by war, or by horses, or by horsemen." When she had weaned Lo-ruhamah, she conceived and bore a son. Then the Lord said, "Name him Lo-ammi, for you are not my people and I am not your God."

Pondering and Meditation: The prophet Hosea obeys God and marries Gomer, a prostitute, in order to show the people through their relationship the extreme and unexpected love of God. When have you been offered extreme and unexpected love? Find someone today who needs some extreme love and be a Hosea for them.

Prayer: God's mercy is gloriously unfair, that is good news. Amen.

Reflection:

Psalm 85

Lord, you were favorable to your land; you restored the fortunes of Jacob. You forgave the iniquity of your people; you pardoned all their sin. You withdrew all your wrath; you turned from your hot anger. Restore us again, O God of our salvation, and put away your indignation towards us. Will you be angry with us forever? Will you prolong your anger to all generations? Will you not revive us again, so that your people may rejoice in you? Show us your steadfast love, O Lord, and grant us your salvation. Let me hear what God the Lord will speak, for he will speak peace to his people, to his faithful, to those who turn to him in their hearts. Surely his salvation is at hand for those who fear him, that his glory may dwell in our land. Steadfast love and faithfulness will meet; righteousness and peace will kiss each other. Faithfulness will spring up from the ground, and righteousness will look down from the sky. The Lord will give what is good, and our land will yield its increase. Righteousness will go before him, and will make a path for his steps.

Pondering and Meditation: Psalm 85 is a prayer to God by a people in crisis. The Psalmist reminds the people of the numerous times in the past when God restored the fortunes of Israel and offered forgiveness. The Psalmist prays: God do it again. In times of crisis remembering the ways God has brought us through can renew faith and hope. How has God brought you through?

Prayer: God, help me remember because when I remember I cannot help believing. Amen.

Reflection:

Wednesday July 24, 2013

Genesis 18:23-32

Then Abraham came near and said, "Will you indeed sweep away the righteous with the wicked? Suppose there are fifty righteous within the city; will you then sweep away the place and not forgive it for the fifty righteous who are in it? Far be it from you to do such a thing, to slay the righteous with the wicked, so that the righteous fare as the wicked! Far be that from you! Shall not the Judge of all the earth do what is just?" And the Lord said, "If I find at Sodom fifty righteous in the city, I will forgive the whole place for their sake." Abraham answered, "Let me take it upon myself to speak to the Lord, I who am but dust and ashes. Suppose five of the fifty righteous are lacking? Will you destroy the whole city for lack of five?" And he said, "I will not destroy it if I find forty-five there." Again he spoke to him, "Suppose forty are found there." He answered, "For the sake of forty I will not do it." Then he said, "Oh do not let the Lord be angry if I speak. Suppose thirty are found there." He answered, "I will not do it, if I find thirty there." He said, "Let me take it upon myself to speak to the Lord. Suppose twenty are found there." He answered, "For the sake of twenty I will not destroy it." Then he said, "Oh do not let the Lord be angry if I speak just once more. Suppose ten are found there." He answered, "For the sake of ten I will not destroy it."

Pondering and Meditation: Are you persistent in prayer?

Prayer: Persist in prayer today.

Reflection:

Thursday July 25, 2013

Psalm 138

I give you thanks, O Lord, with my whole heart; before the gods I sing your praise; I bow down towards your holy temple and give thanks to your name for your steadfast love and your faithfulness; for you have exalted your name and your word above everything. On the day I called, you answered me, you increased my strength of soul. All the kings of the earth shall praise you, O Lord, for they have heard the words of your mouth. They shall sing of the ways of the Lord, for great is the glory of the Lord. For though the Lord is high, he regards the lowly; but the haughty he perceives from far away. Though I walk in the midst of trouble, you preserve me against the wrath of my enemies; you stretch out your hand, and your right hand delivers me. The Lord will fulfil his purpose for me; your steadfast love, O Lord, endures forever. Do not forsake the work of your hands.

Pondering and Meditation: What does it look like to give thanks to God with our whole heart? One of my answers to that question is singing. For me, singing is one of best ways to use my whole heart for God. In worship, even when I do not like a particular hymn or praise song, I sing it with joy and gusto. After all, worship is not about me and likes and dislikes, worship is about thanking God. Also that hymn that I dislike might be the favorite hymn of the person sitting next to me so I sing it for them.

Prayer: I want my whole life to sing for you, God. Amen.

Reflection:

Friday July 26, 2013

Colossians 2:6-15

As you therefore have received Christ Jesus the Lord, continue to live your lives in him, rooted and built up in him and established in the faith, just as you were taught, abounding in thanksgiving. See to it that no one takes you captive through philosophy and empty deceit, according to human tradition, according to the elemental spirits of the universe, and not according to Christ. For in him the whole fullness of deity dwells bodily, and you have come to fullness in him, who is the head of every ruler and authority. In him also you were circumcised with a spiritual circumcision, by putting off the body of the flesh in the circumcision of Christ; when you were buried with him in baptism, you were also raised with him through faith in the power of God, who raised him from the dead. And when you were dead in trespasses and the uncircumcision of your flesh, God made you alive together with him, when he forgave us all our trespasses, erasing the record that stood against us with its legal demands. He set this aside, nailing it to the cross. He disarmed the rulers and authorities and made a public example of them, triumphing over them in it.

Pondering and Meditation: Paul proclaims that through the death of Jesus Christ, the rulers and authorities where disarmed and triumphed over. At face value, the death of Jesus Christ looks like the triumph of the powerful. The Bible is an upside down world where what looks like an end is really a beginning and true power rests in the non-violent witness of Jesus.

Prayer: Teach me, O God, something about your upside down Kingdom today. Amen.

Reflection:

Luke 11:1-13

He was praying in a certain place, and after he had finished, one of his disciples said to him, "Lord, teach us to pray, as John taught his disciples." He said to them, "When you pray, say: Father, hallowed be your name. Your kingdom come. Give us each day our daily bread. And forgive us our sins, for we ourselves forgive everyone indebted to us. And do not bring us to the time of trial." And he said to them, "Suppose one of you has a friend, and you go to him at midnight and say to him, 'Friend, lend me three loaves of bread; for a friend of mine has arrived, and I have nothing to set before him.'" And he answers from within, 'Do not bother me; the door has already been locked, and my children are with me in bed; I cannot get up and give you anything.' I tell you, even though he will not get up and give him anything because he is his friend, at least because of his persistence he will get up and give him whatever he needs.

Pondering and Meditation: Prayer is the means that Jesus used to open his heart to God and to anchor himself in God's desires for him. What is your discipline of prayer? When was the last time you tried something new in your prayer life? If your prayer life feels tired and routine, talk with a Christian friend about that and ask them to pray for you to be renewed.

Prayer: I want to be anchored in you, God, so teach me how to pray. Amen.

Reflection:

Sunday July 28, 2013

Luke 11:9-13

"So I say to you, Ask, and it will be given to you; search, and you will find; knock, and the door will be opened for you. For everyone who asks receives, and everyone who searches finds, and for everyone who knocks, the door will be opened. Is there anyone among you who, if your child asks for a fish, will give a snake instead of a fish? Or if the child asks for an egg, will give a scorpion? If you then, who are evil, know how to give good gifts to your children, how much more will the heavenly Father give the Holy Spirit to those who ask him!"

Pondering and Meditation: Jesus proclaims in this passage that we will receive the Holy Spirit. At his baptism, the Spirit descended upon him like a dove as he came up out of the water, now he proclaims that God will give the Holy Spirit to those who ask. Make it your mantra today to ask for the Holy Spirit to be poured out upon you. Do it repeatedly throughout the day and see if this mantra makes a difference in your day.

Prayer: God pour out your Holy Spirit on me today. Amen.

Reflection:

AUGUST

REV. ANN R. LAPRADE

This month the Scriptures remind us of our partnership with God and the many blessings that result from that partnership. We are created for a purpose and are called by the One who created us. We have the choice of whether or not to respond – that is the essence of free choice granted to us.

There is wisdom and help available to us in our efforts to respond faithfully and deepen our understanding, if we avail ourselves of that wisdom, born of God and expressed by those whose experience with God is represented by and written about in books of the Bible. When we despair regarding our ability to have an impact as one among many, there is the guidance of Ecclesiastes. If we become too invested in a particular outcome, there is the experience of Luke, whose account of the journey of Jesus and his followers includes Jesus' ministering to many along the way. When we experience a loss of vision, there is the prophecy of Isaiah, which, though expressed in the context of vision, also includes reminders that experienced reality often contrasts with vision. There is the progressive understanding of the psalmists, who may, like us, often begin their conversations with God by expressions of despair, but, by their endurance in the quest for understanding, come to an appreciation of God's goodness and cause for rejoicing – so they show us a way through moments of uncertainty.

The relationships we are blessed to enjoy with one another and with God may strengthen not only our resolve, but also our delight in the many wonders of this world and the signs of God's presence. We can be blessed to be a blessing. I hope that you are empowered through the readings for this month to deepen your understanding of that unique partnership with which you are blessed.

Hosea- 11: 1-3, 8-9

When Israel was a child, I loved him, and out of Egypt I called my son. The more I called them, the more they went from me; they kept sacrificing to the Baals, and offering incense to idols. Yet it was I who taught Ephraim to walk, I took them up in my arms; but they did not know that I healed them. How can I give you up, Ephraim? How can I hand you over, O Israel? How can I make you like Admah? How can I treat you like Zeboiim? My heart recoils within me; my compassion grows warm and tender. I will not execute my fierce anger; I will not again destroy Ephraim; for I am God and no mortal, the Holy One in your midst, and I will not come in wrath.

Pondering and Meditating: In this passage, it is evident that the strength of God's compassion is surpassing divine displeasure. A part of the expression of that compassion is a harkening back to a time of intense relationship between Israel and God, when God used Moses to lead Israel out of Egypt and into the Promised Land. There is divine memory of extreme love. There is also the ache of giving that is not received but rejected. We know what it is like to extend ourselves and be rejected. To the degree that we love, to that degree we continue to give, whether or not the gift is appreciated. How will you reach beyond anger to exercise compassion?

Prayer: Gracious God, thank you for continuing to embrace us, even when we turn away from your powerful and enduring love. Help us to reach beyond both anger and feelings of rejection that we may reach a place where compassion grows and wrath recedes. Amen.

Reflection:

Ecclesiastes 2:18-21

I hated all my toil in which I had toiled under the sun, seeing that I must leave it to those who come after me -- and who knows whether they will be wise or foolish? Yet they will be master of all for which I toiled and used my wisdom under the sun. This also is vanity. So I turned and gave my heart up to despair concerning all the toil of my labors under the sun, because sometimes one who has toiled with wisdom and knowledge and skill must leave all to be enjoyed by another who did not toil for it. This also is vanity and a great evil.

Pondering and Meditating: The author of Ecclesiastes is writing to address fundamental issues about what it means for an individual to be a small part of a greater whole. On what basis does one act if the outcome of that action cannot be controlled? That is part of the human struggle – to recognize that life is not always fair and the basis of faithful action is not entirely tied to outcomes. It is vain to suppose that we alone fully determine our fate. It is difficult work at times to continue to do the right thing and difficult to recognize that we are limited in our ability to make an impact. However, the difficult work of humility can bring the relief of knowing that we cannot be all things to all people at all times. Sometimes we must rest.

Prayer: God of power and majesty, help us to take pleasure in our work and in our play. May we recognize our limitations, not as a reason for despair, but as a cause for rejoicing – for in you there are limitless causes for rejoicing and abounding love for all of creation. Help us to believe that and let go of our illusions – and our despair.

Reflection:

Colossians 3: 1, 9-11

So if you have been raised with Christ, seek the things that are above, where Christ is, seated at the right hand of God. Do not lie to one another, seeing that you have stripped off the old self with its practices, and have clothed yourselves with the new self, which is being renewed in knowledge according to the image of its creator. In that renewal there is no longer Greek and Jew, circumcised and uncircumcised, barbarian, Scythian, slave and free; but Christ is all and in all!

Pondering and Meditating: The theological issues raised in the Book of Colossians are also issues that deal with how to live in the midst of the new reality that is Christ. To abide in that new reality requires honesty and a willingness to be changed. The author of this book makes an important distinction between the human capacity to seek change and the divine ability to affect change. Followers of Christ are called to accountability, with the understanding that, ultimately, the main labor required of followers is to clear away all that may impede renewal in those who seek the "things that are above." It is Christ in us, rather than our own efforts, through which amazing transformation happens. What clutter do you need to clear away in your life so that spiritual renewal may take place? Are you honest with yourself, as well as with those around you?

Prayer: God of that which is seen and that which is unseen, open our eyes and our hearts to the new life in Christ in us and in others around us. Help us to clear away all that clutters our thinking and separates us from you. Amen.

Reflection:

Luke 12:13-15

Someone in the crowd said to him, "Teacher, tell my brother to divide the family inheritance with me." But he said to him, "Friend, who sent me to be a judge or arbitrator over you?" And he said to them "Take care! Be on your guard against all kinds of greed; for one's life does not consist in the abundance of possessions."

Pondering and Meditating: However much Jesus sets his sight upon the destination, he continues to minister along the way. He does not overlook those concerns and persons right around him in his intention to go to Jerusalem. So, when someone from the crowds that tended to gather around him makes a "request," Jesus responds rather than ignoring the call. He takes the demand for an equal division of a family inheritance to a different level of understanding – as an opportunity for a reminder that one's life does not equal the amount of one's possessions. As you rush from one activity to another and attend to one responsibility after another, do you pay attention to concerns and people you may encounter along the way? Are you attentive to the opportunities in everyday life where God's wisdom may be revealed in unexpected and marvelous ways?

Prayer: God of wonder, inspire us to seek you everywhere. Remind us that as Jesus ministered to those he encountered on his journey to Jerusalem, so we are called to pay attention to the journey as well as the goal. May we be alert to unexpected signs of your presence and evidence of your grace in the day to day life we are privileged to lead. Amen.

Reflections:

Luke 12: 16-21

Then he told them a parable: "The land of a rich man produced abundantly. And he thought to himself, 'What should I do, for I have no place to store my crops?' Then he said, 'I will do this: I will pull down my barns and build larger ones, and there I will store all my grain and my goods. And I will say to my soul, Soul, you have ample goods laid up for many years; relax, eat, drink, be merry.' But God said to him, 'You fool! This very night your life is being demanded of you. And the things you have prepared, whose will they be?' So it is with those who store up treasures for themselves but are not rich toward God."

Pondering and Meditating: Jesus tells this parable in the context of a dialogue he is having about what ultimately matters. He points to a reality in which every person participates – death. Listeners are reminded that no one knows when death will come. The human tendency to overlook the fact of death often goes with a preoccupation with acquisition of material goods. It has been said that a good indicator of our priorities can be found in how we use our monetary resources. What does your use of the financial resources with which you have been entrusted say about what is important to you?

Prayer: Wise and Loving Creator, your generosity is boundless and your wisdom ageless. Help us to keep the realities of life and death before us as we make decisions according to our priorities. Thank you for life. Amen.

Reflection:

Saturday, August 3, 2013

Psalm 107: 1-3

O give thanks to the Lord, for he is good; for his steadfast love endures forever. Let the redeemed of the Lord say so, those he redeemed from trouble and gathered in from the lands, from the east and from the west, from the north and from the south.

Pondering and Meditating: People have returned from exile. The psalmist gives thanks for their return and for the fact that God has not only brought them home, but has saved them from imprisonment, illness and chaos. The psalmist also reminds those who have been saved to give thanks and not take the enormous generosity of God for granted. Indeed, there is cause to acknowledge the fact of God's action in the midst of human reaction to the stresses and strains of life. Again and again, a call to God gets a response, and peace apart from specific circumstances that may or may not warrant such peace. Ignoring God's guidance can cause people to lose their way again. It is not that God needs praise and thanks, but that people benefit from attending to and responding to the abundant love of God. What acts of compassion have you undertaken today?

Prayer: Steadfast and loving God, we thank you that, no matter what our circumstances may be, no matter how many times we have fallen short or wandered away, no matter how often we fail, still you are there for us and respond to our call. Help us to believe that and to trust in you in all circumstances. Free us to cry out to you when we need to do so and guide us into a place of peace that we may in turn help to guide others to you and tell the story of your love for all people. Amen.

Reflection:

Psalm 49: 1-2, 10-12

Hear this, all you peoples; give ear, all inhabitants of the world, both low and high, rich and poor together. When we look at the wise, they die; fool and dolt perish together and leave their wealth to others. Their graves are their homes forever, their dwelling places to all generations, though they named lands their own. Mortals cannot abide in their pomp; they are like animals that perish.

Pondering and Meditating: This psalm's message is not limited to a particular group or a particular place, but applies universally. This can be understood as either good news or bad news, depending upon one's perspective. On one hand, people work hard to distinguish themselves and it is humbling to read that all share in the same fate. On the other hand, there is peace in acknowledging that only God endures forever and there is no point in pretending otherwise. There is every point in giving up pretenses and knowing what ultimately matters. To do otherwise, saps energy that could otherwise be used for compassionate action. The intention of the psalm is not to discourage but to encourage by dismissing all that is not of God. Just as Buddhist monks meditate upon their own death near funeral pyres, so there is enlightenment for those who face the truth unafraid. What truth do you need to face and what fear keeps you from doing so?

Prayer: God of courage and strength, increase our courage and enable our willingness to face whatever life brings our way. Help us to take refuge in you and not in pretence. Remind us there is no point in pretending, for you see through every pretence. Amen.

Reflection:

Monday, August 5, 2013

Isaiah 1: 1

The vision of Isaiah son of Amoz, which he saw concerning Judah and Jerusalem in the days of Uzziah, Jotham, Ahaz, and Hezekiah, kings of Judah.

Pondering and Meditating: The vision as it is described is often in contrast to the realities out of which it rises. The call it articulates makes clear differences between God's people and the empires and principalities. Isaiah, whose name means "may Yahweh save," expresses a wide range of emotional response to Israel's lack of fidelity to the values that distinguish God's people from the world around them. That which is expected is made clear: "...cease to do evil, learn to do good; seek justice, rescue the oppressed, defend the orphan, plead for the widow." (Isaiah 1: 16b-17) Even with a clear vision, God's people find it difficult to live that vision. What commitments have you made that you find particularly difficult to maintain? How do you get yourself back to a place where you once again live out of a vision of God rather than values centered on short term gains?

Prayer: Enduring and faithful God, you have given us the capacity to envision a way of life that is different from that of empires and principalities. You have graced us with broad imagination that can imagine a world where people do good, seek justice, rescue the oppressed, defend the defenseless and plead for those without a voice. Help us to live out of that vision and reject that infamous phrase "we've never done it that way before." Strengthen our resolve and our commitment to each other as people of God, part of the vision of Creation. Amen.

Reflection:

Tuesday, August 6, 2013

Genesis 15:1-6

After these things the word of the Lord came to Abram in a vision, "Do not be afraid, Abram, I am your shield, your reward shall be very great." But Abram said, "O Lord God, what will you give me, for I continue childless, and the heir of my house is Eliezer of Damascus?" And Abram said, "You have given me no offspring, and so a slave born in my house is to be my heir." But the word of the Lord came to him, "This man shall not be your heir; no one but your very own issue shall be your heir." He brought him outside and said, "Look toward heaven and count the stars, if you are able to count them." Then he said to him, "so shall your descendants be." And he believed the Lord; and the Lord reckoned it to him as righteousness.

Pondering and Meditating: God promises to shield Abram from harm. However, Abram's concern is deeper. He expresses an essential loneliness and God again responds to him by directing his attention to the heavens, challenging him to count the stars, which cannot be counted. The countless stars in the heavens remain beyond our ability to number them all. In the same way, God's generosity is great beyond measure. God's covenant embraces deep human needs for continuity and community. When is the last time you gazed into the night sky and considered the countless creations of God?

Prayer: God of the endless heavens and countless stars, your creations are amazing and full of meaning. Help us to look with deeper understanding, that we may read the signs and wonders all around us and experience unity and continuity as gifts from you. Amen.

Reflection:

Hebrews 11:1-3, 8

Now faith is the assurance of things hoped for, the conviction of things not seen. Indeed, by faith our ancestors received approval. By faith we understand that the worlds were prepared by the word of God, so that what is seen was made from things that are not visible. By faith Abraham obeyed when he was called to set out for a place that he was to receive as an inheritance; and he set out, not knowing where he was going.

Pondering and Meditating: The book of Hebrews continues to serve those who are going through hard time. We are reminded of Abraham as a model of faith. It is rather extraordinary that he set out on that journey, even though he didn't know where he was going. Imagine in this age of global positioning systems with their multiple ways of tracking one's movements, what it might be like just to get in the car and go, because of a word from God. Would you have enough faith to start out on a journey without knowing the destination? Are you able to look past your plans and routines in order to accept God's guidance?

Prayer: God of our mothers and fathers, steep us in the traditions of our faith. Help us to grow rooted and strong so that no hardship or difficulty can unbalance our resolve. Give us appreciation for the richness of the history that has brought us thus far along the journey. Remind us that Abraham set out "not knowing where he was going" and, guided by this example, free up in us a sense of adventure about our faith journey. In the name of one who risked all for our sake, Amen.

Reflection:

Thursday, August 8, 2013

Luke 12:32-34

"Do not be afraid, little flock, for it is your Father's good pleasure to give you the kingdom. Sell your possessions and give alms. Make purposes for yourselves that do not wear out, an unfailing treasure in heaven, where no thief comes near and no moth destroys. For where your treasure is, there your heart will be also."

Pondering and Meditating: Again, Scripture reminds us to not be afraid. One of the reasons we so often become overwhelmed with fear – or experience chronic fear at the edge of our consciousness, is because of anxiety around real or potential loss of some kind. Material loss can have a significant effect on our everyday life. Material dimensions of our life have real influence on our outlook and attitude. Economic challenges and difficulties can take their toll on our psyche. However, if we can also acknowledge the influence and importance of non-material riches, our spiritual wealth increases, and our internal resources for addressing everyday concerns may also increase. What can you do today to increase your attention to spiritual wealth? Is your treasure where your heart is?

Prayer: Thoughtful God, always able to see through pretense and guide us to a deeper understanding, help us to put our sights on goods that have no expiration date and no built-in obsolescence. Show us how to go deeper and deal in eternal good. Increase our awareness of where our treasure is and our willingness to go there. Amen.

Reflection:

Friday, August 9, 2013

Luke 12:35-36, 39-40

Be dressed for action and have your lamps lit; be like those who are waiting for their master to return from the wedding banquet, so that they may open the door for him as soon as he comes and knocks. But know this: if the owner of the house had known at what hour the thief was coming, he would not have let his house be broken into. You also must be ready, for the Son of Man is coming at an unexpected hour.

Pondering and Meditating: In this text, people are being called to a state of alertness. That state could be prolonged. It is not known when circumstances might change. One never knows when Christ will come again. Whatever preparations have been made, circumstances may unsettle those preparations. We know from experience that our security systems are never fully adequate. Breaches of security are not uncommon. Our only real security is to be found in our spiritual preparations. We never really know when God is going to show up. Despite our attempts to predict and prepare, God has a way of surprising us. Are you willing to allow in yourself the vulnerability required of those readied for God's presence? How flexible are you?

Prayer: God of surprises, open us to your amazing and unexpected presence. Help us to be alert for "God moments." May we put our trust in you and be willing to encounter the Holy in fresh ways. Thank you for the variety of life and all the ways in which you reveal yourself to the world you have created. Help us to be ready for whatever may come our way. Amen.

Reflection:

Psalm 50:1-5

The mighty one, God the Lord, speaks and summons the earth from the rising of the sun to its setting. Out of Zion, the perfection of beauty, God shines forth. Our God comes and does not keep silence, before him is a devouring fire, and a mighty tempest all around him. He calls to the heavens above and to the earth, that he may judge his people; "Gather to me my faithful ones, who made a covenant with me by sacrifice!"

Pondering and Meditating: God is Love. God is also Judge. How do we acknowledge multiple aspects of the Holy One and come to terms with the various dimensions of the Creator? There is that sentiment stated "God loves me, but God isn't finished with me yet." The existence of and need for judgment is simply an indicator that we are still going on toward perfection and require assistance to reach the goal. This psalm is also a reminder that God's judgment is not confined to the individual level but is inclusive of groups, including nations. What groups are you part of that might be experiencing God's judgment? Do you experience both divine love and judgment?

Prayer: God of judgment and Sustainer of justice, show us how we may grow closer to you and engage with your world. Remind us that we are not on our own, but are part of many groups, including the Body of Christ. Sustain in us recognition that we have a responsibility to those bodies of which we are a part to help them (and us) grow and deepen in our spiritual life and social awareness. Amen.

Reflection:

Sunday, August 11, 2013

Psalm 33:12-13, 16-17

Happy is the nation whose God is the Lord, the people whom he has chosen as his heritage. The Lord looks down from heaven; he sees all humankind. A king is not saved by his great army; a warrior is not delivered by his great strength. The war horse is a vain hope for victory, and by its great might it cannot save.

Pondering and Meditating: Psalm 33 begins with a call to rejoicing and some instructions about how to do that. Even if we don't play the harp or the lyre, we can all sing a new song, one that expresses our delight in the new life that comes with allowing oneself to be open to new ways and new information. Happiness, not just satisfaction, comes to those who choose God in response to being chosen by God. How are you consciously and continuously choosing God each day? What new song do you sing – or want to sing? What will it take for you to find your voice?

Prayer: God who delivers us from ourselves, as well as our hubris, create in us new hearts and new spirits, so that we might take on the new with enthusiasm and curiosity, knowing that transformation means changes in the ways we operate, respond to people, and even adapt our thought processes to an orientation to Christ and desire to become more like him. Remind us there is no getting away from you, God. The psalmist reminds us that the Lord looks down from heaven on all people, not just some and sometimes. Continually renew our spirits. Thank you for our times of happiness. Amen.

Reflection:

Monday, August 12, 2013

Isaiah 5:1, 5-7

Let me sing for my beloved my love-song concerning his vineyard; My beloved had a vineyard on a very fertile hill. And now I will tell you what I will do to my vineyard. I will remove its hedge, and it shall be devoured; I will break down its wall, and it shall be trampled down. I will make it a waste; it shall not be pruned or honed, and it shall be overgrown with briers and thorns; I will also command the clouds that they rain no rain upon it.

Pondering and Meditating: The prophet Isaiah composes and sings a love song concerning his vineyard. How much more difficult it is to prophecy the destruction of this same vineyard. It seems an extreme reaction. I mean, surely, there is a way through the need for destruction in order to reach reconciliation. However, sometimes circumstances come to a point of no return. While redemption is always possible through God through whom all things are possible, breaking down that which generates evil rather than good can be a faithful act. Are there situations, which you know and in which you are involved in such a way that the elimination of that which is currently in place, is a faithful response? Are there relationships in your life, which are toxic to the point where you will be poisoned if you stay in those relationships?

Prayer: God of Love, sustain us when we need to make difficult decisions that are hard to speak and even more difficult to carry out. Give us courage to make a difference and enable us to know the difference between evil and good, so that we do not confuse the two. Amen.

Reflection:

Jeremiah 23:23-26, 29

Am I a God near by, says the Lord, and not a God far off? Who can hide in secret places so that I cannot see them, says the Lord. Do I not fill heaven and earth? says the Lord. I have heard what the prophets have said who prophesy lies in my name, saying, "I have dreamed, I have dreamed!" How long? Will the hearts of the prophets ever turn back -- those who prophesy lies, and who prophesy deceit of their own heart? Is not my word like fire, says the Lord, and like a hammer that breaks a rock in pieces?

Pondering and Meditating: The prophet Jeremiah has a strong word to share. He makes a distinction between dreams and God's word, spoken faithfully. He challenges those who claim divine revelation but whose words come from their own thoughts and imaginings rather than from divine insight. There can be revelation in dreams but dreams can also be misleading. God's word, revealed in many forms, is sufficient and does not need the fantasy of dreams as a supplement, according to Jeremiah. How can you tell the difference between false prophets and those who lead you to deeper relationship with God?

Prayer: Mystical and mystifying God, we turn to your word, secure in the knowledge that your word is sufficient for us. Help us to be open to the mystical dimensions of Christianity but also to seek closer relationship with you and others of the Body of Christ, as means of testing whatever mystical experience may be granted to us. Grant us acceptance that our understanding alone is incomplete. Amen.

Reflection:

Wednesday, August 14, 2013

Hebrews 12:1-2

Therefore, since we are surrounded by so great a cloud of witnesses, let us also lay aside every weight and the sin that clings so closely, and let us run with perseverance the race that is set before us, looking to Jesus the pioneer and perfecter of our faith, who for the sake of the joy that was set before him enduring the cross, disregarding its shame, and has taken his seat at the right hand of the throne of God.

Pondering and Meditating: We do not make the Christian journey alone. We go forward, surrounded by generations of the faithful who have gone before us, encouraging and supporting us every step of the way, giving us examples of faithful and courageous living. They are important to development as disciples and sources of hope for those times when living as Christians is particularly difficult. Some of these witnesses are known by many, others are known by just a few. They are all important for us as we continue in this adventure that is life. Supreme among these is Jesus, the "pioneer and perfecter of our faith." Who are some people who have helped to show you the Way? Who are some witnesses who have expressed, by word and act, their Christian commitment in ways that strengthened your conviction?

Prayer: God, our Creator and Sustainer, grant us the peace that comes from knowing that we are not alone. Help us to remember and to rejoice in that cloud of witnesses, the souls of those who have gone on before us. Grant us the privilege of one day becoming part of that cloud of witnesses for those who come after us. Amen.

Reflection:

Luke 12:49-51, 56

I came to bring fire to the earth, and how I wish it were already kindled! I have a baptism with which to be baptized, and what stress I am under until it is completed! Do you think that I have come to bring peace to the earth? No, I tell you, but rather division! … You hypocrites! You know how to interpret the appearance of earth and sky, but why do you not know how to interpret the present time?

Pondering and Meditating: Christianity does not always call for us to do the popular thing, but rather the right thing. Living out Christianity often brings controversy as well as disagreement, even among followers of the faith. Some of Jesus' harshest words are reserved for hypocritical behavior. Yet, it is not a simple matter to understand that which is God's intent for us in our experience of everyday living. For instance, we often disagree amongst ourselves. Hopefully, and prayerfully, we work toward resolution of those differences. Do you allow the sharp-edged sword of truth to cut through your pretenses and denial? Are you open to answers other than those you already know?

Prayer: Passionate God, instill in us the conviction you require of us, that we might be true to the mission you have given us. Focus our commitment and, at the same time, broaden our willingness to listen and to learn from others as well as from you, so that we do not miss the possibility of new revelation and greater wisdom. If we have lost our passion for the faith, may we be given the kindling we need to rekindle that faith. Amen.

Reflection:

Psalm 80:1-2

Give ear, O Shepherd of Israel, you who lead Joseph like a flock! You who are enthroned upon the cherubim, shine forth before Ephraim and Benjamin and Manasseh. Stir up your might and come to save us!

Pondering and Meditating: The psalmist prays for deliverance and calls upon God for help. God is referred to as a shepherd and certainly capable of saving those who cry out. How many times have we cried out for God, wondering where is the response we seek? In times of doubt and distress, we wish for an answer and for the help we seek to come quickly. It is hard to remember that God answers in God's own time and not our own. Even when we recognize divine power and might, we might also desire for divine response to be what we want it to be. Although we are promised a relationship with our Creator, as we seek to be in relationship, we are not promised a particular timeline for that to develop. Although we are promised salvation, as we seek salvation, we are not promised salvation in a particular format. What are your expectations of God? What do you believe to be God's expectations of you? Are you more concerned with the former or the latter?

Prayer: Just and loving God, as the psalmist cries out, "Stir up your might and come to save us!" so we also desire at times to be saved. Sometimes we pray to be saved from ourselves. Help us to pray in ways that make us attentive to your call in our life. May we ask less of you and more of ourselves, knowing that we are made in your image? Amen.

Reflection:

Saturday, August 17, 2013

Psalm 80:1-2, 18-19

Give ear, O Shepherd of Israel, you who lead Joseph like a flock! You who are enthroned upon the cherubim, shine forth before Ephraim and Benjamin and Manasseh. Stir up your might, and come to save us! Then we will never turn back from you; give up life and we will call on your name. Restore us, O Lord of hosts, let your face shine, that we may be saved.

Pondering and Meditating: How often do we try to make deals with God? The psalmist calls upon God to come and save. Then, once this has been done, there is that promise to never again turn away from God. If life is restored, then there is the willingness to acknowledge God's existence and call upon God. Whether we are fully conscious of such thinking, our faithfulness may at times find its limits based upon what God has already done for us, or what we hope will happen by divine intervention. The deep richness of a faith which is rooted and grounded in God's goodness is difficult to grow and experience. To give without expecting anything in return is a sign that we are entering a satisfying dimension of our faith life. How often do your prayers center upon gratefulness and thankfulness alone? Are you able to rejoice in what God has done without asking for more? At what moments are you most appreciative of God?

Prayer: Faithful and enduring God, rescue us from insatiable appetites and help us to appreciate what we already have through you. Increase our awareness of the needs of others. We thank you that you hear us when we pray and that you answer that prayer. Help us listen to the needs of others, even those unspoken. Amen.

Reflection:

Sunday, August 18, 2013

Psalm 82:1, 8

God has taken his place in the divine council; in the midst of the gods he holds judgment. Rise up, O God, judge the earth; for all the nations belong to you!

Pondering and Meditating: God exercises judgment not only among God's people, but over all the earth, according to the psalmist, who calls upon this superpower to act in such a way as to pronounce judgment regarding all the nations. God is a superpower far superior to all others. The fervent hope of the psalmist is for God to provide justice among all nations. While we desire justice, the justice we desire is often more focused on others than on ourselves. To call upon God as the sole judge is to recognize an authority and to give allegiance to God before all others. How loyal are you in the face of competing allegiances? Are you willing to accept divine judgment if that judgment was to be upon you as well? Are you able to refrain from judging others and to leave that to God?

Prayer: Holy One, our Judge and our Redeemer, broaden our thinking to include the recognition that you are God of all nations and all peoples, including but not limited to our own. We give thanks that you created this world and called it good. Help us to focus on and to aid in bringing out the goodness in ourselves and in others. Assist us as we seek to be faithful and enable us to leave the judging to you. Help us to recognize our tendency to rush to judgment and, in light of that recognition, resist that tendency. Amen.

Reflection:

Jeremiah 1:4-9

Now the word of the Lord came to me saying, "Before I formed you in the womb I knew you, and before you were born I consecrated you; I appointed you a prophet to the nations." Then I said, "Ah, Lord God! Truly I do not know how to speak, for I am only a boy." But the Lord said to me, "Do not say, 'I am only a boy'; for you shall go to all to whom I send you, and you shall speak whatever I command you. Do not be afraid, for I am with you to deliver you, says the Lord."

Pondering and Meditating: Jeremiah declares himself inadequate to speak as a prophet because of his age. Scholars think that he was 13 or 14 when he began his prophetic ministry. What is translated as an exclamation (Ah, Lord God!) some believe to be better translated as a denial (No, Lord God!). The answer that comes back to Jeremiah denies his inadequacy and assures him that the right words will be given to him, when the time comes for him to speak. The words of the prophet were to be the words of God. God chooses all kinds of people to speak and be representative figures. This passage of Scripture is a reminder that young people are not only the church of the future, but are the church of the present. God gives speech to those of all ages and all stages of life. How willing are you to listen? How willing are you to speak, if called?

Prayer: Discerning God, may we be attentive to your word as it comes to us from others. Remind us that you choose whom you choose. Help us to listen, both to the wisdom of youth and that of age. Amen.

Reflection:

Tuesday, August 20, 2013

Isaiah 58:13-14

If you refrain from trampling the Sabbath, from pursuing your own interests on my holy day; if you call the Sabbath a delight and the holy day of the Lord honorable; if you honor it, not going your own ways, serving your own interests, or pursuing your own affairs; then you shall take delight in the Lord, and I will make you ride upon the heights of the earth; I will feed you with the heritage of your ancestor Jacob, for the mouth of the Lord has spoken.

Pondering and Mediating: Sabbath was not a luxury – it was a spiritual necessity, in order for people to be able to receive the good God would give. Isaiah includes the observance of Sabbath along with giving food to the hungry and satisfying the needs of the afflicted as essential spiritual disciplines. Yet, Sabbath observance is relatively rare in our age. We are busy people – the concept of taking an entire day of rest, of Sabbath, is foreign to our functioning. We think we are invincible and indispensable until a crisis occurs or we become exhausted, or both. Are you willing to return to the discipline of Sabbath, even though it means disconnecting from the illusion that you are indispensable, even for a day? Do you understand the concept of Sabbath to be an essential spiritual discipline or a luxury for those with the time for it?

Prayer: God of Creation and Recreation, renew in us an understanding of the gift you would give us in the observance of Sabbath. Amen.

Reflection:

Wednesday, August 21, 2013

Hebrews 12:25-27

See that you do not refuse the one who is speaking; for if they did not escape when they refused the one who warned them on earth, how much less will we escape if we reject the one who warns from heaven! At that time his voice shook the earth; but now he has promised, "Yet once more I will shake not only the earth but also the heaven." This phrase, "yet once more," indicates the removal of what is shaken -- that is, created things -- so that what cannot be shaken may remain.

Pondering and Meditating: When life is turned upside down and we are shaken to the core by unexpected or expected circumstances, what is it that remains? What remains can be that which is essential, that which cannot be shaken. Hebrews calls for gratefulness, because even when all created things are removed, still God's signs and symbols continue. We cling to an illusion of stability and often seek to create an environment which suggests both stability and consistency. The unexpected reminds us how fleeting such an environment, is, when it is constructed by human hands and not by God. Is your sense of well-being dependent upon your physical circumstances or your participation in God's realm? Where is your center?

Prayer: Holy and limitless God, instill in us gratefulness for your generosity and appreciation for your enduring presence throughout all circumstances. Help us give thanks for created things and, at the same time, recognize their fleeting nature. Amen.

Reflection:

Thursday, August 22, 2013

Luke 13:10-13

Now he was teaching in one of the synagogues on the Sabbath. And just then there appeared a woman with a spirit that had crippled her for eighteen years. She was bent over and was quite unable to stand up straight. When Jesus saw her, he called her over and said, "Woman, you are set free from your ailment." When he laid his hands on her, immediately she stood up straight and began praising God."

Pondering and Meditating: Usually, Jesus asks what it is that is wanted. Only when people articulate their desire for healing does he heal them. In this case, Jesus sees this woman, calls her to him and announces that she is healed. He lays his hands upon her, and it is so. Her first action is to praise God. It is a seemingly straightforward sequence of events. It is the beginning and the end of this story which are somewhat out of the ordinary in terms of biblical accounts of healing. Usually those healed are at first more interested in their changed physical circumstances. When you experience healing of some kind, is your first response one of praise to the Healer? Do you respond to God's call – even before all the specifics are made clear?

Prayer: Great Healer, sustain us in days of trouble and increase our faith, that we may take comfort in your constant presence in our lives. Help us to be ready, when the call comes, whatever it may be. May we delight in you always and never neglect to give thanks, in the spirit of hope that we receive as God's people. Amen.

Reflection:

Friday, August 23, 2013

Luke 13:14-17

But the leader of the synagogue, indignant because Jesus had cured on the Sabbath, kept saying to the crowd, "There are six days on which work ought to be done; come on those days and be cured, and not on the Sabbath day." But the Lord answered him and said, "You hypocrites! Does not each of you on the Sabbath untie his ox or his donkey from the manger, and lead it away to give it water? And ought not this woman, a daughter of Abraham whom Satan bound for eighteen long years, be set free from the bondage on the Sabbath day?" When he said this, all his opponents were put to shame; and the entire crowd was rejoicing at all the wonderful things that he was doing.

Pondering and Meditating: Although it would be easy to blame the leader of the synagogue for his seemingly callous response to a woman who has been freed of her affliction, perhaps it is useful to consider times we may have responded in similar ways. Are you responsive to spiritual needs of others that may not be expressed in a traditional manner? Are you as attentive to the spirit of the Word as to the letter of the Law?

Prayer: Great Healer, grant us insight into your ways, which may or may not express themselves within current religious structures. Amen.

Reflection:

Saturday, August 24, 2013

Psalm 71:1-6

In you, O Lord, I take refuge; let me never be put to shame. In your righteousness deliver me and rescue me; incline your ear to me and save me. Be to me a rock of refuge, a strong fortress, to save me, for you are my rock and my fortress. Rescue me, O my God, from the hand of the wicked, from the grasp of the unjust and cruel. For you, O Lord, are my hope, my trust, O Lord, from my youth. Upon you I have learned from my birth; it was you who took me from my mother's womb. My praise is continually of you.

Pondering and Meditating: The substance of this psalm suggests that the author is writing out of the context of a long relationship with God. Despite that longevity, there are still difficulties that cause the psalmist to seek refuge and call for help. This is a reminder that, although we may be blessed with a long-standing relationship with God, we are not exempt from difficulties at any point of our faith journey. How long have you been in conscious relationship with God? In what sense has your relationship with God made a difference in your life?

Prayer: God of the ages and God of our age, may we continue to deepen our relationship with you, through all circumstance and at all times. Grant us the comfort of knowing that you are with us always. May our faith be centered in you and not in our expectations of you. Amen.

Reflection:

Sunday, August 25, 2013

Psalm 103:1-6, 8

Bless the Lord, O my soul, and all that is within me, bless his holy name. Bless the Lord, O my soul, and do not forget all his benefits -- who forgives all your iniquity, who heals all your diseases, who redeems your life from the Pit, who crowns you with steadfast love and mercy, who satisfied you with good as long as you live so that your youth is renewed like the eagle's. The Lord is merciful and gracious, slow to anger and abounding in steadfast love.

Pondering and Meditating: To ask a blessing is to request God's favor and goodness upon others, and/or upon oneself. God's goodness takes many forms and can be received in all circumstances. So, human affinity with the Lord includes an understanding of reciprocity. People ask for and receive blessings, so part of the equation is to continue those blessings by seeking to return them and multiply them. God blesses us and so we seek to bless God, not because we consider ourselves beyond a need to receive, but because we are in partnership with God. Do you understand yourself to be in partnership with God? What does this mean for your life? How can there be reciprocity between humans and their Creator? What blessing do you most desire for yourself?

Prayer: God of blessing, we thank you for the blessings you are generous to give to us, including those many blessings of which we are not aware. Create in us greater awareness of the partnership with you with which we are blessed and how that partnership can empower us to make a difference in this world. Amen.

Reflection: